(J. Woodley)

Stephen Harris trained as a journalist, working as a reporter for the *Auckland Star*, the *Dominion* and the *National Business Review*, a presenter and editor for Radio Deutsche Welle in Germany, and later as the Political Correspondent for Radio New Zealand. In 2001 he joined the Ministry of Foreign Affairs and Trade, recently completing a three-year assignment as Deputy Ambassador in Berlin. He and his family are now based in Wellington.

Under A Bomber's Moon

The true story of two airmen
at war over Germany

Stephen Harris

EXISLE
PUBLISHING

For my family

First published 2009; reprinted 2009

Exisle Publishing Limited,
P.O. Box 60-490, Titirangi, Auckland 0642, New Zealand.
'Moonrising', Narone Creek Road, Wollombi, NSW 2325, Australia.
www.exislepublishing.com

National Library of New Zealand Cataloguing-in-Publication Data

Harris, Stephen, 1962-
Under a bomber's moon : the true story of two airmen at war over Germany /
Stephen Harris.
Includes bibliographical references and index.
ISBN 978-0-908988-23-5
1. World War, 1939-1945—Aerial operations, British. 2. World War,
1939-1945—Aerial operations, German. 3. Airmen—Great Britain.
4. Airmen—Germany. I. Title.
940.544941—dc 22

Website for this book: www.underabombersmoon.com

Text design and production by Janine Brougham
Cover design by Alan Nixon
Maps by Fran Whild
Printed in China through Colorcraft Limited, Hong Kong

Contents

Maps

ACKNOWLEDGEMENTS

A project carried out while living and travelling in foreign countries is a great way to make friends, and assumes greater significance when one of those countries is a former bitter enemy of my own. Many people have contributed to this story, some featuring in its pages, others because they wanted it told, but still more purely out of generosity or extraordinary professionalism. There are too many to name, but some deserve special mention because their help sustained me along the journey and made a significant contribution to the finished product.

First, the 'home team'. My parents, Ian and Jill, spent many hours critiquing and editing early drafts and helped me to keep to my path despite many tempting sidetracks. To them I owe my greatest debt. My children, Laura and Martin, cheered me on, even on 'boring' research trips by car. Jocelyn, my wife, made perceptive comments on the later drafts. Earlier, when I was struggling to point the project in the right direction, Lloyd Jones helped me to define the job ahead. Michael Gifkins, his agent, protested only a little at having a complete stranger thrust upon him by Lloyd, and gave me the benefit of his years of professional experience, always with great humour. Max Lambert, author of *Night After Night*, contributed his extensive knowledge of Bomber Command and, with a sub-editor's sharp eye, weeded out several factual errors and inconsistencies. He regularly drew on the encyclopedic Errol Martyn, author of *For Your Tomorrow*, a book that honours the New Zealand losses of Bomber Command with a thoroughness I doubt will ever be surpassed. Ian Watt, my editor at Exisle, has applied a sure but delicate hand towards publication.

Judy Hill, Col's niece, got the whole thing started by transcribing his diary in the mid-1990s, thus breathing life back into his story 50 years after his death. In Britain, Jan Burke and Gordon Galloway, whose fathers had been among Col's crews, made available a wealth of material that lit up several of the episodes in this book. Fred Coney of the Mildenhall Register put me in touch with them and welcomed me to the 149 Squadron reunion in 2008, where Jim Coman DFC, a veteran former wireless operator with that squadron, provided many technical explanations from his experience on two tours.

Second, my thanks to those people whose professional help went well beyond what I could reasonably have hoped for. Frank Simpson, the Air and Naval Attaché at the British Embassy in Berlin, made possible my visits to Col's former airbases in Britain, streamlining bureaucratic processes that I might otherwise still be grappling with. Once I was there, Jerry and Ruth Neild at Lakenheath and Rick Fryer at Mildenhall ensured the visits were both highly enjoyable and informative. I owe some of the most useful research gleanings to a curator at the RAF Museum, Hendon, Gordon Leith, who responded fully and promptly to every query. In Berlin, Holger Steinle of the German Technology Museum was equally supportive of my project, while Jan Heyen and Cornelia Loeser at the New Zealand Embassy helped to dislodge occasional obstacles. Wilhelm Goebel of the Gemeinschaft der Flieger Deutscher Streitkräfte (the Association of German Military Airmen) put me in touch with several of the former fighter pilots interviewed for this book.

Which brings me to my heartfelt thanks to the Germans who told me their stories. In Penzlin, Hartmuth Reincke and Kurt Köhn led me to the site of Col's demise. Paul Zorner shed further light on that fatal night and many of his own experiences. Otto-Heinrich and Irmgard Fries not only told their stories of triumph and trauma, but did so with an openness and generosity that helped me to understand some of the qualities of resilience that enabled Germans to pick themselves up from defeat and build the country I know and admire.

Stephen Harris

GLOSSARY

Ack-ack – anti-aircraft fire.

Bordschütze – air gunner.

Bordfunker – Luftwaffe wireless and radar operator.

Corkscrew – a bomber's evasive action, flying a twisting roller-coaster.

Dead reckoning – navigation by calculating position and course, factoring in wind strength, sometimes with references to visual landmarks, or 'pinpoints'.

Düppel – *see* 'Window'.

Endgültig Krähe – 'final crow', or operations scrubbed. Vorläufig Krähe meant remain on standby, in case the weather improved sufficiently to fly.

Fasanen – 'pheasants', meaning weather clear for operations.

ETA – estimated time of arrival.

Flak – acronym for Flieger Abwehr Kanone, or anti-aircraft cannon.

Freya – German radar installations with a range of about 120 kilometres.

Funkfeuer – radio beacon signals to help German pilots locate their airbase.

'Gardening' – air operations to lay mines at sea.

Gee – standard British navigational device from early 1942, for navigators to fix their bomber's position by vectoring radio signals from three transmission stations in Britain.

Jägerkreis – social organisation for former German military airmen, similar to the Returned Services Association.

Lichtenstein Gerät – German on-board target finding radar, comprising three (later two) screens, which indicated the bomber's distance ahead, its bearing and altitude in relation to the fighter.

H2S – revolutionary on-board navigational and target finding device enabling a bomber and its user to track the terrain below, independent of radio position-fixing signals from Britain.

Loops – radio position signals, using the 'loop' aerial just rear of the cockpit canopy. 'Ropey loops' were readings 180 degrees to the signal source, i.e. in the opposite direction.

Nachtjäger – literally 'night hunter' of the German night fighter force.

Nachtjagdgeschwadergruppe – Night Fighter Group.

Oboe – British navigational and target finding device that improved precision by guiding bombers to target along an arc 'scribed' by tone signals that varied in relation to the target location.

Pauke, Pauke! – meaning 'drumbeat': Luftwaffe fighter pilot's report to ground control that he was commencing an attack. Similar to 'tally-ho' used by RAF pilots.

Pinpoint – a visible landmark to plot position.

Plattenbau – tenement blocks, mainly in the former East Germany, constructed from prefabricated concrete slabs.

Radar – Radio Detection and Ranging, first developed in Britain in 1935.

Raumjagd – Luftwaffe practice of guiding individual fighters, assigned to a particular defensive zone, onto individual bombers detected by radar. This guided hunting was also referred to as zahme Sau, or 'tame boar'.

Schräge Musik – upward-firing cannon on German night fighters, mounted rear of the cockpit and angled forward at 70 degrees.

This enabled the attacker to approach a bomber undetected and to open fire from beneath its undefended belly.

SN2 – updated German on-board radar, which used a longer-wave radio frequency that helped to overcome the distorting signals of 'window'. The forward-mounted antennae necessary for SN2 were larger and thus caused more wind-drag, impeding performance.

Staffel – Luftwaffe squadron.

Stellplatz – parking position for Luftwaffe aircraft.

Viktor – German ground control acknowledgement over radio, similar to 'Roger' in English.

Vorläufig Krähe – 'provisional crow', meaning German night fighter crew should remain on standby, in case the weather improved sufficiently to fly. Endgültig Krähe – 'final crow', or operations scrubbed.

Weidmannsheil! – Luftwaffe salutation meaning happy hunting!

Wilde Sau – literally 'wild sow', but usually referred to as 'wild boar', and meaning the free-range hunting by night fighters without guidance from ground radar. By contrast, zahme Sau fighters were guided into close contact with bombers by ground control.

Wehrmacht – German army.

'Window' – metallised strips strewn from bombers to distort German tracking and on-board radar with decoy showers. The German name for 'window' was Düppel.

Würzburg – German localised radar, with a range of about 40 kilometres.

Zahme Sau – *see* Raumjagd.

Part One

BEARINGS

CHAPTER 1

JOURNEY AMONG GHOSTS

BERLIN IS FULL OF GHOSTS. Occasionally they leave a sign to show the past is very much still with us. In December 2005 – a year after my job brought me to Berlin – a works crew digging up part of the city's imperial grand boulevard, Unter den Linden, unearthed a British 1000-pound (450-kilogram) bomb that had failed to explode during one of the big wartime raids on the German capital. The bomb, embedded vertically 4 metres under the present-day road's surface, forced its closure for four hours.

Ten years earlier, while working as a journalist for Radio Deutsche Welle, I made a programme about a team of a dozen munitions experts who, 50 years after the Second World War, worked full time locating and defusing leftover ordnance in and around Cologne. Aerial photos of most German cities taken by the United States air force in 1945 reveal the extent to which the Allies took the war to the homes and factories of the Third Reich. Little wonder the physical remnants, too, of this trauma are still working their way to the surface.

Though I did not know it when I worked in Cologne, my time getting to know this city founded by the Romans was the first small step in a quest. While I was there, my mother sent me a copy of the diary written by her uncle, Frank Colwyn (Col) Jones, while he was flying operations over Germany. He died raiding Berlin in

1944. I could not then – and still cannot – reconcile the evil that Nazi Germany unleashed across Europe with the decency and moral seriousness of my many German acquaintances. Nor could I place the answering destruction the Allies rained down from the air within the fundamental reasonableness of the Commonwealth nations. My great-uncle's story, mostly in his own words from his diary and extensive letters home, forms the starting point and the core of this book, and of my own quest. It tells of adventure, terror, tragedy, devotion to duty, deep camaraderie and humour. His part in this story is of a journey across great distances from his home in Auckland, New Zealand, via Canada to Europe, which he crisscrossed over two years with deadly intent. But it is also a journey of discovery – of England, a country and people he regarded as his own – and of his realisation that his young, new world had grown apart from Britain in more than just distance. He never made it home.

My journey traces his, but from a very different beginning and from a distance of more than 60 years. My travels have taken me to all the cities he bombed and many more. Along the way I have had many conversations with people who remember those times as intensely as if they happened yesterday. A neighbour – a teenager in Berlin at the time it fell to the Russians in May 1945 – warned me the time was 'not ripe' to write about such a subject: Germany needed still longer to come to terms with its past, he said. He was in the minority. Contrary to Basil Fawlty's warning, many Germans *do* like to talk about the war in an informed way. It destroyed their country, along with others, and shaped both their lives and the map of the Europe they live in today.

Many exhaustive analyses tell of the destruction wrought by the bombing of Germany, complete with an endless statistical rendering of the houses and factories levelled, people killed and aircraft brought down on both sides. I could not do a more thorough job and I have no intention of trying. Instead I have, in my journey, tried to understand the human impact on both sides. Our family lost an esteemed and accomplished member with a bright future. He was among millions who died fighting a just cause, 55,500 of them while serving with Bomber Command.

But what of those who 'started it'? The American poet Henry Wadsworth Longfellow wrote: 'If we could read the secret history of our enemies we should find in each man's life sorrow and suffering enough to disarm all hostility.' It was impossible for me to live so many years in the modern Germany and not be driven to find out what it was like for this country, having 'sown the wind', to 'reap the whirlwind', as the Chief of Bomber Command, Air Marshal Sir Arthur Harris, described it.[1]

As I so often found when making radio documentaries about Germany in the mid-1990s, I did not have to step far off my path to meet people who had experienced extraordinary episodes in their country's history, and were happy to tell me their stories. Given the subject of my inquiries, my name even turned out to be an ice-breaker, as 'Bomber' Harris is second only to Churchill as the British name that Germans most associate with the war. 'No, we're not related,' was often my answer to their first question. Some of those I talked with remember the events of the 1940s with crystal clarity, because they spent several formative years of their youth never knowing whether each night would be their last. I have focused my discussions with these witnesses to history on two of the German airmen sent up to destroy the bombers before they could pulverise and burn their cities. Their experiences were typical of those related by others with whom I have talked.

One of them in particular, Otto-Heinrich Fries, recorded his experiences some years later. He never published them, but with a humbling generosity made them and his photographs available to me, with the tacit expectation that I would try to capture what it was really like to fight and lose a war and much more besides. Leutnant Fries and Flight Lieutenant Col Jones were sometimes pitted against each other in the night sky above German targets. Though they never clashed directly, as far as I could determine, they shared the experience of destroying the enemy and of being shot down by him. Both were decorated for their skill, tenacity and bravery, and both were completely devoted to their tasks. Both paid a high price for this dedication. Some two dozen interviews with

Professor Dr Otto-Heinrich Fries and his wife, Irmgard, during 2007 and 2008, plus discussions with several other former night fighters, helped me to understand this personal cost.

Where did my journey start? My great-uncle Col's account of his part in the first thousand-bomber raid on Cologne, in May 1942, burned in my mind while I worked there in the mid-1990s. The magnificent cathedral on the Rhine stood out from the rubble in 1945, even though it had been struck by a dozen bombs during successive raids. When I arrived in Berlin in 2004 I knew Col had died bombing the city and lay buried there, just two bus-stops from my home. From my home office window I could see the Teufelsberg, Devil's Hill, one of the few areas of high ground in this flat city, but one created entirely from the rubble of 400,000 Berlin homes flattened by Allied bombers and Russian artillery. Beyond a natural curiosity about my great-uncle's experiences, however, and what he might have contributed to Berlin's suffering and Germany's defeat, I saw no prospect in a busy working schedule of starting to piece the two broken remnants of these stories together.

That changed after I visited the town north of Berlin where Col's bomber was destroyed in February 1944. When I went there in early October 2006 with my two children, I left a greeting and a request for information in the visitors' book of Penzlin's Lutheran church, which was grandly garlanded from the previous weekend's Harvest Sunday. The brick interior diffracted the warmth of the autumn afternoon sunlight and seemed to breathe more spirit into the harvest offerings. On the pillars running up each side of the nave, large oak panels bore the names of dozens of Penzlin's sons who had died in the First World War. Nothing pointed to the town's experience in the Second World War, and my attempts to gain some knowledge via the internet and messages left with Penzlin's 'archivist' had come to nothing. I asked a German colleague to phone again for me, but again, nothing, except for a contact to an amateur Luftwaffe museum established at a former airfield, Rechlin-Lärz, nearly an hour's drive away.

During the war some 2000 top engineers worked in secret at Rechlin-Lärz to develop Nazi Germany's airborne weapons – not just aircraft, but also the initial experimental rockets that became the infamous V1 'doodle-bug' flying bombs. They fired the prototypes into nearby woodland; today the area is a popular recreational nature reserve. I contacted the museum and made an appointment to visit, driving there on a gloomy November day with my parents, who were visiting from New Zealand. We hoped it might throw some light on the region's role in defending Germany against the wartime bombing onslaught – possibly even what happened to Col's aircraft – but we found little at the museum to encourage us. We left our car on a parking area of broken asphalt demarcated only by a low chain linked to posts sunk into concrete-filled car tyres and picked our way across a neglected expanse of boggy grass. We had become lost en route, were 'blitzed' by two speed cameras lurking in dead villages with no other evident source of revenue and finally found the airfield on a road that led to a crane-nesting area. Despite the fact we were running so late and had had to phone ahead and apologise, our host greeted us with affable familiarity – a trait I have routinely found more often in eastern than western Germany, where it sometimes seems punctuality is revered above hospitality.

Bernd Neumann cocked a snook at history when, soon after the Berlin Wall was erected in 1961, he went against the tide of thousands fleeing to the west and instead headed east. In his early twenties at the time, he opted to join his sweetheart in the nearby town of Müritz. And here they still were, Frau Neumann greeting us briefly and leading their little dog out through the clutter of engine parts to the front of the building, where part of a vivisected Soviet-era MiG jet fuselage gaped on the broken tarmac, alongside various other rusting carcasses. Bernd Neumann sat us down at a table in what served as his office, crammed with a desultory array of aviation paraphernalia, including a mannequin fully kitted out as a wartime German paratrooper – the scourge of the Anzacs at Crete – and still menacing, with its Schmeisser machine gun trained on our coffee mugs.

As the little dog's extended family of fleas set to work above our socklines, Neumann explained his involvement in establishing the museum after the Russians departed in 1990 in those aircraft that still flew. Job prospects since die Wende – the changes following Germany's unification in 1990 – have been thin for people of his generation in this and many other parts of the former East Germany, so he and some friends had put much of their time into this project. He led us through the display rooms – mainly models of the aircraft developed there during the war, but also remnants of aircraft, uniforms, rescue equipment and a small room furnished to show the typical barracks accommodation of a Luftwaffe officer.

I asked the origin of the photo pinned to the doorway showing a handsome young airman. The pilot, here sporting a shiny, black flying jacket and liquorice-whip hairdo, had landed briefly at Rechlin-Lärz in the closing days of the war to reload bombs for his single-engine Focke-Wulf fighter before taking off to attack a river crossing established by Russian soldiers. The pilot had survived the war and settled in Hamburg. Could this, I wondered, be my way into finding out what it was like to be on the other side, taking off each night to stop people like Col Jones dropping *their* bombs?

My curiosity pricked, I emailed the curator asking if I could contact the elderly former pilot and attaching a translation of the letter Col's mother, Emma Jones, received informing her of the circumstances surrounding his death. Neumann promised to make some inquiries. His reply came back two weeks later, saying the pilot had died some weeks before. But he put me in contact with Wilhelm Goebel, a former colonel in the post-war German air force. Goebel co-ordinated Jägerkreis, a networking circle of former German airmen, and published a bi-monthly bulletin called *Flieger Blatt*.

I left a message for Goebel, which he returned one Saturday morning as I watched my daughter's soccer match from the sideline. Two senior US army officers attached to their embassy in Berlin – fellow soccer dads – stood at my side; they must have wondered about the nature of the conversation. I told Goebel of my search for information about the fate of Col's bomber. I also wanted to talk to some of the former Luftwaffe airmen who might provide some perspective from the opposing side. Goebel offered to place a small notice in his publication if I could send through what we knew about the circumstances surrounding Col's death. He then gave me

Professor Fries's name and number, plus a contact for the Berlin Jägerkreis chapter.

I contacted Professor Fries early in 2007. Over the phone his voice was high-pitched, obviously elderly, but what struck me more was its warmth and his immediate invitation to me to come and talk. He gave me precise directions and I set off one dark and misty March evening for his home in south-west Berlin. The hand I shook had spent a few years flying deadly machines and then years designing buildings, including his own house. It was soft and slightly clawed by arthritis. At 89, Otto-Heinrich Fries was a little stooped and moved stiffly. Yet once we sat in the companionable glow of a standard lamp and settled into the soft lounge furniture, with Irmgard Fries offering nibbles and wine from the vineyards of her husband's childhood home, the still-sharp mind of one of Hitler's élite airmen began to reveal its secrets, and with astonishing recall. I knew immediately I had found one path to the past. Would it cross my great-uncle's?

CHAPTER 2

DITCHING

THE EPISODE THAT HOOKED ME and made me want to find out more came halfway through Col's first tour of operations. By his 16th op, Col had already had some narrow escapes, but nothing compared with what happened coming back from bombing Essen in the early hours of 6 June 1942. As events unfolded, the crew's chances of survival seemed to get steadily worse. That most of them made it home to fight another night is a story not only of skill and determination but also of tremendous luck – luck that had an echo 66 years later as I tried to track down those involved. As if the dead had returned to discuss a shared adventure, I found a recording of Col's skipper for that trip recounting the dramatic episode soon afterwards in a BBC radio broadcast, supporting Col's vivid, written description almost blow for blow. And my search also took me down a path to another of his former crewmates, still alive, who had played another part in trying to ensure their survival.

Col's ill-fated op to Essen on 5–6 June 1942 was the third time he had bombed a city that was to suffer 272 such bombing raids during the war.[1] Lying in the industrial belt of the Ruhr River valley, north-east of Cologne, Essen was within easy range of Bomber Command. Bomber crews called this unfortunate strip 'Happy Valley' because they returned to pound it so often. Col's adventure began when he took off at five minutes to midnight as a fill-in navigator on 149 Squadron Stirling OJ-'T' Tommy. His diary describes what happened that night.

This was an epic and a tragic trip. Essen again and coming back shot to pieces, lost the rear gunner, collided with a Wellington, shot up by a fighter, went down in the sea and none the worse. Funny thing, I was not down to fly and just went across to tell Mac [McKiner, Squadron Navigation Officer] that I was going for a swim. But he said that they were two navigators short and would I fly with either Tony Ballauff or Eric Whitney and I said Eric. So it was arranged. The crew was: Eric Whitney [pilot], then a Flight Sergeant, but commissioned soon after; Paddy Martin wireless operator/air gunner; me; Bob Shields engineer; Geoff Cheek wireless operator; no mid-upper [gunner] and Keith Roderick in the rear.

Curiously enough, when we compared notes subsequently, we all admitted to a premonition that it was going to be a 'shaky do'. The first thing was that we swung on take-off and landed up in a bunker. Got her back on the runway. Undercart found to be all right, so we started again. No trouble. Paddy Martin map read us across Germany and we saw Duisburg in the moonlight – saw the docks.

Got to the target – pretty hot, too; and just as we were weaving in, before we had dropped our load (incendiaries) they hit us. However, we coped and turned on the southern route for home. Bloody Gee box [navigation device] packed in so we were just making a general direction, aided by the occasional ropey loop.[2]

Just about somewhere near Antwerp it all started and everything happened at once. Out of the blue a terrific crash followed hard after by another. Direct hits by flak. Flying controls affected. At that stage Geoff was in the mid-upper watching for fighters. When the excitement of the crash had passed he told us that simultaneously with being hit by flak, a Wellington [RAF twin-engined bomber, nicknamed 'Wimpy'] had dived out of control and hit us at the rear with an engine. Personally, I think we were more likely to have been hit by a wingtip, but he says he is sure, so there it is.

Then we were hit again, and the combined result of the collision and the flak almost buggered the flying controls completely. In a quiet interval(?), Geoff made his way down to the rear of the kite to see what had happened to 'Moonbeam' Keith, because there was no answer on the intercom. He had to pick his way over the holes in the floor of the fuselage – they gaped everywhere. In the dark he fell into the space for the mid-under [ventral turret, not installed]. The blast of the flak had forced the doors open and he thought he had gone right through. That is one of the worst experiences I think I have ever heard. When he picked himself out of there, he fell over the flare chutes. Then he looked for Keith – and all he saw was a great gaping hole in the rear of the kite. The turret had completely disappeared. Poor old Keith must have gone with it. Still, he would never have known what hit him, because Geoff said the Wimpy came down from above.

After that I don't know how many times we were hit by flak. To make matters worse, we discovered that the flak had caused fires in the bomb doors. We managed to put them out, with a small fire extinguisher, or perhaps they went out themselves. Anyway there was no sign of flame and no smell of smoke. Then we received two more direct hits by flak, one shell burst inside the kite about two-thirds of the way down the fuselage and another in the bomb aimer's position. That one wrecked the front turret, in which fortunately no-one was sitting at the time. Somewhere about this time, Eric ordered us all forward to try and keep the nose of the machine down. It wanted to climb, having no fore and aft stability, but did not have the speed. We were staggering along at between 95 mph and 105 mph – a few miles an hour above stalling speed – and that is a fact. When I looked at my air speed indicator I thought it had been put out of action when it read that, but then I noticed Eric's read the same.

We threw out everything moveable – spare ammo; the navigator's chair, hoping it might hit something on the ground (even his cushion, which was silly); we tried to get the gas [cylinders] out, but they were jammed and shot away so that they would not shift. Only Geoff was aft of the armour plating door, and he was protected by his own armour plating. I think the fact that we all had that protection saved us from what came next.

We were attacked by a fighter – a twin-engined machine. I shall always associate the noise of ripping silk with fighter attacks, because that is what the noise of the bullets hitting the fuselage sounds like. The fighter made three attacks, one from behind, one from underneath and one from behind and slightly to the side. We had no guns to fight back with because the rear turret had gone, the front turret was useless and the mid-upper would not operate because the oil feed had been broken and the guns would not fire. God knows why someone was not hit. For some reason the fighter then left us. Why the fighter did not carry on his good work, God only knows, because we could do nothing; we could not return his fire; could not do evasive action; only climb and stall, climb and stall. I don't know why. No-one knows why, but there were no more attacks. By that time we were just about 10,000 feet and wondering what was going to come next.

The skipper's radio account describes how he experienced the same sequence of events up to this point. Finding the recording was one of those strokes of luck that makes me believe in a guiding hand. While researching this book, in May 2008 I visited a Lincolnshire airbase where I bought a CD containing short BBC broadcasts made during the war, of Royal Air Force (RAF) bomber crew recounting hair-raising experiences.[3] When I slipped it into the car's player as I drove south, I could scarcely believe what I was hearing: the voice of Pilot Eric Whitney, on 18 June 1942, describing how, 12 nights before he, navigator Col Jones and their crew had ditched in the Channel. Having worked in radio, I knew what I had found was pure gold. What he was saying was valuable enough, but actually *hearing* him recount it was even more precious: it was as if the past had flagged down my car and got into the seat beside me. On the four-minute recording Whitney's reading is stilted and he stumbles at each page-turn, but the essential character of this 23-year-old, who had shown such extraordinary skill and leadership in saving himself and his crew, comes through strongly. What struck me was the modesty of his young voice which, from its unperturbed tone, might have been describing missing a bus. Even on paper, his account of what happened is still vivid after all these years and matches Col's in even the smallest of details:

The first thing was a terrific jolt. There were two bursts of flak right under the front gunner's feet. He went down into the bomb aimer's compartment and found it in a mess. There were two big holes and a small fire burning. The front gunner grabbed the fire extinguisher and put the flames out quick. What happened next came in such a rush that it's difficult to know in what order it all occurred. The nose of the aircraft went up. The wireless operator told me that he thought we had been hit by an enemy aircraft diving out of control, which had struck our rear turret. I sent everyone into the nose of the aircraft to keep it down. I got no reply when I called up the rear gunner, so I sent the wireless operator back to see what had happened to him. He told me that the whole of the rear turret had gone. He looked straight through the hole where the turret had been and saw an enemy fighter coming up to attack; he told me so. It wasn't too good, because we couldn't take any evasive action. We had been knocked about too much for that. There was a rattle like hail and cannon shells ricocheted off the fuselage in every direction. The enemy made three attacks in all. Cannon shells burst along the whole length of the fuselage, inside and out. The front turret and the mid-upper turret were both put out of action, so we had nothing to hit back with. But then the night fighter left us; I suppose he had used up all his ammunition.

Most of our flying controls were shot away, so there wasn't much I could do with the aircraft and practically all I had left were the four engines and – as the last resort – the dinghy. But all the time the wireless operator was signalling base. I headed out to sea, steadily losing height. I put it up to the crew whether to bale out over enemy territory or paddle home. They were all for paddling. The navigator kept on working out our position right up to the last moment, so that when we did hit the sea we could send off a message with our exact position in it. I'm sure that this is one of the things that saved our lives.

Col's account of the few minutes before impact continues:

When afterwards we looked at the rear of the armour plating, it was pitted and dented, while the fuselage looked like a colander. All this time I had been struggling to make Gee [navigation device] go; no joy at all, right from the target. Eric asked me where we were, and I told him we were over the coast. That was a line, but what was the use of adding to his difficulties? I knew we were a good 10 miles inside Holland. At this stage, after the attack by the fighter, we had no flying controls at all, only the four engines, which by the mercy of God were not hit at all. Eric asked us if we wanted to bale out, but Paddy Martin replied for all of us when he said 'bugger that. Home for us.' Then we saw the coast coming up and got hit again. We were all cooped up in the relatively confined space between the armour-plating doors and the pilots' seats; and I know that for my part I was just waiting for the floor under us to be hit. For some strange reason it wasn't, though it was literally the only part that wasn't.

We crossed the coast and Eric thought that possibly we might make England and bale out there. We were all in favour of that. If only we could make England, baling out would be nothing. But we didn't. The compasses had been shot away, but for some strange reason the repeaters [compass indicators] still jerked around. When Eric saw that movement, he followed his repeater. It led him round in a circle. We flew over the enemy coast again. I did not notice because I was desperately trying to get the [Gee, radio position-fixing] box to go, our need of it was so great. But I looked up and there, the moon was ahead of us, instead of being behind – Eric noticed it at the same time, so out we went to sea again. We had barely made the complete circle before we noticed, but each mile was precious. I can remember the pilot calling to himself, or to the machine, 'come on Tommy,' (the machine was T for Tommy) 'you have never let me down before. Don't let me down now.'

The time has come to say something about Geoff [wireless operator]. I don't think a man deserved a gong [medal] more. When we were struck by the Wimpy, Geoff was in the mid-upper and was thrown violently against the top of the turret, receiving bad concussion. He was also wounded in the arm by shrapnel. But throughout, he coped. His set was broken; his trailing aerial was shot away. He mended one and replaced the other. From the time he was told to send out an S.O.S. and get a fix from Hull, he stuck to his set. He not only got a fix, carried out the necessary S.O.S. procedure, but he sent the full account of our adventures. He never weakened.

Just about the time that Geoff got his fix the Gee picked up again. And I managed to get a fix, but the set was spasmodic – had been, in fact, all the way from the target. Moreover, I think that the set was damaged in some way in the battering we received. None the less, the fix I got agreed to within eight miles of the fix Geoff got, so they more or less tallied. When we had got some 12-20 miles out to sea, and the kite was simply staggering through the sky, Eric finally decided that we could not make it. He told us he would have to come down in the sea. That the machine could have flown in that condition was a miracle. The only thing that was not shot up were the four engines. The pilot had to fly the half-out-of-control, 23-ton machine solely by the throttles. He had no other controls – they had all gone – and he brought her down in the sea like that. He will get a DFM [Distinguished Flying Medal] for it as sure as God made little apples. He is only 23 years old, but no-one could have done a better job.

Curiously enough, I was more relieved than anything else. It seemed an end from one period of uncertainty and terrific tension, after which anything was a relief, and a welcome relief. As soon as Eric had made his decision, the crew went to work. It was good crew drill and each man knew exactly what to do. I can say that with more force, as I was not a regular member of the crew, Maurice White (afterwards Squadron Bombing Leader at Lakenheath) was the regular navigator. The pilots' escape hatch [in the cockpit canopy, above the pilot's seat] was opened by Paddy Martin, or Bob Shields, I am not sure which; Paddy opened the top escape hatch [just behind the aerial mast, aft of the cockpit] and got the ladder down. Both Paddy and I made sure that the front escape hatch [just behind the bomb aimer's position on the 'chin' of the aircraft] was closed properly – bloody necessary, because if that were forced open the nose would not rise again if the kite did not land level – and either Paddy or I opened the astrodome [mid-ships, above the wings].

Whitney on BBC again:

When we were well out to sea and still coming down gradually I told the crew to take up dinghy positions and prepare to crash-land on the sea. The front gunner opened the escape hatch and threw out the ladder. Then he took up his position by the dinghy release handle. Just before we crashed we all grabbed hold tight. Everything the crew did worked wonderfully, and so did the drill. After we had hit the water we all got into the dinghy without getting any more than our feet wet. We started a log of the dinghy's voyage. The navigator wrote down: 0315 landing, 0330 set course for base. We reckoned that with the wind and the drift we could get back to England in 60 hours if we weren't picked up before.

Col:

Then we took our places for landing. Bob, Paddy and I got our backs against the draught-proof door and our feet against the rear main spar, Bob and I on the starboard side and Paddy on the port, where he could be near the dinghy release cable. Eric turned the kite back into the moon and used the path of the moon on the water as a flare path. After what seemed like an hour of waiting we landed. I remember thinking that the impact was much slighter than I had anticipated. I had imagined that the crash would be awful. Actually, it was pretty bad; but when I had a nasty feeling that this must be the end, it was over. Bob Shields fell on top of me and hurt his ankle; but that was all. When Eric was about to ditch, the machine had a bank of about 30 degrees to starboard. Just before impact, he managed to reduce the bank to some 5 degrees, so that the starboard wingtip struck first. The impact slewed the kite round through 180 deg; but the wing held. Only the extreme tip was broken.

As soon as we struck, water came in and swilled round our seats. Some came through the holes in the floor of the fuselage; but some cascaded from on top, I deduce from the top escape hatch. I think the nose must have gone down and under the water, letting the water come over along the top of the fuselage; but of that I'm not sure. As soon as the kite stopped jumping about we were on our feet and at the foot of the escape hatch ladder. Paddy, Bob and Geoff and I were there. I remember vividly that we all stood aside waiting for each other to go first. I forget who actually did, but I know someone out on top tried to help Geoff Cheek out. Poor old Geoff. I don't think that anyone realised how bad he was until then. He tried to get up the ladder, but fell back, hitting the left side of his mouth on the side of the ladder, cutting it rather nastily.

We all helped him out, and I remember as I got out how nice the dinghy looked sitting there behind the wing, and how damn lucky we were that it had not been holed. Then I had an awful thought. Did not see Eric and thought he was unconscious in his seat. Dreaded the thought of going back to look for him but thought that someone should. Then saw him. He had got out of his own escape hatch. We all got in – but before that I looked along the fuselage and saw the wreck that had been an aeroplane, but still flew. Every 2ft 6" [76 centimetres] was a cannon shell hole and in-between were the marks of .303 bullets. I have said that the floor was nearly as much hole as whole and that is not an exaggeration.

We all got in and cast off. The first thing we did was to paddle round to the rear to see if we could see anything of poor old Keith. There was not a sign – no bloodstains, nothing. But I go too fast. We were in a hell of a hurry to abandon old 'T' Tommy, because the only other Stirling ditched had floated for 90 seconds. We were working on that basis. Why it floated longer I don't know, because the fuselage was a mass of holes; but this much may be said: there was no rear turret thus lessening the weight aft and the tanks were nearly empty, giving added buoyancy to the area presenting the greatest surface to the sea. Anyway, we saw the old hull silhouetted against the moon track for two hours after we landed. The dinghy floated up over the trailing edge of the wing, which was submerged. We all clambered in; and I got my flying boots full of water. I was the last in and Paddy broke us adrift.

The British Air Ministry's official flying manual for pilots and flight engineers of Stirlings contained a detailed section on emergency procedures, in which it listed the items the crew should have found in the dinghy as they paddled off into the night: 28 tins of water, seven tins of emergency supply rations; one Very (flare) pistol – 1-inch bore, plus 18 tins of cartridges (these were missing from their dinghy); three fluorescine sea markers (dye to spread in the water); one first aid outfit; one sponge; two paddles; one mast aerial and flag; two tins of matches   Col's account continues:

We came down at 03.15 in the morning and we set a course by the pole star for England. I made a rough log, and the entries were: 0315 landed; 0330, set course for base. We steered north-west and we did not care a damn what part of England we were going to hit. The sea was warm and calm, so we were not very uncomfortable. We paddled hard to get away from the vicinity of the aircraft, because we thought she might just have been seen to come down. When we had put about two miles between it and us, we set about organising ourselves. Two of us paddled and three rested. Decided to paddle in 15-minute spells and to adhere to that. Eric put in the water purification tablets so that the water would be ready when needed. Then he rested. We also made Geoff rest because, though he protested, he was not fit. Eric went to sleep and Bob, Paddy and I paddled.

We steered NW by the Pole Star, making about 2 mph. We decided that the wind was more or less with us. Keeping up like that, we continued until 9 am, when we decided to halt for breakfast. We sang a little, but not until day came. We knew we were not far from the enemy coast, so we wanted to put as much distance between us and the coast as possible by daylight. The stars paled and gradually the sun came up. It was a lovely day and we reckoned that, since the wireless operator had sent over to our base our position when we landed, that we had a fair chance of being picked up. If we weren't, we reckoned on making England in 60 hours.

We investigated the rations – hard biscuits, thirst-making and unpalatable food cubes. We munched a biscuit, but divided the rations on the assumption that we would be 60 hours in the dinghy, by which time we counted on being home. We had a cigarette – I had none, but the others did – though they were wet, how good they tasted. Then we started again, 15 mins on; 15 mins off. We concluded that we could not be rescued before noon, because it would take that long for base to get organized. We counted on Jock Watt [Col's regular skipper] coming. To digress, actually he did – and that against orders. He was told he couldn't so he said he was going air testing – and ordered his crew to wear Mae Wests [life jackets]!

In February 2008 the son of Stan Galloway, one of Col's former crew-mates, sent me an excerpt from his father's scrapbook. It recounts what happened that day in the words of Al Shoreman, one of Jock Watt's other regular crew members, as they flew out in search of Eric Whitney's missing crew. I had tracked down Shoreman and Galloway with the help of the 149 Squadron Association. In response to the letters I sent to the addresses the association provided, I received an email from the son, Gordon Galloway, in November 2007, explaining that his father had died just that week. Al Shoreman's daughter, Jan Burke, however, phoned from England to say her father was still alive, though in 24-hour care and unable to recall events with any predictability. Col flew 13 operations with Shoreman, including the first thousand-bomber raid on Cologne in May 1942, also with Jock Watt as skipper.

Recalling this aerial search many years later, Shoreman got Colwyn Jones's name wrong, remembering him as 'Colin Davies'. Shoreman's logbook records a 'navigational flying test' in Stirling 'V' Victor, piloted by Watt, taking off from Lakenheath just after midday on 6 June – while Col's dinghy was still adrift in the Channel. Shoreman's account, written years later and pasted into Stan Galloway's scrapbook, brought his part in this episode to life. Jumping on board their Stirling, Watt's crew – supplemented by the crew's mascot, a dog named 'Section Officer Archibald', that was invariably the first to welcome the crew on its return from operations – defied orders and headed out to sea:

On the night that Eric Whitney ditched, our aircraft skippered by S/Ldr Jock Watt was the last home. Colin Davies, a New Zealand bomb aimer [and] the replacement on our crew, was flying in that aircraft. We were so fond of Colin that in no time we were so eager to go out again on a search and rescue mission. Geoffrey Cheek had radioed the position some 10 miles from the Dutch coast, so without waiting for permission and with two volunteers from dispersal [ground crew] the aircraft was refuelled. Up front and standing next to Jock Watt was Section Officer Archibald and as Jock was a law unto himself, authorisation didn't exist as far as he was concerned, no record exists about this detail, and as log books were not sacrosanct in those days I have no record of when this operation was carried out. What I recall most vividly is commencing our search by overflying the Dutch coast then carrying out at zero feet our blanket search. Although we did not sight the dinghy a Sea Otter did. Eric Whitney and Colin Davies [Colwyn Jones] were awarded DFCs [Distinguished Flying Crosses] and Geoffrey Cheek the DFM.

But by the time Watt, Shoreman and their crew returned to base around 1 p.m. on 6 June, the five men in the inflatable dinghy had been given the first reliable hope that they might be rescued, as Col's written account explains:

At 10.30 we stopped and took off our wet clothes, hanging them on the side to dry. Fortunately the day was hot and sunny, so we were not cold. Had another smoke and on again. We also heard heavy gunfire from the French coast. It afterwards transpired that there was a heavy sweep over France that morning, which personally I think accounted for no Jerry planes coming out. There was a good deal of haze about, so visibility was not too good. Then we all heard a sound. Yes! It was the sound of an aeroplane and coming from the English side. Gosh we were frightened to breathe. No luck. It did not see us and we never saw it either. Well, we just set to and kept paddling on. We heard planes three times that morning. One of us would hear one first, and I can still see the look of concentration on the faces of the others as we listened – and hoped. But they never saw us. By 12.30 we thought that they had searched for us and must have reported failure. It was not a very pleasant thought but we did not give up hope. We reckoned we could make it.

Anyway, when noon came and went we began to paddle with new

earnestness, hoping to put as much distance between us and the enemy coast. I forgot to say that several times during the morning we tried to set off the distress signals, but they would not work. We forgot the Very pistol and cartridges. About this time, we hung the green stain stuff over the side so as to show where we were drifting if any plane happened to see the trail in the water. We had also had the sail up for some hours by this time. Then, at 1 pm, we heard another plane. The noise of the engines became louder – and louder. He saw us, and we him. We all waved like madmen. For a moment we wondered, feeling so damn small. Then he altered course. We knew we had been seen. Eric, who had been so capable up to that time, so confident, so calm, buried his head in his arms on the side of the dinghy and cried like a child – aftermath of strain.

The Beaufighter flew over us; the pilot waved. He made a wide turn, put down his wheels and flaps to lessen speed and 'bombed' us with a haversack of provisions. The bag broke open and out popped a small package within stretching distance of the dinghy. The package was a tin of 50 Gold Flake [cigarettes]. We knew we were saved and that our actual rescue was only a matter of time. We all had a good deep drink of water.

On the BBC almost two weeks later Whitney elaborated: 'At one o'clock a Beaufighter spotted us and dropped supplies. The supplies came down so close that we were all splashed. The front gunner said "Very good bombing!" and it was, for all we had to do was to lean out and pick up the package. Then we just relaxed, because we knew we would be picked up.'

Col again:

The 'Beau' circled us for a while presumably to send our position back and then off he flew. I have never felt so happy in my life. We just sang and laughed at nothing at all, and talked the most ridiculous nonsense. We waited on and on, because we knew that he would send back our position to his base and that our rescue was assured. The only thing was that we thought that Jerry fighters might find us and use us as live bait target practice. Still, that did not happen.

After that we all relaxed and had a good sleep. Time went by, hour after hour, until I began to wonder what had happened. Then we heard engines.

Out of the sun darted six Spitfires. They dived on us and waved to us and circled and kept circling until the rescue launch loomed out of the distance and we knew we were safe. Picked up at 4 pm; 13 hours in the dinghy.

Whitney:

At four o'clock we heard planes again and saw six Spitfires. Four of them circled around us and the other two went back to guide the air sea rescue people to us. Then, at ten past four, we saw a small spot on the horizon. It came nearer and turned into a cloud of fast-moving spray. In a moment or two the air sea rescue craft came alongside us and stopped. We all climbed in. They treated us very well. They were the kindest chaps imaginable and we were very glad to see them…. All the way back the Spitfires circled around us. Then we saw white cliffs ahead and we knew we were nearly home. When we landed no-one could do enough for us; they treated us like lords.

Col:

Again hard to describe our relief and thankfulness. They gave us tea laced with rum. I went to bed. Landed Ramsgate; tea at the naval mess – boiled egg. Taken to Manston [airfield, Kent]; slept in the sick bay; wonderful treatment; corker food – eggs and bacon. Flight Wing-Co Charlton-Jones flew down the next day and took us home. Party in the mess; week's leave. Boy o Boy!

No-one would believe us when we said we saw butterflies in the dinghy. Fact, though!

Whitney's logbook is held by the RAF Museum in Hendon, north-west London. The pages relating to that escapade are sparse on detail: 'Crew F/Sgt Jones. Operations Essen – 24x90x4 incendiaries. Hit by Wellington. Rear turret & gunner missing. Hit by flak inside aircraft. Attacked three times by night fighter. Landed in sea. 13 hours in dinghy. Picked up by high speed launch.' Attached to the logbook is a photograph of the five crew pulling the dinghy alongside the launch. Prints of this same photo and one of Col boarding the rescue craft were sent home to New Zealand in Col's photo album after his death.

As far as I could determine, Col was the only other crew member of 'T' Tommy that night who did not survive the war. The same scrapbook page that carried Al Shoreman's recollection of Watt's 'illicit' search for Col also has a brief note, undated but clearly some years after the war, from Eric Whitney in Warwick. The small item in the scrapbook conveys Whitney's best wishes to a gathering of the Goldfish Club of former airmen who had also survived a crash landing in water. It says: 'I was pilot and captain of 'T' Tommy, a Stirling of 149 Squadron Lakenheath and "ditched" 03.15 5/6th June 1942. We were picked up by an HSL (high speed launch) from Ramsgate at 16.05 hrs. 6/6/42. The crew was under the command of F/Sgt Roberts and they did us proud. Thank them for my life, and I wish you all, all that you wish yourselves. Yours sincerely, ERIC WHITNEY, Bilton Cottage, Oxhill, Warwick.'

The aircraft that sheared off 'T' Tommy's rear turret, killing 21-year-old Sergeant Keith 'Moonbeam' Roderick, was not a Vickers Wellington bomber, as the crew had initially thought, but a Messerschmitt ME110 night fighter. Its pilot, Oberleutnant Petersen, and radio operator parachuted to safety.[5] Roderick's body was later washed ashore on the French coast and is buried at Langemarck, Belgium. On the night he died his crew must have reflected, as they too were carried by the tide, how close they had come to joining him. I imagine them looking back in awe at 'T' Tommy's huge silhouette against the moon's path, amid the slap of paddles in a calm sea so eerily silent after the frenzy of just minutes before. Col had flown in 'T' Tommy on three previous bombing operations, never dreaming he would have its 'seaworthiness' to thank for his survival. He had left one island more than 18 months before to fight for another, and his journey to that point had been as much on the ocean as over it.

CHAPTER 3

LANDFALL

ALWAYS THE SEA. When Col left Auckland on the Union Steamship Company vessel *Awatea* for wartime service in November 1940, he had just finished documenting in meticulous detail the building of several Maori war canoes, or waka, to mark New Zealand's centenary celebrations in 1940. He had been asked to do so by the Maori princess, Te Puea Herangi, whom Col had come to know while researching his MA thesis on the impact of the missionaries on Maori social life.[1] Col was by then at the *Auckland Star*, having joined the staff in 1929. According to Maori spiritual tradition, as a woman Princess Te Puea could not be involved in the building of these waka, so she asked Col to be her eyes in the bush, to chronicle this massive undertaking of felling the giant totara and kauri trees and dragging them through dense tracts of forest to where they could be hewn, carved and bound into war-like form.

By November 1939, just three months before the centenary celebrations, only two of the six waka had been completed. Col's narrative of this back-breaking, inspiring project was among the unexpected discoveries I made in 2007 as I sifted through the suitcase full of documents and photographs that contained the remnants of Col's life. In his manuscript, Col noted the importance of the seven main canoes of the initial Polynesian migration to New Zealand centuries before: 'The craft have been personified until the canoes rather than their crews are counted as ancestors. So intimately are these canoes interwoven with the legend, tradition and proven history of the people that, to a nomadic people, they have come to mean something the same as the Royal Navy to Britishers.'[2] With the canoes unfinished, the manuscript remained unpublished as he sailed back in the direction from which the waka of the original Great Migration had come. But Te Puea and Col had formed a bond during the waka project, which she acknowledged by giving him a greenstone tiki (neck pendant), with the words 'This must return to the tribe'. This treasure, posted to Col in 1941 at his final training base in Scotland, sat unclaimed for weeks because the mail clerk there failed to tell him it had arrived. Col was probably wearing it the night he died, as it was not among his belongings returned to New Zealand.

Frank Colwyn Jones was born in Auckland on 21 April 1908, the second of three children of Frank and Emma Jones, who had both endured the four-month trip from London to New Zealand by sailing ship, she in 1874, he in 1898. The children grew up on Northcote Point, linked to Auckland city only by ferries until the Auckland Harbour Bridge was built alongside it in the late 1950s. Col and his two sisters, Florence and Gwen, spent a childhood roaming the expanse of two wide, tidal bays on the Waitemata Harbour and playing among the pohutukawa trees clinging to the Northcote cliffs. The young Frank – Colwyn or Col to his family and friends – did well at Northcote Primary School and then at Auckland Grammar School in the mid-1920s. Active in many sports, he played wing for the First XV team that won the Auckland schoolboys rugby championship in 1926.

His mother, the fifth of 11 children, was an avid reader, but had been forced to end her formal education at 12, when her parents took her out of school to help look after her six younger siblings. She was determined her children would have the chance she was denied of a good education. Col fulfilled those hopes by earning a Diploma of Journalism in 1930, graduating Bachelor of Arts in 1932, then in 1935 completing a Master of Arts degree part-time while working as a journalist.

By the mid-1930s Col's father, Frank Jones senior, had lost his job as a publishing company executive in a boardroom struggle and left his family to move to Taranaki, breaking off contact. With money tight, Col and his elder sister, Florence ('Lass') supported their mother, Col living with her in Mission Bay and Remuera and paying the bills from his reporter's wages, which rose from £7 to £32 a month during the 11 years he worked his way up the ladder at the *Auckland Star*. From Auckland Grammar and university sprang a close circle of friends, several of whom also died in the war. Among the others, some rose to the top of their professions, including a later headmaster of Auckland Grammar, Henry Cooper, and Martin Sullivan, who became Dean of St Paul's, London, in the 1960s.

Since overseas travel from New Zealand was then both much more expensive and more difficult than it is today, Col thought he might as well be paid for the privilege. In the early 1930s he covered the Governor-General, Viscount Bledisloe's, Pacific tour for the New Zealand Press Association, an experience that encouraged him to apply for the Colonial Service. He missed out. But then came war. He was already a territorial (reserve soldier) in the intelligence section of the army's 1st Battalion, Auckland Regiment when he applied for the Royal New Zealand Air Force (RNZAF) in December 1939. Then 31, he was already a good 10 years older than most of the RAF crew he later flew with. By September 1940 he had begun basic training at Levin, north of Wellington. He had resigned as financial editor of the *Auckland Star* to enlist, knowing he might not return, but judging the risk worth it for the cause: the survival of the land from which his parents had emigrated the century before. As was so typical of New Zealanders of his generation, he was fiercely loyal to the Crown and wanted to prove himself worthy of the empire to which the Dominion of New Zealand belonged.

Col left Canada to cross the Atlantic for Britain in May 1941. Six months earlier he had spent three weeks aboard *Awatea* crossing the Pacific via Suva and Pearl Harbor to reach Vancouver in November 1940. He then made his way by train over the frozen Rockies and spent five bitterly cold winter months completing training as a navigator and bomb aimer at Ontario and Manitoba. Here the vastness of the Canadian landscape – 'miles of flat dam' all' – was mirrored by expansive night skies washed with the magical play of the Aurora Borealis, the Northern Lights. Some close friendships with other New Zealanders began here and ended only with their death in war. Col also wrote of the Anzac spirit they shared with the many Australians training alongside them – a bond tested during fiercely contested 'friendly' rugby games played between the runways, first in Canada, later in England.

Soon after his ship's convoy sailed from Halifax in May 1941, Col got his first taste of war. The German U-boat menace was then at its peak. The mighty battleship *Bismarck* was roaming the Atlantic and had just sunk the Royal Navy's biggest battleship, *Hood*. Elsewhere, too, the British Empire was being overwhelmed by the German onslaught. London had weathered the storm of the Blitz, but Col embarked for Britain knowing Anzac and British troops had been driven out of Greece and were making a desperate stand against German paratroopers on the island of Crete. Against this bleak backdrop he began a letter home on 24 May 1941 describing his crossing:

We left Halifax a little over a week ago – I had better not mention any dates – and after a little time on board sailed. Other ships in the convoy had started earlier to go down the harbour, but we picked them up, and began the long journey. We go as slowly as the slowest ship, and believe me that is slow, because some of the ships are as aged as the ark and look something like it. Looking back, I remember that I have written letters from queer places, but none queerer than this. Here we are, in the middle of a convoy, with ships on either side of us and behind us and ahead, and all we can see is precisely – nothing. Ever since we left Halifax we have had little but fog. Visibility is about 50 yards, and we can't see the nearest boat. All we can see is grey, swirling swathes of mist, clammy and heavy, so heavy it is almost rain. As I write I can hear the hoarse, anxious cry of the ship's sirens, answered by other calls from other ships. The boat, indeed the whole convoy, has the strictest blackout regulations. If you go on deck when it is dark, it is impossible to see your hand before your face, and if you go far from the door out of which you came it is dam' hard to find it again.

We have learned a lot about fog. Almost as soon as we left we ran into the beginnings of fog, and until yesterday CENSORED we were never quite free of it. For a considerable time – some days in fact – we could not see anything at all. All we heard for hours and hours on end was the hoarse bellow of ships' sirens. That must have been how they kept contact. We must have been somewhere near the CENSORED to have had fog. Everything was wet, including our spirits. Then yesterday we got up to find that the weather had cleared. What a thrill! We could see the ships which had been only noisy ghosts for the past few days. We examined them closely, as though they had been new-found friends. We have speculated what cargo they are carrying. We don't know, though in a few cases the deck cargo is discernible. They are all low in the water, though, as though there was no empty space on board.

We heard with interest last night of the battle off Greenland. Wasn't it a terrible thing to lose the *Hood*, the largest battleship afloat? Then we remembered that Greenland is not a deuce of a long way from where we were at the time. We have followed with added interest the attempts to catch and destroy the *Bismarck* and her escort. We have heard nothing definite yet; but we don't expect they will come our way. We hope not. The Atlantic looks too cold to go messing about in a boat for hours. I'm comfortable where I am, thanks very much. We have since heard that the *Bismarck* was sunk – dam' good job too.

Thursday 29th May. Whenever the news is broadcast, there is always a large group round the wireless, seamen and airmen alike. Everyone is vitally interested. We are having a struggle for Crete, aren't we, and Crete seems to be very important for our position in the eastern Mediterranean. The Captain told us this morning that we would be going straight to England. He also told us that our course since hearing of the naval battle near Greenland was like a dog's hind leg – that we had cruised all over the place out of the way of that locality. You ought to have heard the cheers that went up when it was learned that we had sunk the *Bismarck*. It seemed an eye for an eye after losing the *Hood*. Still, our losses in the Mediterranean since then have been heavy. I hope we can fix the Nazis in Crete.

A few days later. We are in the danger zone proper now, and our escort seems to have an added caution. We are said to be within the range of the German Stuka dive bombers, while we have been within range of submarines for some considerable time. To look over the side, however, I find it hard to realise that there can possibly be any danger. The sea is as calm as a millpond – has been all the way, in fact.

A day or two ago we had an obstacle race on board. We had to tear all over the place, through lifebelts, up ropes, down ropes, under little, narrow hurdles, along a spar, up planks made greasy with soap – in fact into all sorts of queer places. There were 16 teams of four members entered, and our team won. It was a gruelling race; but we won, so that was a good thing. There was a lot of excitement during which everyone crowded round the course and cheered. I was an entrant, and I shall never enter another one. I was stiff and sore for days – still am, in fact. Our team won a prize of £1, which we divided, thus adding the princely sum of 5/- to the exchequer. We have a picture tonight – 'Wells Fargo' – which I shall attend. Anything for a break, you know. Honestly, there is nothing more to say, so I shall end this letter and write to you as soon as we have landed. Give my love to everyone, and tell them that we have endured the Battle of the Atlantic with complete success.

On arriving in Britain, Col was posted to Lossiemouth, on Scotland's Firth of Moray, to an operational training unit for final instruction as aircrew. During these four months he spent each leave in London, where he explored a city battered but not beaten. Amid the Blitz damage, he encountered a fighting spirit that primed his own determination to strike back at Germany. He described his feelings in a letter written on 12 June 1941 to his mother, who had lived there as a small child.

I have stood and watched the life of London flow past. I felt that I had come home. I felt that I belonged here. This was part of me. It must be part of all those who are proud to realise that they are British. They are a wonderful people, Mother, a wonderful people. I have seen them mending the roads, I have seen the people skirt the gaping holes in the road. I have seen the quaint signs in the windows: 'Our windows are smashed; but that's nothing to the smash in our prices.' I have seen afternoon teas served on the pavement because the interior of the tea-shop was hardly presentable. I have seen the stained and blackened ruins of many buildings. I have seen the twisted iron girders, the rubble that once was walls. I have seen one side of a wall shorn away, disclosing a bed and a table, and a towel over the chair. All this I have seen – but I never heard a word of complaint, never a word of bitterness, never more than a passing, light reference to the bomb damage. They are a wonderful people.

I have seen the people sleeping in the tube stations and it is scarcely credible, hundreds of them, lying side by side like sardines in a tin; men, women and children. Some of them had air-inflated full length cushions; but others simply put down a piece of paper over the hard concrete. You had to step over rows of sleeping bodies to get to the train. Apparently the rights of property are coming to be enforced there. Each person has his or her place, and if anyone happens to bag it, there is the devil to pay. We passed two old buffers who were sitting on the stairs. The same two were there on three nights. They were smoking foul-looking pipes, and despite the fact that hundreds of people passed between them as they sat on either side of the stairs, their conversation was in no way interrupted. As they sat, all they could see from their level was an unending passage of trousered and skirted legs, like a forest of human trees. They just talked on through the tree-trunk legs.

There were three of us, all Aucklanders. Gordon Harrowby, Percy Stewart and me, and between us we remembered enough of the famous places to fill in about two hours. It is not permissible to say much about the bomb damage; suffice it to say that though it is apparent and bad in parts, it is not bad when the size and unconcerned life of London is measured against it. But it made everyone who saw it fiercely eager someday – and not long now, perhaps – to repay it sevenfold. If the people had moaned about their loss it might not have been so bad. But they didn't. They hardly mentioned it. It seemed such a shocking, needless and brutal thing. Still, we have done the same to Germany, and as time goes on we will do more and more.

We went to the Abbey and to the Houses of Parliament. It is not possible to see much of the Abbey because a bomb struck part of it. But we saw the Tomb of the Unknown Soldier – 'They buried him among the Kings because he had done good towards God and towards His House.' It is impossible to speak coherently of one's feelings at being there. They were so chaotic, so overwhelming. But I knew a deep pride that I was British, and before I left I went towards the altar in the same hall as the Unknown Soldier lies and I prayed. I am not given to praying, as you know. Nor am I religious in the accepted sense; but there was something that needed expression. I did not ask that we should win the war, but simply that this place, which of all others is the greatness of England, might be spared. We all felt the same. None of us had much to say when he came out. We went past St. Margaret's Church and there opposite, or nearly opposite, was Big Ben and the Houses of Parliament. As I left I said to myself that I had been inside the Mother of Parliaments. We gave the world a parliament, you know; and if Britain fell tomorrow the fact that she has done even that much would make her the greatest of nations.

When Col wrote this letter Britain was at the low point of its war – alone and being pushed back on every front. Crete fell to the German paratrooper assault in late May 1941. Then on Sunday 22 June, less than two weeks after Col sent off this letter, Germany made a crucial mistake: it attacked the Soviet Union, providing Britain with vital breathing space and thrusting into its arms a huge ally in the fight for survival against the Third Reich. By the end of 1941 the United States, too, was pulled into the conflict on Britain's side when, after Japan's surprise attack on the American naval base at Pearl Harbor on 7 December, Germany quickly joined its Axis partner and declared war on the United States. Thus within six months Germany had decisively tipped the military balance against itself. Although the Japanese military tsunami had yet to break on Pacific shores by the time Col next wrote to his mother, in late July 1941, he saw new hope for Britain:

I have been to London again. We got a week's unexpected leave and three of us made the most of it. The Luftwaffe has been leaving England alone since the Russian affair began, so I have not seen an air raid. I don't want to see one either. It is a good thing that London has had a respite. By Jove, haven't the Russians been putting up a good show. Nearly everyone here has been surprised; and the better the show they put up, the better for us, for we are striking hard every day and night at Germany in the air, and doing tremendous damage.

What interests me at the minute, though, is what Japan is going to do. If her fleet moves down towards the Dutch East Indies, there will be war, and the USA will come in. I am convinced of that; and I think America is preparing for that contingency. We can deal with Japan all right. Russia seems to be holding Hitler up. Good. We are giving Germany hell with the lid off every night and have been doing so for the past month. Good again. We are getting some of our own back.

In October 1941, nearly a year after leaving Auckland, Col completed training as an observer – a combination of navigator and bomb aimer. From Lossiemouth he was posted to Mildenhall, northeast of Cambridge, to begin operations with 149 Squadron. Already, however, the risks he was about to face had been brought home to him by the loss of a friend he had trained with since boot camp in New Zealand, and with whom he had spent his early leaves in London. He wrote about this to his mother on 25 November 1941.

I learned today that a great friend of mine, one of the lads who trained at Levin and in Canada with me, has gone. He went missing [en route to] Berlin and nothing has been heard of him since. There is a chance that he may be a prisoner, but it is a slender chance. His name was Gordon Harrowby. We were together nearly all the time in Canada and all the time at Lossiemouth and we used to spend our leaves together. Gordon was a hell of a fine chap – quiet, sincere, steady and determined as well as being a first class navigator. I know that because I used to fly with him in Canada. I used to call him the 'fat boy' because he was always eating and always hungry. He always had money because he was careful with it, and when I ran short at the end of leave, Gordon would always have some and would always hand it over. He was generous to a fault. I rather miss him. When I tell you that Gordon has gone, don't think that I'm in any danger of going. I'm not. I have a feeling about this war. If I was going to be killed in any accident, I have had plenty of chances, as you know. Remember the time I fell from the tree in Birkenhead?

Of the three Aucklanders who explored London together on those early leaves only one, Percy Stewart, survived the war.

At Mildenhall, Col became firm friends with Barry Martin, another observer he had known since they were mustered together in Levin. This friendship carried them through many of the highs and lows of 1942, and seems also to have influenced Col to return to operations after he completed his first tour and was transferred to non-combat duties. How this camaraderie between two young New Zealanders took root in English soil, so far from the land of their birth, is a story of both discovery and shared action. My journey to understand theirs brought me through the gauzy gloom of an autumn day in 2007 to the gates of the first two airbases that had launched them into the darkness to bomb Germany.

CHAPTER 4

HOME BASES

THE HEART OF BRITAIN'S bomber fightback against Germany was once a bog – but a bog with a proud history of resistance to invaders. After the Norman Conquest in 1066, a band of Anglo-Saxon rebels led by Hereward the Wake waged a guerrilla war against the invaders from a base in the surrounding marshlands. This tidal, partly swampy terrain gave him plenty of room to range freely. It once stretched from the Wash, above the elephant's ear of the Norfolk coast, to west of Cambridge, but the fens had been drained between the 17th and 19th centuries to increase the area of land for cultivation.

It was into the middle of this huge, dried-up puddle that Col Jones and Barry Martin arrived in the autumn of 1941, when the threat of German invasion had abated but the progress of the war was still against Britain. Their airbases were action stations from which Col flew three dozen bombing operations over enemy territory. But they also launched him on many exploratory visits throughout England on a journey of kinship that coloured his experience of war – his sense of what he was fighting for – just as strongly as trading destruction with the enemy. Col ranged widely across Suffolk and Norfolk on a bike bought with a £10 birthday gift from his mother, until it was stolen from his base. He wrote many letters home about the discoveries he made in the old villages and castle and abbey ruins, and almost as many describing the pubs and their quaint regulars visited along the way. I was curious to discover what remained of these bases more than 60 years later, to see what remnants of Col's time there I might find, and whether any sense of 'Fortress Britain' he described so evocatively still lingered.

Long before Hereward the Wake, since at least the Iron Age, others had lived and fought in this area. In 1997, excavations for the foundations of a dormitory at the United States Air Force base of Lakenheath unearthed the intact remains of a Saxon horseman and his charge. Underneath what had been the most recent occupants' softball pitch, careful sifting by archaeologists also freed the remains of some 270 Anglo-Saxon burials, contributing to a rich haul from that vicinity of weapons and jewellery dating from between the fifth and seventh centuries AD. Other finds revealed evidence of human settlement from prehistoric times, the Iron Age Celts around 300 BC, Roman occupation through to early medieval settlements during the sixth to ninth centuries AD.[1]

Col's and Barry's first two bases in Suffolk, Mildenhall and nearby Lakenheath, were smack in the middle not only of an historical treasure trove but also a growing hive of Allied airfields. By 1945 these numbered some 670 in Britain, of which 120 were Bomber Command airfields, almost all in the east. This was a springboard of staggering proportions for striking back at an enemy massed just across the water, but Col hardly seemed impressed when he wrote to his mother in April 1942 about Lakenheath:

Though Mildenhall was in the centre of an area of rich, black earth, this dump is pure sand. I had never realised that such a place could exist in England. When the wind blows there is a regular sand storm. I think it would be a good idea if someone were to come out clad in Arab clothes and riding on a camel. We are not sure whether we have been transported to Libya or to the Sahara. The sand gets everywhere, in the food, in clothing, in our sleeping quarters and living quarters – and in our noses and ears. We are miles from anywhere; but as we have little time, that does not matter so much.

To make matters worse, his new billet was a box-like prefabricated hut – a Spartan contrast to the comforts he had enjoyed during his first few months with 149 Squadron, before it transferred from Mildenhall in February 1942. When Col wrote to his mother in January from his lodgings in a mock-Tudor manor a few miles from Mildenhall, he was soaking up some unexpected luxuries, and the prospect of starting operations seemed far from his mind:

The other night another New Zealander on the station, one Barry Martin of Christchurch, turned on a rare treat – fried oysters. He scrounged some flour from the mess, made a batter from it and some other ingredients best not mentioned or known, and fried the oysters in batter in some rancid butter. Despite the sound, they tasted grand. They reminded me somewhat painfully of the days at home when we used to go into a grill room and have lovely steak and fried oysters and stacks of bread and butter.

(Wednesday) Last night we had a marvellous supper. Barry Martin had been sent a lot of tinned stuff from home and among the tins was one of tomato sauce and another of lambs' tongues. In our room we have managed to secure a radiator and an electric hot water jug, both of them against regulations, but very handy just the same. About 9 o'clock, after we had been yarning for some two hours, the cry went round for supper. Barry Martin is something of a cook. In fact, we told him he would make a good wife some day. He heated the tomato sauce, or some of it, and into the sauce he put the tongues. Then he thickened the mixture with some flour which he had scrounged, and let it heat. Then we shared it and ate it out of cups. I have not tasted anything so delicious for a long time. Then when that was finished, we put on the hot water jug and while that was heating we made toast. I had pinched some bread from the mess, so all was well. We opened one of my tins of butter, and then in the fullness of time had hot buttered toast and cups of tea. It was very good.

True to this spirit of high living, Mildenhall has a stately cachet to its name, in contrast to many other nearby airbases with such bogworthy names as Little Snoring, Sculthorpe or Strubby. Built in the early to mid-1930s, Mildenhall's layout of well-proportioned brick buildings and spacious, tree-lined parade squares reflected the rising status of the RAF when military strategists regarded air power as a key element in the conflict many by then saw as inevitable. At

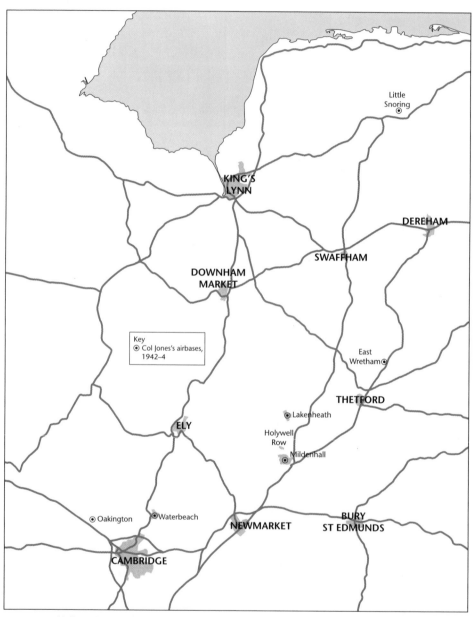

Map 1: *Suffolk and West Norfolk*

a popular level, aviators were revered for making the world seem smaller through such adventures as the 18,000-kilometre Great Air Race to Melbourne, which started from Mildenhall in October 1934, and the record-breaking England to Australia flight by New Zealand woman aviator, Jean Batten, earlier that year.

When I visited in October 2007, I was astonished by the sheer scale of the US military presence there, which had largely replaced the British soon after the war. Today Mildenhall is home to US Air Force C-130 Hercules heavy lift transporters and KC-135R four-engined air tankers, but the core of original buildings from the 1930s and 1940s – the part that interested me most – remains much as it stood seven decades earlier, and with most still in use. One addition is noteworthy: the stained glass windows in the chapel, depicting the military history of the base. When I later attended the 149 Squadron reunion at Mildenhall, in May 2008, a highlight of the remembrance service was seeing the window dedicated to the Commonwealth airmen based there during the war. It features, below a moose, a green tiki and the Maori words 'ake ake, kia kaha' (for ever and ever, be strong). Here was a piece of our past, remembering not only individual 'colonials' like Col, who flew with RAF squadrons, but also 75 (NZ) Squadron, which operated from Mildenhall in 1940–1 and again for a few months in 1942. And in a jumble of photos pulled out for me in its archive I discovered a picture of RAF ground crew loading bombs aboard Col's first Stirling, 'N' Nuts, in early 1942 – a precious find indeed.

During my first visit to Mildenhall, in 2007, I climbed its control tower to get a rough sense of what bomber crew saw as they came in to land. Despite the extent of the runways and tarmac areas, which compare in size with Stansted airport near London, Mildenhall seemed just one patch in a pancake landscape. From my vantage point, the counties of Suffolk and Cambridgeshire merged into one under an awning of puffy, cumulus cloud, the horizon undisturbed by any feature to break its natural curvature. Although the flatness denied the bomber crews the navigational landmarks they so often needed, East Anglia provided the ideal landscape for such a concentration of British and American airbases.

At Lakenheath, some 10 minutes down the road by car, I toured a sprawling complex that extended well beyond workshops, hangars, administrative buildings and dormitories to encompass housing clusters, gymnasiums, schools, a hospital – all thoroughly American down to the greenbacks used in the small shopping centre and the catfish and fried chicken I was served in the cavernous canteen at lunch. Outside, a strike force of F-15 fighter-bombers was busy on exercises, thundering through the air.

When Col and Barry arrived there from the comforts of Mildenhall at Easter 1942, Lakenheath was far from complete – just one of scores of new airbases springing up to cater for the growing strength of Bomber Command. Lakenheath was initially intended purely as a decoy field to lure German bombers away from the fully operational bases of Mildenhall and nearby Feltwell. The Germans twigged to the ruse and dropped a wooden bomb there in response, but the joke backfired on the Luftwaffe when the RAF developed Lakenheath into one of the busiest airbases in the region. Towards the end of the war it even came under consideration as a site for London's new airport, before Heathrow got the nod instead. Today Lakenheath is the biggest US military base in Britain, accommodating 12,000 personnel and families, plus 600 British personnel, and is unrecognisable as the sand-blasted wartime airfield from which Col and Barry flew most of their first tours of 30 operations.

Apart from the excitement these operations brought, leave was their release from this desert, and Col and Barry got away when they could. Early on, when they routinely spent most of these leave periods together, it was unusual for British fellow crew to invite them home on leave. As these English comrades headed off to their homes, Col felt the distance from his own family in New Zealand even more keenly. An organisation founded by Lady Frances Ryder to open the homes of Britain to 'colonial' servicemen helped to fill this gap. Col's time with a variety of generous hosts strengthened an instinctive bond he felt with England, but also cast into sharper relief the altered profile of a New Zealander one generation distant from the land of his parents. Col commented on some of these differences in a letter to his mother, after a visit with Barry to Bude, on the west coast of Cornwall, in January 1942. This was a bleak time for the British Empire, which was about to be sent reeling yet again, this time by the fall of Singapore to the Japanese:

We had no idea where we were going, and when we arrived we found that we were the guests of the headmaster of Clifton College, Bristol, one of the great public schools of England. The college was evacuated from Bristol when the bombings were at their height there. We had a wonderful time. It was an experience to live in the intimacy of an English public school, and to see the life from the inside of both masters and pupils. As independent New Zealanders, we maintained a most independent view about English social customs, education and their conduct of the war. We said that we thought that England did not understand the meaning of democracy. We added that the standard of education of the masses was deplorable, infinitely lower than in NZ – which is incontrovertibly true. It was a bit of a shock to us to hear the headmaster agreeing with us. In fact, he is something of a social reformer. The opinion we formed after being at the place a week was that what England needs is not to drag down the standard and tradition of the great public schools, but to lift other schools up to that level. We found the same sympathetic view as to the need for lifting the educational standard expressed by the housemasters, to whom we talked just as freely. One housemaster spoke about the crushing bonds of tradition. All the worst aspects of that had to be broken down, he said, before England could rise. He thought that the war would do much to help, in the long run. His wife thought the same.

One night the headmaster had the school's surgeon down as a guest. He was one of Bristol's famous surgeons, Professor Short. He piled into us over our views of the Pacific situation. We told him what we thought about the falsity and paucity of the information given to Australia and NZ as to the situation in the Far East. He did not agree with us over some aspects which we presented. We told him that while none could disagree with the broad lines of Britain's policy, we based our criticism on the fact that our countries had not been informed of the weakness of defence in the Far East. Then we had a really good argument. We said we did not think that England was getting down to the job of a war with her full potentialities.

Col had written about defence issues for the *Auckland Star* but now his criticism of the British military collapse in South East Asia also reflected a deep concern that his family in New Zealand suddenly stood in the path of the Japanese advance, while he was half a world away fighting Germany. The distance that separated them was brought home to him by frequent disruptions to mail, as each letter in either direction now had to cross a world at war. Many letters went missing or took months to arrive. Col wrote in frustration on 7 January 1942, a month after the Japanese attack on Pearl Harbor and several other targets, including Wake Island, which up until then had been a transit port for ships carrying mail to New Zealand:

I have not started this letter for some few days, as I have been trying to find out whether the state of affairs in the Pacific has made any difference to the air mail, but so far I have been unable to find out anything definite. I have written to New Zealand House to ask them, but have not yet received any reply. By the time this letter is finished, though, a reply should have come. I suppose you are a little worried just now at the initial success of the little yellow men. We do not seem to have done much, do we? – and the same is true of the Americans. But in a little time, we'll have them. You'll see. It seems to me they have been hoping to provoke the American Navy into some rash retaliatory action; but the Yanks have been wise enough to realise the lure, and to have refrained from any such action. The position in the Philippines must be worrying for the Americans; but just at the minute they are wise to be content to lose a little for the sake of winning in the end. The same is true in Malaya, though there I reckon that the British should be kicked firmly in the pants. Mr [Robert] Menzies [Australia's Prime Minister] was told by people there that Malaya was not prepared. Yet when he approached the Imperial Government, he was put off. The plain fact is that we were not prepared; and in my opinion the fact that we had to send munitions to Libya is not the complete answer. There is a considerable body of criticism over here about the position in Malaya, while what Australia thinks is plain for the world to see.

Col and Barry Martin spent another leave together in May 1942, in the lap of rural privilege north-west of Birmingham. Col described this interlude to his mother just days before his plane ditched in the English Channel:

We went to a little place in Shropshire called Mucklestone. We stayed on a farm and had a wonderfully enjoyable, quiet time. One evening, we went rook shooting. We both performed creditably with a .22 rifle, but not so well as our hostess who was a crack shot. One unfortunate incident rather spoiled the evening. Our host was shot through the leg by a small bore rifle. It was not a bad wound, and he was not greatly inconvenienced, though he had to stay in bed for a while. However, we spent the rest of the evening with the person on whose farm the wood was. We had a wonderful supper – forgive me if I seem to dwell on food, but it was so different from our mess – consisting of cheese and biscuits with plenty of butter, a home-made cake and some coffee. We enjoyed it and ate so much that I felt slightly ashamed. He had a lovely old home, which looked out over a shallow valley filled with all the greens of which spring is capable. Evening was just falling, and with the first of the shadows and the last of the sun, no greater scene of peace could have been imagined. The swallows have come. Aren't they graceful? They seem to zig-zag through the air like a dart shot from a bow. I saw one chase and catch a large blowfly. It followed the fly through each desperate turn the fly made. Finally, there was an extra sharp turn, and the swallow was on its way home.

This was Col's second trip to Shropshire that month. The first time he had arrived in a Stirling bomber – for a wedding.

The wedding was that of the navigator of the crew, whose place I have recently taken. He has finished his operational trips and has celebrated that happy event by getting married. The captain of the crew, a squadron leader, was his best man and he flew the entire crew (who had been invited to the wedding) over from our station to the little village of Church Stretton, just some 13 miles south of Shrewsbury. It was a perfect day for flying to begin with, but the really delightful part was the drive from the aerodrome to the village, a distance of some 25 miles. It led through some lovely lands, through Shrewsbury itself, past winding, lazy rivers and down some peaceful valleys. Shrewsbury, as much as I could see from the car windows as we passed, was full of old buildings, timber and plaster, and in heavy, weather-beaten stone, while winding through the middle of the city, crossed by many bridges, is a river. The day was perfect, not a cloud in the sky, not the littlest of wind, and as warm as a summer's day at home. As we came near to Church Stretton, we passed between two lines of hills into the loveliest valley I have seen in England. To begin with, the hills made it seem more like home, and then the scattered hamlets, with their tiny fields and trim hedges, with their carefully tilled fields, gave the place an atmosphere of peace. The war was far, far away.

Everywhere were trees, freshly green, with the sun glinting through them, making their leaves more yellow than green. We came to the church, passing from the yellow glare of the sun, to the quiet and peace and dimness of the ancient, Saxon church, where the only light came through the stained glass windows beyond the chancel. The church itself was a mass of spring flowers and spring green, which threw into great effect the old oak pews and the 700-year-old oaken rafters, put there by Saxon or Norman workmen, when the world was young. It was a quiet wedding, utterly peaceful, with the organ music passing gently out of the open door to the equally peaceful village street outside. We went out to wait for a car to take us up to the bride's parents' home. We stood there in the sunlight watching the gnarled old trees in the churchyard. They were nearly as old as the church, yet the spring had made them as young as the smallest child in the congregation.

Then, past ancient church and ancient trees, down the winding village street lazed a flock of sheep. They passed by the church gates; they passed the doorway of a shop selling sweets and tobacco. They stopped to nibble the odd blade of grass which grew between footpath and road. A little cloud of dust rose after them, subsided, and as their bleating grew fainter, the softness of the organ crept out again into the village peace. I thought that in this place, as at Lake Waikaremoana, was to be found 'that peace that passeth understanding'. I thought of the serenity, the happiness, the calm of such a village; and then I knew that this was something about the English life that Hitler could never break; and I knew, too, that the happiness of the couple who had just been married was what we were fighting for. I have not realised more forcibly before how much the fight was worthwhile. You would have loved it all. The serenity, the quietness, the peace. The war was not in the same world as this village, which dreamed in the afternoon's content.

Col saw himself in the people he met; the footsteps he followed were those of his kin. This process of recognition was undiminished to the end, even as personal links were severed by the death of many of his friends. His last letter to his mother, received by her after his death, evokes this love of England as strongly as any he sent home during the two and a half years he lived there. When he wrote it in February 1944, Col had just arrived at Oakington, between Cambridge and Ely, to begin a second tour of operations.

The names of the hotels, the country inns, I mean, continue to intrigue me. In Ely, for example, there is one called 'The King Charles in the Oak'. Another I saw, miles away from anywhere, was called the 'Lock and Keys'. The 'Hart and Hounds' was another. Some of them are set just in the back o' beyond. Goodness knows what they do for custom. They are thatched and tumble-down, but surprisingly warm and cosy inside. After dinner the locals come down and play the odd game of darts. Sometimes, if we drop in in the evenings, we challenge them, to their delighted amusement. These old chappies, with one foot in the grave and the other on a banana skin, who are tottery about the knees when they walk, and who seem scarcely able to see, have eyes like hawks when it comes to throwing the dart in the right place. Probably they could not multiply three by four, but they are razor-edged when it comes to adding up their score at darts.

Some of these inns are very old. In some, a tall man would have a job to stand upright, while he would certainly hit his head on one of the rafters. We went into one in the course of a cycle ride last summer in which the rafters were the original roughly squared oaken beams, black with age. I could not understand what my host was saying at all. He might honestly have been speaking a foreign language. I don't think the war has changed their way of living a bit.

I visited the Ely Cathedral again the other day. It is a magnificent old place. Inside the flag stones are worn and pitted with the marks of over hundreds of years of people just walking over them. The roof is lost in shadows, and the light comes so faintly through the stained glass. It just depicts the age of this ancient land. Each little village in this part of the country has its tremendous church built of stone, themselves hundreds of years old. The churches are in size out of all proportion to the number of people who attend; but there they are, and there they will remain for hundreds of years yet.

I felt a breath of Col's delight while wandering through the coolness of Ely Cathedral in the summer of 2007, the low angles of the late afternoon sun enlivening the stained glass windows. During vespers in the Chapter House, the young choir's expressive faces provided a curious counterpoint to the headless, shattered figures around the walls, vandalised on Henry VIII's orders during the anti-Catholic violence of England's Reformation. On my way out, and with a lurch of surprise, I came upon the stained glass windows commemorating the airmen who flew from the stations dotted about the surrounding countryside. What a lonely, welcome sight this grand cathedral must have been to so many returning bomber crews, straining to make out their airstrip as the new day rose like Ely's twin towers in the early morning mist. Col would no doubt have found some solace in knowing he has an enduring place in Ely Cathedral: his name is entered in an elegant, calligraphic hand in the four-volume Roll of Honour recording the 14,820 airmen of 2, 3, 8 and 100 Bomber Command Groups who died while serving at airbases in the region.

CHAPTER 5

A LUCKY ENEMY

BY THE TIME Col wrote of his last visit to Ely Cathedral, Otto Fries was only starting to become a truly dangerous adversary. Though he had begun pilot instruction a year before Col, they had both completed their training at the same time, December 1941. Although 10 years younger, Otto shared with Col an energetic intelligence, a devotion to family, a fierce patriotism and an unstinting dedication to the job. In other times, different circumstances, the two men might have become the most natural of friends rather than the best of enemies. It is hard today to reconcile this time of killing with a relative who lives for me through his writing and with his former enemy, whom I came to know so well.

Professor Otto-Heinrich Fries always greeted me with warmth and a gentle whimsy that made the reason for my visits to his Berlin home seem unnatural, almost rude. But during more than two dozen conversations over 18 months he never shied away from what it had meant in human terms to shoot down at least 18 bombers and the people in them – people like Col Jones. One night Professor Fries's grandson joined our conversation as part of a school project on the 'morality of killing in war', and I observed him grilling his Opa in a way that made even me squirm. Younger Germans appear to have few qualms about passing judgement on the wartime generation. But the elder Fries took all questions in his stride, rolling many of them back gently with the implicit counter, 'What would *you* have done?' Otto saw he had a job to do, one for which he had received two years of the best training in the world. Using this great skill, and in control of a sophisticated killing machine, his task was simply to prevent enemy bombers from destroying his country's cities and the people who lived in them. Usually he tried to shoot down the bombers in a way that improved the crews' chances of getting out, but they rarely escaped. He lived with this knowledge, even while taking pride in his service to his country.

Otto was blessed with resilience from an early age. As a 17-year-old he was working in his school holidays at Ludwigshafen, at the chemicals company, IG Farben – later the makers of Zyklon B gas, used in the extermination camps. He kept his drinking water in a fridge with several similar bottles, randomly placed there for cool storage. When he rushed down to the cafeteria for a break one day he grabbed what he thought was his drink. One big gulp made his error devastatingly clear: He had swallowed calcium hydroxide, which burned his oesophagus and stomach so badly that he spent the next year in a clinic and had to receive special treatment intermittently for years afterwards – into his seventies. Even in peacetime, Otto was a survivor; and it was his luck as much as his skill that enabled him to make it through the war.

Otto Fries frequently talked about his childhood village, Herxheim am Berg, which sits on the rolling hills west of the Rhine, south of the cathedral city of Mainz. I travelled there one perfect autumn day in September 2007 to add my own impressions to his descriptions – and to put a scenic backdrop to the wines he always served when I visited him in Berlin. I was quickly seduced by the village charms: the vineyards the Fries family had owned formed a crossword-puzzle of small Weinlage (vineyard) allotments straddling the main road. I strolled through these and down the narrow streets to a point where I looked east from a stone-walled terrace, dappled by broad, rusty-leafed chestnuts, towards the twin industrial cities of Mannheim and Ludwigshafen, which straddle the Rhine. Two hot-air balloons drifted north above carpets of golden vines. The idyllic scene was worlds away from the infernos that raged in these two cities – and most others along the Rhine – as Bomber Command relentlessly struck back at Germany's westernmost cities from 1940 onwards.

Otto grew up there between the wars, when Herxheim am Berg was in a part of Germany patrolled by the French, who were keen to rub German noses in their First World War defeat. His grandfather always pulled him away from the fence when French military convoys passed along the town's main road in front of the family home. The French were the Erbfeind – the hereditary enemy. Otto Fries recalled how every autumn of his childhood a pig was slaughtered for a feast. The men gathered around the large table had all served on the Western Front – Otto's father near Verdun, where he was once buried in his bunker for three days after the French detonated an underground mine. For the men of the village the central topic of conversation at these annual feasts was always the Schmach von Versailles – the humiliation of Versailles. Otto grew up knowing there was an historical score to settle with the western powers.

This was typical of the simmering anger and a growing delusion across Germany that it had *not* lost in 1918, but had merely agreed to end hostilities. By this reasoning, the Armistice on 11 November had been twisted into an 'unjust' defeat by the vengeful western allies, aided and abetted by the German left – the Communists and the Social Democrats. This resentment gave rise to the Dolch-Stoss-Legende, the myth of being stabbed in the back. A malign weed took root and strangled the new seedling of Weimar Republic democracy. The resentment was made worse by vicious war reparations, particularly to the French, which deepened the humiliation of defeat and aggravated shortages of all essentials. Malnutrition was commonplace and was exacerbated by the Royal Navy blockade of German ports, which continued even after the Armistice. Hyperinflation during the 1920s and the mass unemployment of the Depression that followed opened fresh wounds. The sense of grievance and betrayal played into the hands of a demagogue like Hitler, enabling him to unite behind him the extreme elements on the right, ingeniously to paper over their contradictions and to portray his evil ends as consistent with restoring national pride – and reclaiming Germany's rightful seat in the dress circle of nations. 'Hitler meant something to us,' Professor Fries told me. 'He created jobs, trust in the future, he fixed the economic crisis. We had the feeling the country was going upwards and forwards.' Much has been written along these lines, but when Professor Fries spoke of these times in his childhood and adolescence it was heart muscle contracting, not a turning of photo album pages to show a neat ordering of events long past. Even in July 1944, with Germany headed towards inevitable defeat, he remembered being angry at the unsuccessful attempt to assassinate Hitler with a briefcase bomb planted in his military headquarters near the eastern front – the 'July Plot'. Otto felt it was too late in the piece to be taking such 'dilettantish' actions. What could these fools be thinking of, with Germany's back against the wall?

As an 18-year-old, Otto had celebrated along with other Germans when their troops marched across the Rhine in 1936 and restored 'honour' to their lands on the west bank. Under the Versailles Treaty of 1919, the year after Otto was born, these lands were placed out of bounds to the German military. Germany was also forbidden an air force under the Versailles Treaty, but the Nazis created the Luftwaffe in secret once they came to power in 1933. The Luftwaffe's later role in such Spanish Civil War outrages as the bombing of Guernica, in the Blitzkrieg victories of 1939 and 1940 and in the bombing of England during the Battle of Britain in summer 1940 quickly proved why air power in the hands of Germany had been seen as such a threat.

By the end of 1938 the new Luftwaffe had cut its teeth in Spain, and Germany had annexed Austria and the Sudetenland in western Czechoslovakia. Otto was by then a student of chemistry at the famous University of Heidelberg. In going on to higher studies, he was a rarity from his village, which did not even have a high school. His mother, armed with proof of his academic potential, had presented herself at the high school in the larger neighbouring town, Bad Dürkheim, and insisted they admit Otto to continue his education. Her boy was bound for the headwaters, and it seemed that the stronger the opposing current, the more determined Otto became. Bad Dürkheim's school did not extend to the upper forms but, at 17, Otto was among a handful selected to go on to Gymnasium, or grammar school, to sit the Abitur university entrance exams. This would have been beyond the means of his family, but the Nazis had made it possible, opening a separate tributary into the academic stream to children not tagged for higher learning by a privileged family background. Given the humble surroundings in which he had grown up, his elevation by the Nazis to view wider horizons, and his indoctrination through the Hitler Youth, Otto's loyalty was hardly surprising. When Germany triggered a Europe-wide war by attacking Poland on 1 September 1939, Otto was keen to become part of the élite Luftwaffe and volunteered immediately, even though it meant cutting short his university studies. When, however, he said he was a chemistry student at the university, the recruitment officer in Heidelberg told him to go back to his studies, as Germany would need plenty of chemists. As Otto left, disappointed, the woman secretary advised him to return in a couple of weeks and say instead he was studying law; lawyers were expendable. The advice worked a treat and by October 1939 he was in uniform.

The postcard scenes that greeted me at Herxheim am Berg were no less picturesque the day Otto flew over his home for first time in late August 1942. His squadron had been scrambled the night before to intercept bombers bound for a target in southern Germany. Otto and his Bordfunker, or radar and radio operator, Fred Staffa, finished their flying for the night well south of their own base of St Trond, or St Truiden, which is near Brussels on the road south-east to Liege. They landed at the large Luftwaffe airfield of Echterdingen, near Stuttgart in the south-west of Germany, and turned in at the barracks there, flying back to their own airbase the next morning. At this stage, before the introduction in 1943 of a more sophisticated and demanding version of on-board radar, and before RAF night fighters began attacking the Luftwaffe fighters over the continent during the hours of darkness, Otto and Fred flew without a rear gunner as third man. They were firm friends by then, having entered training at the same time. Although the two were schooled for different roles, each quickly recognised in the other a reliable partner, which was a prerequisite to success and sometimes survival. Fred was from the German-speaking Sudetenland, the Bohemian part of today's Czech Republic, and it was he who gave Otto his nickname, 'Otakar' – after a 12th-century Bohemian king, Otakar Przemyszl.

That August morning in 1942, after taking off from Echterdingen to return to St Trond, Otto followed the Neckar River past his old university until he reached the Rhineland Palatinate Wine Road that runs from north of Karlsruhe to just south of Worms, on the Rhine. Herxheim am Berg lies roughly at the halfway point of this Pfalz Wine Road. Cruising at an altitude of 200 metres, which was normal then for overland flights, Otto could easily make out his fellow villagers working among the vines. As he circled three times – strictly against Luftwaffe regulations – he saw the vineyard workers flourishing their headscarves. Otto could see his mother waving to him from the front step of their home.

Otto's aircraft, a twin-engined Messerschmitt ME110, was the aircraft used most widely by the German night fighter force and the type that attacked Col's aircraft several times, including the night he ditched in the Channel.[1] The ME110 had been savaged by the faster, nimbler Spitfires and Hurricanes during the Battle of Britain in the summer of 1940, but the German aircraft's range, stability and capacity to deliver a fatal blow to the much larger bombers made it an ideal night fighter. It was also the plane in which Otto Fries was first shot down and later scored his first victories.

That first shooting down came only weeks after his low-level flight above his village. Otto was stalking a bomber returning from Nuremberg – a raid Col Jones took part in. It was the first time Otto had come into contact with a Stirling. Crammed into the metre-wide cockpit of his ME110, Otto was aghast at the bomber's size – its fuselage high-sided like a ship and the length of two tennis courts. The size belied the Stirling's agility, which Otto experienced when he closed on the bomber too quickly. He was forced to veer away so sharply that he exposed the flat undersurface of his wings to the bomber's gunners, who shot him from the sky. He and Fred parachuted to safety. It was the first of many duels in which Otto's respect for the enemy's skill grew.

For a full year after this first encounter in August 1942, Otto had not a single contact with a bomber. Each lost opportunity merely confirmed his sense of impotence, compounded by the practice at that stage of scrambling Luftwaffe pilots in order of seniority. This gave a select few officers first claim on being guided in to a target by the combat leader on the ground, whose radar system and target plotting table were set up to direct individual pilots to the vicinity of single bombers. Frustrated at being, in effect, grounded because of lack of seniority, Unteroffizier (Corporal) Fries applied in writing to his commandant to become an officer, so that he would have the chance to do what he had been trained to do – attack bombers. In early 1943, after 14 weeks of intensive training, Otto was promoted to sergeant. Finally, in August 1943, he became a Leutnant, an officer. But by then the growing pressure on the German air defences from the massive build-up of RAF Bomber Command strength – compounded by the daylight raids by the United States Army Air Forces (USAAF) – had forced a fundamental rethink of the Luftwaffe night-fighting strategy: to have a chance of combating the bomber stream, every available aircraft would need to be deployed.

On 11 August 1943 a newly promoted Leutnant Fries got the chance he had been waiting for. Just after 1 a.m. he took off from St Trond and headed east. Initially he was sent on a wild goose chase, hunting a machine that turned out to be another German night fighter coming in to land. Around 2.30 a.m., however, the ground control directed him towards a new object detected by the regional radar. Otto almost repeated his previous error, again closing too quickly in his enthusiasm and overrunning his slower quarry, which initially disappeared into the darkness before Fred was able to pick it up again on his radar 10 minutes later. The three screens of Fred's Lichtenstein radar console showed an object some 700 metres ahead and above them and slightly to the left. Otto reported the sighting to ground control: 'Parsival from Eagle 98 – I have contact with the enemy, over.'

In a single co-ordinated action, Fries activated his guns by retracting the covering of the two undernose 20-millimetre cannons, levered up his seat to bring his line of vision to the level of his reflector-gunsight and adjusted its illumination in preparation for bringing it to bear on the target. Fred guided him closer, to 500 metres; Otto slowed to avoid overrunning the bomber.

'Up a bit, a little to the left, distance 400,' Fred coaxed him in.

Otto flipped the safety cover forward from the cannon release button on the top of the control stem. The teaspoon-like cover hinged forward onto the 'shin' of the control stem, to create a squeeze-trigger for the four 7.92-millimetre machine guns mounted in the upper nose.

'A bit higher, just to the right, 300,' said Fred.

Otto strained to make out a shape in the darkness, blinking hard and trying to distinguish the horizon. 'Where is he exactly?'

'Slightly to the right, slightly above us – you must see him – distance about 250.'

At that point Otto noticed a star snap into blackness and reappear. Then, a thumb's-breadth above the horizon, he saw the shadow in front of him, as thin as a knife blade with five knots in it – the fuselage flanked by two engines on each side. Otto accelerated and could now make out the red glow of the exhaust flues and the twin tails of a Lancaster. 'I see him!'

Then to ground control: 'Parsival from Eagle 98 – I have contact'.

'Viktor, understood – Weidmannsheil – happy hunting.'

The bomber hung unawares above the smaller fighter.

'Why don't you open fire?' Fred cried.

'Softly, softly.' This time Otto was leaving nothing to chance, and focused his calmness as he stalked the bomber.

'If you zoom past him this time I'll clock your noggin with my flare pistol,' Fred said. Out of the corner of his eye Otto could see his Bordfunker, seated behind him, brandishing the butt of his pistol. 'Press the button, will you?'

'Easy, easy! This time I want to get it exactly right!'

The Lancaster loomed like a whale emerging from the deep; Otto felt insignificant in his own Messerschmitt, lurking underneath it. He noted the time – 2.43 a.m. – and radioed ground control: 'Parsival from Eagle 98 – Pauke, Pauke! (drumbeat, I'm going in for the attack)'.

Slowly and with great care Otto eased back the joystick, lifting the ME110's nose so that the vertical line of crosses on his gunsight slid across the wing area between the bomber's two port engines. When the upper edge of the sighting circle was aligned with the Lancaster's leading wing-edge, he opened fire as he continued to slide backwards, the stream of bullets and cannon shells raking fore to aft where the broadest part of the wing encased the main fuel tanks. The thunder and vibration of his own guns seemed to rattle the Messerschmitt to its core, and the cordite from the spent shells filled the cabin with a stench like fireworks.

Despite the temporary blinding by the muzzle flashes of four machine guns mounted in front of his windshield, he could see flames spring to life between the bomber's port engines. His burst having lasted no more than two seconds, Otto flipped his machine to the right in the nick of time, watching the firefly-like tracer bullets from the Lancaster's rear gun turret whip the darkness where he had been moments before. The bomber twisted downwards into the darkness, trailing a ghostly train of smoke. Otto dived after it and drew closer in the web of darkness so that the bomber was held again just above the faint corona of the horizon in his field of vision. He unleashed another burst into the seat of the flames and saw this bloom with greater intensity. Again Otto jinked off to the right but this time the rear gunner made no attempt to return fire.

'Parsival from Eagle 98 – courier [the enemy] has had it!'

'Viktor, understood!'

The bomber yawed and bucked in a futile attempt to shake its pursuer. A bomber trying to extinguish a fire faced enough of a challenge to hide in the absence of cloud cover; this one had no hope, since its wing had become a torch. Otto felt his wings vibrating and noticed he had picked up speed to 500 kilometres per hour in his headlong pursuit of the bomber. They were down to 3500 metres, the time now 2.46 a.m. Otto continued to match as closely as possible the acrobatics of the stricken Lancaster to keep the bomber in his grasp – the swallow pursuing the desperate blowfly.

'He's using a lot of time and juice with his antics,' Fred said.

'Someone's forgotten to put on his parachute,' Otto replied. He slid to port again and fired once more into the burning wing, which started to spray flame like a Guy Fawkes sky rocket, then he darted right. Now the bomber levelled out and hung like a board in the air.

'Time for you to jump, my friend!' Fred had only just spoken when the first shadow rushed past their port wing. Then the second...the third. Otto and Fred counted them off aloud – four, five, six...a pause – seven, the pilot. That was all of them.

The Lancaster suddenly reared up like a marlin trying to throw the hook, twisted slightly to the left, then flipped over its burning wing and plunged straight down into the darkness. Scarcely a minute later – at 2.56 a.m. – Otto and Fred saw the Lancaster erupt in a fireball as it struck the ground. In the reflected light of this inferno they could see seven parachutes strung out like patio lights, disappearing into the night.

'Parsival from Eagle 98 – Sieg Heil!'

'Viktor, understood – congratulations.'

'Thanks. A question: Do you have another courier for me?'

'Eagle 98 from Parsival – all couriers have gone to bed – suggest you do the same.'

As Otto turned towards his base, Fred tried to mask his elation: 'All right, Otakar, you got him, congratulations on your first kill. Now you know how it's done, you won't screw it up next time!'

I asked Professor Fries how it felt to shoot down his first bomber. 'It was a feeling like Christmas, Easter, Whitsun-holiday and my birthday rolled into one – not a scrap of nerves, just joy.' He recalled resetting his course for home and trying in this moment to define his feelings – not just happy and proud, but freed of the 'curse' that had dogged him until now, the depressing sense of non-achievement. But he also felt an indefinable sense of satisfaction the crew had all made it out of the bomber alive.

The pilot and one other crew member of this 97 Squadron

Lancaster made it back to England, three were captured quickly while two remained at large for several weeks before they, too, became prisoners of war. One of the three first captured, Warrant Officer Samuel Ramsden, a 23-year-old Canadian, died just two weeks before Germany's surrender, when his POW column was strafed by aircraft from his own side.

Part Two

COMBAT

CHAPTER 6

FLYING BLIND

DESTROYING A TARGET in the dark was often a battle as much against the elements as the enemy. Both sides in the night war struggled to gain the upper hand against the common dangers of darkness and weather, which claimed the lives of many airmen without the enemy needing to fire a single shot. Adverse weather conditions killed more airmen on some raids than night fighters or anti-aircraft fire from the ground. Weather caused attacking bombers and defending fighters alike to become hopelessly lost, to seize up in mid-air or to crash while struggling to land in atrocious conditions. Bad weather could turn the job of finding the target into a matter of pure luck. Conversely, though, it often gave pilots cloud cover to hide in and shake off attacks by prowling night fighters.

For Bomber Command crews, the dangers of darkness and weather were made worse by the long distances to many targets, usually over large stretches of water and often in shocking conditions. As the war progressed, both sides developed increasingly sophisticated gadgetry to improve their chances both of finding targets in the darkness and of returning home safely. This technological race to 'see in the dark' by developing better navigation tools and the instruments of stealth made both the RAF and the Luftwaffe airmen by turns more deadly and more vulnerable as each side fought to stay a step ahead of the enemy.

By the time Otto Fries downed his first bomber in August 1943, Col Jones had already finished his first tour of operations and was training bomb aimers and navigators in these arts of warfare. Through several frightening experiences he had learnt how dangerous the weather could be. One took place early into his fifth op, to bomb Essen, on 6 April 1942. Both the target and his Stirling, 'T' Tommy, were the same as when he ditched in the Channel exactly two months later. Col's diary records what happened soon after take-off at 1 a.m., with Flight Lieutenant Reginald Turtle at the controls.

Bugger of a night. Rain and low cloud. Considerable doubt as to whether we should go or not. Wing/Co (Spence) asked Turtle what he thought about it and Turtle said the weather was just about flyable. Group [command] gave last minute instructions that we were to fly low out to sea under the cloud and then climb when we had passed it.

But Turtle had other views. He decided to climb through it. We had got to 10,000 ft about 15 miles from the English coast, when we got flat into the middle of bad static and icing. I saw rings of fire round the props, fire playing along the fuselage. The front and rear gunners saw their guns alive with fire in front of them, while the rear gunner saw a living line of flame where the trailing aerial ought to have been. Later that was burned off.

Then she began to ice. I saw the lightning in a quick glance, because at that stage I was busy working out a fix – days before Gee [radio position-fixing device]. Got it set when became aware that the kite was bucketing about a hell of a lot. Then I saw the ice. Piling up on leading edge of wings and tail of plane, being chucked off the props and hitting the fuselage with a noise like flak.

Then old 'T' Tommy began to fall and the engines stalled. I thought that only two did but Henry Hammond DFM, mid-upper [gunner] told me after that, for a second, all four went. Anyway we dropped like a stone and it took Turtle and Tony all their time to pull it out at 4000 ft. They did not get control properly until she had got down to 400 ft. Rowly told me he thought his feet were going to touch the roofs of a small town we got over. Must have come 15 miles at a hell of a pace. I have no idea how long this lasted. We came home after that but our compasses were unserviceable and we wandered all over East Anglia trying to find base. Skipper could not steer a course, because the machine went in a curve.

Then we had to jettison bombs on Lakenheath. We did a bombing run at 2000 ft – and three of them, 1900 lb, went off! Set safe too. Nearly blew us out of the sky.

In December 1942, the Stirling flown by the commanding officer of 75 (NZ) Squadron, Wing Commander Victor Mitchell DFC – a man Col knew well and admired – was not so lucky when it struck bad weather. His aircraft was one of four Stirlings in that squadron alone that failed to return to Mildenhall entirely because of weather.

Only a minority of bomber crew downed by night fighters over the continent or water survived – the few thousand picked up from the 'drink' during the war by air-sea rescue craft is an indication of how many others perished in the cold seas or were simply lost without trace. Col flew several 'gardening' operations to lay mines in German-controlled waters, but this was far from straightforward. Even without the threat of German flak ships sitting in wait to defend important waterways, bombers on mine-laying operations faced plenty of natural hazards. Flying just above the sea at night – and sometimes in fog or rain – a bomber could fall victim to the smallest miscalculation and plunge into the sea, with almost no chance of the crew surviving.

Jim Coman, a former wireless operator I met at the 2008 reunion of Col's 149 Squadron, said that while mine-laying he used the 80-metre-long weighted aerial, which trailed 15 metres beneath his bomber, as a means of judging the aircraft's height above the water. One type of mine designed to float unseen beneath the surface had to be dropped from an exact – and very low – altitude to become effective. On such flights if the cable aerial hit the water, Coman would tell the skipper to climb immediately.

Col, as observer, initially performed the joint role of navigator and bomb aimer, and so had to find the way to the drop-zone, release the mines, then set the course home again. He referred to these many tasks in a letter home in November 1941, in which he described the observer's combined duties:

He uses wireless aids to get what are called fixes, that is, he knows he is on a certain position on the map at a certain time. Then he also uses the stars, which is called astral navigation, by which he can also fix his position. Then he looks at the map and then at the ground, and when he sees something on the ground that he recognizes on his map, like a big town or a prominent bend in a river, or a place where two railway lines cross, then he knows where he is. This last method is pinpointing. Of course, you can't always see the ground, and then you have to make certain allowances. But that in the main is how you navigate. The observer has also to release the bombs, which he does by pressing a little push button on the end of a cord. He also has to take photographs if any photographs are required; but in the main the camera is more or less automatic, and all you do is to press another button. In special circumstances he might also be required to man one of the guns on board. I sometimes think that his duties are so many that if there was anything to cook on board he would also be asked to do a job of work in the cooking line.

The roles of navigator and bomb aimer were later split, as navigation tools became more complicated and thus needed more concentration. By the time Col began flying operations in January 1942, however, his tools of trade had not improved much. The first significant advance, used on operations from March that year, was called Gee. It enabled bombers to establish their position by cross-referencing radio pulses transmitted from three separate points in Britain. By midway through Col's first tour of operations in 1942, Gee was becoming a standard tool for navigators. These pulses could not be picked up over the horizon, so Gee was limited in range – a definite drawback when attacking eastern targets, where the potential to get lost was in any case greater. This inability to peek over the earth's curvature also disadvantaged lower-flying aircraft, like the Stirling. And the Germans eventually found means of jamming Gee signals.

Even by the time Col had completed his first tour towards the end of 1942, the tools of navigation had not improved at nearly the pace achieved later in the war. A more advanced over-the-horizon navigational aid called Oboe superseded Gee and improved accuracy, but the big breakthrough came at the end of 1942, with a revolutionary device known as H2S. This enabled navigators to 'see' the terrain below without reference to guiding signals anchored to fixed points in Britain, and was therefore not limited in range. The picture H2S gave the navigator would satisfy most children's expectations of what a radar screen should show – a constant scan of the land below, with areas of water appearing dark on the screen, open country as an indeterminate fuzz and built-up areas as bright blobs. Rough though it seems today, from January 1943 this device dramatically improved bombers' chances of survival and success. It boosted the confidence of bomber crews just as their casualty rate was reaching appalling new levels.

But for the period in 1942 when Col flew most of his ops, he and other navigators were still relying heavily on dead reckoning – calculating the position, where possible with the help of visual landmarks, or 'pinpoints' – and factoring in wind speed to try to determine its effect on both the plane's course and the way the bombs would fall to the ground. He drew on this experience on his longest trip of the war, to Genoa, on 23 October 1942. His diary describes a round trip of nearly nine hours, which he flew in another 'T' Tommy that had replaced the earlier one in which he had crashed into the sea in June.

Wing/Co. asked me this morning whether I would like a trip tonight. Though I had a definite hangover I said I would, which was at least half true. I was keen to fly, but I wished I had felt better. Still....

Then I found out that we were going to Genoa, which heartened me considerably, as I have always wanted to go to Italy. Took with us Flight Lieutenant Simmons DFM, DFC, the Gee expert from group. Had a special Gee aboard. Took off and all was well – but the bloody Gee would not work. Actually did not work until halfway across France. Told Simmy that I did not have time to worry with it, so he struggled with it. The trouble was acute divider trouble and then some.

Well we landed up to port, well to port. Crossed the French coast on ETA [estimated time of arrival] and set course. I think we were all right up to there; but the wind changed then. As I say we went to port and had to alter course. Then far ahead we saw the Alps. I have never seen anything more inspiring. There was 10/10 cloud below us; but the summits were unclouded. They looked so serene, so apart, so lonely and so majestic, bathed in moonlight. Mont Blanc was away to the port beam, the most aloof, impersonal, unapproachable thing I have ever seen. We seemed merely intruders, just a tiny moth in comparison.

We rather skirted the Alps than flew over them and as a matter of fact we were too far to starboard. We flew a little more than mountain top level and over the top of a pass. Far below us we could see ravines, with streams and one road. We saw a ravine broaden out into a valley and branch out into more valleys which narrowed until lost in the labyrinth of peaks. Little villages nestled under the shoulders of the mountains, their households winking so eerily. We flashed a 'V' sign at one village, and to our astonishment the answer came back – again the 'V' sign. We thought that perhaps it was wishful seeing, so tried again. Again the same result. Wizard! Simmy thought the occasion of crossing the Alps appropriate for yodelling through the intercom. But though the thought was good, the result might have been more tuneful.

Well, we passed the Alps and turned east on the last leg, across the plains of Lombardy. Saw the coast far ahead and knew that all was well. Arrived there and Simmy acted as bomb aimer. We found a good deal of cloud there, so finally had to bomb on a dead-reckoning run [i.e. reliant on calculations rather than sighting the target or, later, with the help of electronic target-fixing]. I think we got Genoa, though a great many fires were at Savona, which must have been pretty well destroyed.

The ack-ack fire was negligible. Think the Ities [Italians], poor negligible quantities, must have fired their guns by remote control – piece of string tied one end to the trigger and the other leading to the nearest shelter where they were. Few fighters seen. We saw none, but one crew said they saw a biplane – bloody cheeky, attacking a Stirling, I thought. That reminds me, we saw a fighter as we crossed the coast, but I doubt whether it saw us. We lost each other in the cloud. Finally we turned for home. Altered course to miss Turin, but came back more or less on course. Saw the same awful beauty of the Alps – saw, too, the cloud disappear as we left the coast and reappear as we crossed the Alps.

Big wind change coming back across France. Backed down to about 156 degrees. [Wind] lowered in speed from approximately 60 mph at 7000 ft going to 18–25 mph coming home at the same height. Hit the coast where we wanted to, and no-one fired at us, though the clouds broke as we came to the coast. Got a pinpoint and set course. Another wind change and Gee refused to work; hit the English coast at the wrong place and had to fly along it. Then we finally did set course on the home leg but we got too far to starboard and had to go to port. Then we hit base head on and all was well. So ended the only trip I did in October.

By then, October 1942, Bomber Command's boffins were putting the finishing touches to the terrain-scanning H2S. The first H2S units entered operational service at the start of 1943, but within a month the Germans retrieved one of these devices almost undamaged from a bomber shot down near Rotterdam and began developing counter-measures. Since the technology was so far ahead of anything Germany's engineers were yet working on, however, the Luftwaffe was slow to detect H2S's Achilles heel: because the revolutionary new device operated like bats by bouncing signals against objects below, these signals could also be turned into a kind of homing beacon in the darkness, helping to lead the night fighters onto them. Once the Luftwaffe grasped this fact, it gained crucial ground in the stealth race.

While the engineers on both sides of the conflict raced to improve their own airmen's night vision and to throw sand in the eyes of the enemy, pilots like Otto Fries battled the elements night after night. Darkness was the medium through which he and Fred Staffa sought out their quarry. To see and not to be seen required luck as well as skill, and the natural conditions on a given night could determine success or failure. They called the moon 'the traitor', because it enabled them to be seen by bomber crews – better pitch blackness in which to creep up on the massive aircraft undetected. But the moon could also charm and mesmerise. Several times Otto witnessed moon rainbows, when the moon shining from behind beamed its light into fine, misty rain ahead, creating a surreal archway of ghostly light that seemed to lure them on. But even the ideal complete darkness was far from a void. High above any cloud, Otto was spellbound by the majesty of the star canopy, which seemed so much wider and more tangible at that altitude – to touch the stars! Sometimes a fine layer of mist hung like a veil between the aircraft and the stars. Otto experienced these moments with 'an infinite feeling of freedom'.

Ice posed a threat to the bombers, but seldom caused problems for the German night fighters sent up to intercept them, mainly because conditions that produced icing above the continent were usually regarded as unflyable for other reasons anyway. Cold and altitude posed more of a danger to Otto on the four occasions he had to bale out. Beginning his free-fall from as high as 8 kilometres, he knew not to open his parachute until he was below 4 kilometres, from which point he could breathe without oxygen and would have less time exposed to the freezing elements. On each occasion he knew when he had fallen to the survival level: 'I had a feeling for heights.'

Otto Fries's airfield at St Trond was the base for 5 Squadron, First Night fighter Group – 5 Staffel, Nachtjagdgeschwadergruppe 1, or 5NJG1. While on readiness there, the crews began every evening with a briefing from the weather forecaster – the 'weather frog' or 'Meteorolügner' ('met. liar'), as they referred to him. Sometimes these Luftwaffe crews sat helplessly listening to the RAF bomber stream passing overhead towards a target, while the defenders remained grounded in Belgium because poorer weather over the continent prevented them from taking off. Endgültig Krähe – final crow – meant no flying that night; vorläufig Krähe – provisional crow – meant remain on standby in the readiness room in case the weather cleared enough to take off and intercept the bombers on their path back to Britain. Fasanen – pheasants – meant clear for operations, but that did not necessarily imply ideal flying conditions. Wind often pushed aircraft of both sides off their course, though Otto had great faith in the saucer-sized Knemeier circular slide-rule he carried with him to factor in the wind-effect and adjust course. As long as the cloud level did not drop below 150 metres, visibility was considered adequate for taking off.

The term 'visibility,' however, referred only to a lack of atmospheric obstacles. First the pilots had to guide their aircraft through the darkness into that void, aided by sparse runway lights, their instruments – and their training. One green light on the control tower ushered the fighters from the Stellplatz – the parking position on the tarmac apron – to the start of the runway, where twin green lights would signal each to take off. Three green lights, hooded from above and set 50 metres apart, guided the accelerating fighters along to a white light at the 200-metre mark. After a gap of unpunctuated darkness, twin red lights appeared every 50 metres, threaded to the next pair by a row of red lights, until the end of the runway at 1600 metres.

When taking off, Otto accelerated with the joystick pushed forward to keep the Messerschmitt hugging the ground. Then, as he felt the tail rise with his speed at about 140 kilometres per hour, he gradually pulled the joystick back until he 'hopped' the plane into the air with a small jerk of this control column. Now the night held him – but not securely. A string of red lights marked an artificial horizon 2.5 kilometres from the end of the runway, another line at 5 kilometres, another at 15 kilometres. During the time it took to close this distance, Otto had to complete an intense routine of checking all his instrumentation – the artificial senses he needed to trust more than his own in the darkness. 'Taking off at night was a struggle between feeling and reasoning. We always said feelings belonged back here,' Professor Fries told me, patting his bottom.

Otto knew the danger: he often had the strong feeling the aircraft was banking away; the urge to 'correct' the roll was strong, but the instruments said it was flying horizontal, so he resisted the urge. The take-off routine of checking instrumentation and engaging mentally with it proved too much for many less experienced pilots, however, in the intense couple of minutes before the end of the 15-kilometre guided section tipped them into the blackness. Many lacked the practice of multiple take-offs needed to make the procedures seem second nature, and had not benefited from the rigorous training for instruments-only flying that early recruits like Otto had received. The newer men often allowed their own senses to override what their instruments were telling them and ploughed into the ground. Flying accidents took an increasingly heavy toll.

Taking off was perilous enough, but landing again in the darkness presented far greater risks. If the weather closed in while the crews were aloft, their options for getting back on the ground again diminished. On one occasion Otto brought his aircraft down when the clouds hung only 80 metres off the ground – low enough to shroud the 93-metre Statue of Liberty's torch or to swallow the top of London's Big Ben, above the clock faces. Short on fuel or with engine problems or damage inflicted by a bomber's defending gunners, night fighters were frequently forced to put down when and where they could. Others unable to find their own base or land there owing to bad visibility often located an airfield away from the densest cloud and stayed there for the night, returning to home base in daylight. They located these alternative airfields either from distinctive light patterns on the ground or via radio beacons – Funkfeuer – that 'fired' a tone signal audible to aircraft when they were circling a given location and thereby enabled them to be guided in by a radio operator from the ground, to reduce the risk of collisions. Otto landed often with this help and without complications. By then, his eyes were often streaming from the cold air leaking in from breaks in the cabin seal, so that he suffered almost constant eye infections.

Once an airstrip had been located, further signals aided the approach to the runway from 30 kilometres out: a Morse dash or dot sounding either side of a central radio corridor beamed into the air on the approach, then with further signals at 5 kilometres and 2.5 kilometres from the start of the runway. If visibility was clear, Otto and other pilots landing at St Trond could see the elliptical shape of the airfield perimeter from low altitude 10 kilometres away, marked by evenly spaced triangles of hooded red lights and, at the end of the runway, two landing beams angled to direct approaching aircraft down the throat of the landing corridor.

The one advantage night fighter pilots had when landing in the darkness was that their instrument lighting was easier to read. But even this was fraught with uncertainty, as Otto experienced once when he tried to land in impenetrable fog. First the radar failed, then the radio and finally his instruments. He managed to find his airfield and get the aircraft down safely. He and Fred walked away unhurt, but this was just the lucky, improbable ending to a nerve-wracking sequence of events, described in a later chapter, that several times could have killed them that night.

CHAPTER 7

FIRESTORM

I SAW COLOGNE IN FLOOD in January 1995, when the Rhine had burst its banks from Switzerland to the Dutch coast. My view from the tower of the Kölner Dom – Cologne Cathedral – had been onto an expanse of water more like a massive delta than a busy thoroughfare through one of Germany's most densely built-up cities. But the menace of such devastation was its silence, and I could not help measuring it against a far more terrifying scene half a century before when, on a moonlit night, Col looked down on Cologne over a bomb-sight as the city was engulfed in flames. By 1945 the magisterial Dom stood almost alone – damaged but not structurally – amid a wasteland of rubble. An estimated 1.5 million bombs fell within the city limits during 262 air raids in the course of the war, all but erasing a settlement as old as Christianity.[1]

Col was on his second operation to Cologne when he took off at five minutes after midnight on the morning of Sunday 31 May 1942, as part of the biggest air armada yet assembled – the thousand-bomber force. This was to demonstrate a new doctrine of aerial warfare, the brainchild of the Bomber Command chief, Arthur Harris. He called it area bombing, but it has since become known as carpet bombing. In a letter written two weeks later to his sister, Gwen Restall, Col described the scene from above that night.

Flight Lieutenant Col Jones DFC, 35, shortly before his death in February 1944. *(Collection Col Jones)*

Emma Jones with her children in the late 1920s: Col, aged about 20, younger sister Gwen (left) and older sister Lass.
(Collection J. Harris)

Col at work at the *Auckland Star* in the early 1930s.
(Collection Col Jones)

Col Jones, 24, graduates Bachelor of Arts in 1932.
(Collection Col Jones)

RNZAF trainees at Levin, September 1940. Col Jones is standing at far right, Barry Martin seated in the middle row, 3rd from right. *(Collection Col Jones)*

Two of Col Jones's earliest Stirlings: 'T' Tommy in background and 'N' Nuts being 'bombed up', Mildenhall, March 1942. *(Collection Gordon Galloway)*

Col and his crew board a launch after being rescued from the English Channel, 6 June 1942 *(Collection Col Jones)*

Spamming Adolf. Part of the leaflet dropped by Col on his first op, to Emden, reminding Germans of Hitler's 'embarrassing promise' that the war would be won by the end of 1941. *(Collection Gordon Galloway)*

Col's Stirling 'A' Apple after being attacked by a night fighter and struggling back to crash in Kent, August 1942. The people appear to be local residents and an RAF recovery crew. 'A' Apple flew again, but only as a training aircraft. *(Collection John Johnston)*

Lancaster KO-A, sister craft to KO-N of 115 Squadron, in which Col bombed Hamburg on 24-25 July 1943. A week later KO-A was lost without trace on the last raid of Operation 'Gomorrah.' KO-N was itself destroyed in a crash a week after that, killing all seven men on board. *(Collection Col Jones)*

Otto Fries in 1943. *(Collection O-H Fries)*

Otto's boyhood village,
Herxheim am Berg,
west of the Rhine
city of Ludwigshafen.
(Stephen Harris)

Otto (right) and Fred, beside their ME110, 1943. *(Collection O-H Fries)*

A Heinkel HE219 from Otto's squadron, showing underwing markings to avoid being fired at mistakenly by German flak crews. *(Collection O-H Fries)*

Lancaster bomb aimer's position, seen here at RAF Coningsby in 2008. *(Stephen Harris)*

The wreckage of Otto's ME110 the first time he was shot down, in August 1942. *(Collection O-H Fries)*

Otto's second 'kill': a Lancaster shot down at Nettersheim, south of Cologne, in October 1943. *(Collection O-H Fries)*

I was in the Rostock and the Cologne raids and it was a thrill. I find it hard to put on paper exactly how much of a thrill the Cologne raid was. We all knew something was in the wind. First it was a full moon. Second, the weather was good, and third, and most of all, there was a general air of expectancy. Then came the day. We all knew that an extra effort was afoot, because so many machines were being prepared – but we did not know the full scope until briefing time came.

So many crews were going over that it was a hell of a job to get them all into the briefing room. Added to that it was as hot as a boiler room, and I could feel the perspiration trickling down my nose. Everyone was the same, and the room was absolutely packed. The atmosphere was tense as the Wing Commander read out the details. There was a whole lot of detailed instructions from Bomber Command; but we were interested in our own share. We wanted to know what time we were to be on the target, and how long we were to be there and all the rest of it. Then the Wing Co. read out the total number of kites going. Boy, o Boy! It was the day we had all been waiting for ever since the people of London had to take it and do nothing back. There were over 1000. It was a masterpiece of organisation and, God knows, I've moaned about the mess the RAF seem to make of things in little issues. Machines were going from all over the place, and all sorts of machines.

When the briefing was over, all the crews going ran out of the room, singing and dancing. As we observers got our maps ready we were all smiles. Then when the time came to get changed and get into the buses to take us to the aircraft, everyone was singing. The fellows just yelled as they went from the crew-room out to the aircraft. Long before we were due to take off, machines passed over, waves of them, until the sky was filled with thunder. Then the turn of our station came, and away we went. Actually, our crew was among the last to take off, so many hundreds were before us. We could see the target from miles away. We just flew towards it, and then circled waiting for a chance to make our bombing run. We got over the target area, I went down to the bomb aimer's position – the observer always does that at that time – and I had a good look at what was happening below. There were machines everywhere. There must have been German night fighters among this milling crowd; but personally, I saw only British [bombers]. They whipped across in front of us. They nipped from in front and roared away towards the stern. They crossed and re-crossed. Some were some thousands of feet lower. Some were only a few hundred feet. That was what it looked like underneath. The others who could see above tell me it was just like that from where they were. They actually saw three Wellingtons flying wing-tip to wing-tip over the target to drop their bombs.

Eventually we dropped ours, and then got away to have a look. There were literally acres of flames. I don't mean patches of flame and patches with no flame. I just mean that there were acres of a seething mass of fire. I have never seen anything like it – perhaps never will again. The Rhine flows through the city and there is one famous street which has the Rhine as diameter for its semi-circular shape. It is known as the Hohenzollern Boulevard [Hohenzollernring]. It is prominent on any large scale map of Cologne. I could see it – stark black against the orange red of the sea of fire which billowed on either side of it. The moon and the fires were both reflected in the river. Later on I suppose the fires would have been partially shrouded in the smoke; but when we were there, the smoke was not important. It was impossible to photograph the result for some days on account of the smoke. Well, they say that on that one night, we did more damage to Cologne than was done during the whole bombing of London. I can believe it, even though I have seen London. The city must have been a holocaust. It must have been gutted. I think it may be said that we taught the Nazis a lesson that night.

Rostock [on 23 April, three weeks later] was a smaller Cologne. We laid it to waste under the same perfect conditions for bombing. There was a full moon, so that from the coast on the west side of Germany where it merges with Denmark, we simply map-read our way down to the target. It was actually possible to follow the courses of the rivers from Baltic to North Seas. They were just silver ribbons against a black background.

The residents, military and civil defence forces of Cologne had endured more than 100 raids by 30 May 1942 and were to suffer many more before American troops moved into the shattered wasteland in March 1945. Operation Millennium, against Cologne, was the first of a series of thousand-bomber raids Harris unleashed on major German cities over the ensuing three years. It gave an horrific new dimension to people's power to destroy each other – not only in Germany, but also in Japan. Whether this tactic of pounding the enemy into submission succeeded is still debated. It had the opposite effect in Britain. Although the destruction and loss of life during the Blitz of 1940-1 was on an unprecedented scale, the psychology of terrorising the civilian population was the same. But, just as in Britain, the bombing of Germany failed to break the civilian population's capacity to endure, and the destruction was readily twisted by Nazi propagandists into another reason to fight on. But unlike the British, the Germans had a more immediate terror to contend with: that of retribution from the Gestapo, the secret police, for any murmurings – let alone opposition – that could be seen as 'defeatist'.

Beyond debate is the scale of suffering as Cologne emerged from its sleepless night on the morning of Sunday 31 May. The official record shows that 469 people died, 5027 were injured and more than 45,000 were bombed out of their homes. Bombing of some of Cologne's major industrial districts on the east bank of the Rhine was light compared with the concentration on the residential and municipal areas on the west bank. Thirteen thousand homes were completely destroyed; 36 factories were annihilated and a further 70 severely damaged.[2] Public transport was disabled for a week, and extensive damage to electricity, gas supply and water mains also hampered the return to 'normality' for the already bomb-weary city.

The death toll was a new record for an RAF raid, the first to approach the 550 estimated killed in the bombing of Coventry in November 1940. Many aircrew, including Col, saw Coventry's suffering as justification for the retribution Bomber Command was now meting out, but the destruction of the English city paled in comparison with the later losses suffered by Hamburg in July 1943 (40,000 dead) and, in February 1945, by Dresden (at least 40,000) and Pforzheim (between 17,000 and 21,000). In a US attack on Tokyo in March 1945 firestorms killed at least 100,000.

Harris and Churchill regarded Operation Millennium as a tremendous success. It had dealt the target a blow on a scale not previously imagined and signalled to the Germans a new capacity to take the war to their homes. Leaflets dropped on Cologne soon after the raid promised as much, in a message signed off by Winston

Churchill: 'This proof of the growing strength of British air power is also the Sturmzeichen – storm warning – for what is to come from now on in one German city after another. The RAF offensive in its new form has begun.'[3]

Dropping leaflets like this was a common means of adding insult to injury. As a newspaperman, Col must have chuckled at the irony that his first two trips were 'paper runs' rather than bombing operations. The son of one of Col's gunners on those trips had copies of the original leaflets, kept by his father, and he sent me these in 2008. The first, dropped over the north German port of Emden on 14 January 1942, reminded the recipients of Hitler's promise that 1941 would be the year of final victory – 'an embarrassing promise!' – and quoted a string of statements by the German high command claiming the imminent collapse of Soviet forces. The second, dropped over Bremen and Cuxhaven three days later, featured a road strewn with destroyed Wehrmacht equipment – 'the retreat from Moscow' – and questioned the veracity of the comparatively low loss figures on the eastern front cited by Hitler.

If such leaflets could forecast doom, Harris and Churchill were busy trying to make it happen. After Millennium they aimed to repeat a feat of destruction on a similar scale every full moon, giving rise to the term 'bomber's moon', though that policy was later reversed because of high losses of bombers more easily found and picked off in full moonlight. Harris made good on this promise just two nights after the massive Cologne raid, sending 956 bombers to Essen. Then, on 25 June, he dispatched 1067 aircraft to Bremen. Neither raid caused anywhere near the intended damage. Col served as navigator and bomb aimer on both of these follow-up raids, flying in 'E' Edward and again with Watt as pilot and with Shoreman as the wireless operator – two of the same crew who searched for Col when he ditched in the Channel a week after the Cologne raid.

Total bomber losses for these first three thousand-bomber raids amounted to 129 aircraft – or 4.25 per cent of all those dispatched. These losses, unsustainable on bare numbers alone over the longer term, appear even more so considering they were disproportionately high among trainee crews, scraped together to make up the numbers. To achieve his show of strength, Harris was eating into his seed corn as well as testing the endurance of his more experienced crews. As the Luftwaffe did the same in the desperate attempt to counter the growing strength of Bomber Command, the air war over Germany took on some characteristics of the war of attrition on the Western Front during the First World War, when tens of thousands of troops were sacrificed, often for minimal gains, in the belief the other side would run out of men first.

Many air raids shared another feature with this trench stalemate: the bombing was often no more successful in destroying the enemy than 'going over the top' had been on the Western Front. Col's diary records that once he thought he had hit a target square on as bomb aimer; another time the force he was flying with entirely missed the city it had been sent to bomb, and instead caused widespread death and destruction to a neighbouring town of no military importance.

The bombing run Col counted as a bull's-eye was over Paris, his 13th op, just two nights before the Millennium attack on Cologne. His diary and logbook record that Watt cleared the runway at Lakenheath in their Stirling at one minute to midnight on Thursday 28 May 1942.

Will never forget Paris. Bombed the Gennevilliers [Gnome and Rhone aero engine] works on the south bank of the Seine. Two crews from the squadron went out, ours and Bill Barnes'. We got there flying at 6000 ft and the first thing we saw was an unmistakable pinpoint [landmark] just above the target.

We turned on our bombing run, but cloud intervened. As we had been told emphatically that we were not to bomb unless we were quite certain of the target, we made another run. Cloud again. We made five runs altogether, with the same result, so finally we decided to go below the cloud. We got down to 2900 ft and there, right ahead, was the pinpoint. Beyond that were the two bridges across the Seine which were shown on the map. What a thrill! I told the skipper to keep on and not to mind the flak (which was surprisingly heavy) because we might not get another run like it. He put her into a shallow dive, and held dead on. I saw the target come up, nearer and nearer and when it was dead in line I let them go. It is the one time I have actually seen them hit a specific building on a target, but by God! I saw them and so did the rear

Map 2: *Col Jones's targets in Europe*

gunner, F/Lt Morrison DFC, and I was so bloody excited that I yelled down the intercom.

We started the shallow dive at 2900 ft so I suppose we would have bombed at 2600 ft. It occurred to me afterwards that the safety height for those bombs is 3000 ft. However, we were going like the clobbers of hell, so we were away before the blast got to us. Jack Ekelund as 2nd dicky [pilot].

Despite the crew's apparent care to pinpoint the target, and Col's belief he had hit it fair and square, later photos showed little damage to the factory. The bombs from the 77 aircraft taking part seem to have fallen mainly on French houses and caused about 200 civilian casualties, including 34 dead.[4] Harris's introduction of area bombing, using massive waves of bombers, was itself recognition of the *inaccuracy* of night-time bombing. A report in August 1941 assessed the strike rate of bombers by analysing some 4000 aerial photographs taken after more than 100 night raids. It found that at *best* only one bomb in six fell within a 16-kilometre-wide circle centred on the target.[5] In other words, accuracy improved as the war progressed, but right to the end bombing remained a bludgeon rather than a rapier.

Col was open in his diary about one time he simply missed. This was on his 26th operation, late in his first tour, by which time he was already one of the RAF's more experienced bomb aimers. By August he was flying only the occasional op with Watt and had become a regular with the crew of a Canadian pilot, Flight Lieutenant Al Greenslade. They took off at 11.30 p.m. on Tuesday 1 September 1942.

Went to Saarbrücken – quiet trip, though we were plotted [by searchlights] most of the way back home. Nothing happened and hardly a shot was fired at us. Pranged target good and proper and all the crews came back with a great story of a target well and truly blitzed. Then Command told us that we had pranged the wrong place. Bit of a blow, especially as I said I had seen the marshalling yards – the distinctive loop in the river.

More than 200 bombers unleashed their misguided fury on the

small, non-industrial town of Saarlouis, killing 52 civilians, while not so much as a damp squib fell on Saarbrücken itself.

The prospects of bombers hitting the intended target improved in later years as navigation equipment became more reliable and the RAF established the élite, target-marking Pathfinder Force, which Col joined in early 1944. Even so, bombing remained imprecise. Dr Laurenz Demps, a Berlin history professor who, when I met him, was researching the capital's experiences during the war, told me the German defenders knew that around a third of bombers attacking Berlin deliberately dropped their bombs short of the target as they approached over the outer suburbs. He said many bombs missed for other reasons, even when released at the right point over the target: the 'smaller' bombs – those 500 pounds and lighter – that accounted for much of a standard bomb-load until 1944 were susceptible to thermal updrafts, such as those created by industrial activity. As a result, many bombs veered off as they fell towards factory roofs and struck surrounding residential areas instead.

Demps experienced at first hand what it was like being in a residential area of Berlin once the bombs started to fall. He was five, his brother six and their mother raced to get them to safety as the heavy drone of enemy engines grew louder. Frau Demps was intent on reaching the air-raid shelter underneath the large flak tower in the eastern suburb of Friedrichshain. This and a command tower nearby made up one of three major flak emplacements in Berlin: there was another north of the city centre at Humboldthain and a third by the zoo beside Tiergarten Park, just west of the city centre. Each 40-metre tower had a platform on top with an octagonal, concrete turret on each corner sprouting twin 128-millimetre anti-aircraft guns, and with a cluster of rapid-fire 20- and 37-millimetre cannons on a skirting platform running around the building below these turrets. Underneath were the bunkers: steel-reinforced concrete up to 2.5 metres thick that could withstand even a direct hit, as was proven only once at Friedrichshain. The emplacement survived the Allied bombing and Red Army shelling, but shortly after the Russians took it over a suspicious fire destroyed an extensive collection of priceless artworks that had been transferred to the nearby command tower from Berlin museums early in the war for safe keeping. The flak tower itself proved too tough to demolish completely, and today its remnants poke through the earth heaped over it to form a landscaped and tree-shaded mound at the centre of the park. Like Devil's Hill near my home, this rare piece of high ground in Berlin is built on the bones of the city's misery.

The Friedrichshain bunker was a 20-minute dash away for Frau Demps and her two little boys. With a sense of deliverance Frau Demps reached the bunker entrance before the bombs started to fall. But the shelter, built to hold 20,000 people, was full; the warden turned the three Demps away.[6] Back Frau Demps fled, the little boys numb-kneed and scrambling, knowing only their own vulnerability and their mother's panicked will to save them. The gauntlet-run passed between a gasworks on one side of the road and the unbroken façade of apartment blocks on the other. The bombs were now falling all around. By a miracle, they made it back to their home unscathed. The Demps boys saw immediately that in the desperate, short hour between when they had left their home and when they returned, their mother's hair had turned white.

The Demps' experience, during the failed campaign of winter 1943–4 to reduce Berlin to rubble, was already common to many people living in German cities further west. What happened to Hamburg in July 1943 made the May 1942 attack on Cologne seem like a curtain-raiser. Col had completed his tour in 1942, but flew as a bomb aimer the following July on the first raid of the campaign against Hamburg, codenamed Operation Gomorrah. His letters are silent on the raid – he had decided not to tell his family he was doing his best to get back on operations. His logbook, however, shows he took off at 10.30 p.m. on 24 July 1943, in a 115 Squadron Lancaster piloted by a Canadian, Squadron Leader Ian Bazalgette. It must have been an eventful trip, as Col received a Mention in Dispatches for bravery as a result.[7] Unusually, Col made a descriptive entry in his own log: 'First 8000 lb bomb – wizard!'[8]

Like so many of the war's most terrible weapons – the atomic bombs 'Little Boy' and 'Fat Man' dropped on Japan being the most obvious examples – the 8000-pound (4-tonne) bomb had a benign nickname: 'Plumduff'. The more standard 4000-pound bomb went by the name 'Cookie' and it had a variety of different fillings. In some attacks, such as that on Bremen on 13–14 September 1942, these bomb casings contained an incendiary cocktail of benzol, rubber and phosphorus, which exploded in a vivid pink flash and earned this version of the bomb the name 'Pink Pansy'. The 8000-pound bomb dropped by Col on Hamburg contained mainly an ammonium nitrate explosive called Amatex. It was a blast bomb, designed to blow the roofs off buildings and collapse their walls so that the incendiaries showered over the target could feed on the flammable materials inside.

Though Hamburg, Germany's second city, had already endured 99 raids by late July 1943 and was among Germany's most heavily defended cities, the raid of 24–25 July, and the three that followed during Operation Gomorrah, were to redefine 'total war' in a way the Nazi Propaganda Minister, Josef Goebbels, had surely not imagined earlier that year. In a speech at the Berlin Sportpalast in February 1943, in the wake of the catastrophic German defeat on the eastern front at Stalingrad, he had whipped the audience into a frenzy with the words: 'The English say the German people have lost their faith in victory…that they have become war-weary…that they don't want total war, but rather capitulation. I ask you: do you want total war – if necessary more complete and more radical than we can scarcely imagine today? ... Now, Volk arise, and storm break loose!'[9]

Gomorrah was no exaggeration as a description of what befell Hamburg in July 1943. Col had been in the first raid, on 24–25 July, but was not flying on the second raid of the series three nights later, when another force of nearly 800 bombers returned. A rare combination of high temperatures, low humidity and the tinder-dry conditions following a prolonged rain-free spell contributed to the infamous firestorm. The horror left an estimated 40,000 dead, three-quarters of them from asphyxiation. It drove 1.2 million survivors from the city.[10] In 2008 I visited Ohlsdorf Cemetery, in the north of Hamburg, to see the cruciform mass grave of nearly 37,000 victims of the firestorm whose remains could not be identified. Where the two axes of the long, grass burial plots cross is a cenotaph containing a stone sculpture of death's boatman of Greek mythology, Charon, ferrying a clutch of tortured souls across the River Styx to the afterlife. Amid the roses along the edge of each grass strip some families have erected small crosses or plaques to relatives who disappeared that night. Some list up to a dozen names, their birthdates counting down the generations from grandparents to infants, most ending with the same surname and all recorded as dying on that same night in late July 1943. Just across the roadway in this huge cemetery is the Commonwealth War Cemetery containing, among others, 169 of the 554 RAF airmen killed during the bombing of Hamburg.

And what of Operation Gomorrah's Old Testament connotation of a city eradicated for its sins? East Germany's most famous artist dissident, singer-songwriter Wolf Biermann, survived the firestorm as a six-year-old, later describing it as the night his 'life's clock stood still'. He told an interviewer how his mother had welcomed the bombing – even though she lay in its path – just as prisoners in Auschwitz, where Biermann's father had been murdered that year, prayed for the Allies to bomb the extermination camps out of existence, even if they died in the process. 'Not only my father, but our entire Jewish family had been murdered there. The Allied bombers were our friends, as a child would put it: our Verbündeten – our allies – who should free us from the Nazis.'

By some miracle, Biermann and his mother escaped from the Hammerbrook district at the heart of the fire, which suffocated all those trapped there who did not perish in the flames. Amid the consuming carnage, the small boy observed such terrors as phosphorus dropped by bombers and burning on victims unable to douse it by jumping in the canals. Another searing image was boiling, viscous asphalt that trapped those who tried to flee across it. More than one in three residents of this area died that night, most of them women, children or men either too old or infirm to serve in the armed forces – or the terribly brave men tasked with the impossible job of quelling the flames and helping civilians to safety.

Biermann realised one irony only later: the city park where they found safety was the same from which his grandparents and several other members of his Jewish family had been deported to the death camps earlier that same year. 'The only accusation I – and not only I – really level at these Allied bombers is that they could have kept aside a few small bombs to destroy the gas chambers in which my father died. And to smash the rail tracks, and the bridges over which the death trains carried millions of people to the death factories. In a humanitarian sense, the bombs could have been put to better use there than against Dresden. That much is clear.'[11]

One of Col's letters, written in December 1942, shows he knew of the Holocaust at least seven months before he took off on that Gomorrah raid, but there is no indication he thought he was 'saving' German Jews by bombing their cities, nor that he ever considered the merits of targeting the infrastructure of extermination. That 1942 letter indicates he was spurred along partly by his growing awareness of the atrocities Germany was committing to its east, particularly against the Jews, but others show his justification for seeking vengeance was the bombing of English cities and of Warsaw and Rotterdam. He was clearly keen to get 'back on the job' when wrote to his sister on 17 March 1943, four months before Gomorrah:

I can hear the planes go overhead as the lads do their night flying. I'm stuck on the ground. I'd rather fly. Well, at long last we have made one great, big, hell of a mess of Essen. Goodness knows we have been trying for a long time, and now we have done it. I went to that nasty spot five times, and saw it only twice. There is a great deal of haze there. Still, they have had it at last. It is no secret that Germany is going to feel a terrific onslaught by air this summer. What has happened to Essen is going to happen to many other cities. This summer is the beginning of the end – and also the end of the beginning. I would not like to be a German. I wonder when we are going to begin the second front. Soon, I hope, the sooner the better. Then we can turn our undivided attention to the merry little Japs. I still hope to fly over Tokyo and shovel out the odd incendiary. Tokyo will burn, and in it will be the ruins of the Japanese Empire.

CHAPTER 8

ON A WING AND A PRAYER

COL'S DITCHING in the English Channel was the only time he had to abandon his aircraft, but far from the only occasion his life hung on a thread – times he felt the brushing of what he referred to as 'the wingtips of lady eternity'. On several occasions his aircraft was caught in the blaze of searchlights. The triangulation by teams of searchlights created a tepee-like effect of light beams, with the bomber caught where they crossed. Aircrew called this being 'coned', and unless the pilot could pull off a dramatic evasive manoeuvre, the bomber would often be held there, floodlit, while the flak batteries zeroed in for the kill. Col experienced coning for the first time over the Baltic naval city of Kiel in April 1942, and then survived another daredevil exploit near the same city just a few days later. His diary describes what happened after OJ-'D' Donald, flown by Jock Watt, took off on the night of 28 April.

Kiel. We nearly had it. Never thought I should see Lakenheath again – and neither did anyone else. W/Cdr Mitchell (75 Squadron) said afterwards that he was low and saw us coned. Did not give us a hope. It was the same perfect visibility; but when we got a quarter of an hour from the target, the first of the searchlights blinded us. From then on, we were never quite out of them. We were not coned for more than five minutes at a time; but they were always getting on to us.

Kiel is hot – I should say one of the hottest places in Germany. It is nearly as bad as Hamburg and is worse than the Ruhr. We seemed to be the only kite there, because I did not see a searchlight playing anywhere else. They gave us everything they had and as I lay there I could see the black puffs coming nearer and nearer. The others said the same afterwards. Jock Watt said afterwards that he nearly told me to jettison. For him to say that shows how bad it was.

In the middle of it all, with the target still five minutes away, I saw a line of flame shoot past my windows in the bomb bay. We had been attacked by a fighter, who had come into his own flak! Bags of guts, that Jerry! The cannon shells shot over the port wing and just over the skipper's head, while some came on a line with my windows in the bomb bay. Well, if the atmosphere in the crew had been tense before, what the hell was it now? Then Jock Watt showed the sort of man he is. He simply said with a funny kind of half chuckle, 'the cheeky bastard!' Well, though we were still cursing and though we still had the worst ahead, the tenseness went from the crew. Amazing! Just typical of Jock Watt.

Managed to edge him over to port gradually, coping with the searchlights until we managed to let our bombs go; just near the docks. We went like hell out of the target area and never saw the fighter again. Jock went over Denmark at 50 ft just for the sheer devilment. We saw the countryside just as though it had been day and saw houses and hedges and ploughed fields and irrigation ditches and all the rest of it.

They returned to the Kiel area four days later, Col's 11th op.

Seem to be specializing in 'shaky dos'. Went gardening [mine-laying] in Kiel Bay, just south of Langeland. Another perfect night, and I saw the pinpoint [landmark] I wanted 30 miles away. Told Jock to tell me when we had it on our port beam three miles away just in case I lost sight, and we casually lost height down to 600 ft. We had just got to the pinpoint, actually I was just about to say 'bomb doors open' when, out of the blue, as unexpectedly as leave, up it came. Damn! – just immediately behind our spot, if there wasn't a convoy anchored for the night, protected by flak ships. Al Shoreman, wireless operator, counted 13 guns on one ship and both Sandy Hill and Douggie Seagrave opened up as we sailed over. They could not have missed. We let them go, and like a bat out of hell, Jock put the nose down and turned hard port. He did not think he would ever pull out but be did, 50 ft over Langeland.

But we still had one on, so back we went into all the shit and corruption. Tried to let it go. Tried to let the convoy have the two 500 pounders we carried in our wings; but I think we missed with them and the mine stayed on. Looking back, I think we were mad to try to bomb the convoy with 500 pounders from 600 ft because that is asking for trouble. Safety height is 3000 ft.

Came home without incident. The lads saw a horseman on the Danish sands and wanted to open fire, but the skipper said it might be a 'free Dane.' The tide was dead out. Jock told me months afterwards at Waterbeach that when we dived after the second effort, we were 10 ft off the water.

Col's ditching in the English Channel came just a month later, but even after this he did not stay out of danger for long. Less than two months after being pulled from the water he survived an episode that was about as close as any bomber crew came to hand-to-hand combat with ground defenders without actually getting out of the plane. The sequence of events began at one minute to midnight on 28 July 1942, when he took off from Lakenheath with another skipper, Flight Lieutenant Al Greenslade.

Went to Hamburg in 'B' Beer 6hrs 05mins – one of the shakiest trips yet – bad met. – icing – coped with that – came out of cloud only over the target – went down to 10,500 ft – perfect visibility – full moon – everything spread out below.

Intense flak heavy and light – worst searchlights I have ever seen – caught as soon as entered target area. Could never get out at all. There was supposed to be a large raid there, but for a variety of reasons a good many machines turned back. Icing conditions were very bad. We managed to cope with them, and when we got to the target we received their undivided attention. It's bad enough when there are a large number of machines, but to be there alone was a bit awkward. Just as we turned to the target, I saw one lonely kite bombing. It was caught in the searchlights, so that it looked just like a silver moth in a chink of light through an ill-fitting door. That kite got away and in we went. Well, it was a nightmare of a bombing run – the longest bombing run I have ever made. All we did was to dive and twist and climb and weave like a mad thing. I was lying in the bomb bay, where I could see all the searchlights below.

Everything they had was on us; and believe you me, the Germans are good at ground defence. Worked our way into the target by dint of much weaving and dodging – opened bomb doors and let them go – satisfaction of seeing them fall into right place. But still caught in searchlights – could see the heavies below us and see the tracers flying past. Strong smell of cordite from heavy flak. The light tracer was flashing past all round us, and the gunners were giving the skipper instructions where to go. All I could say was that we would have to get further over to starboard, because below on to the left was the river, so we had to get further over to the right.

Just when we were nearing the part of the city we had to bomb, a shell hit our starboard outer engine, so it went on us. Everyone was very calm, and all the engineer said was 'well, skipper, you had better feather that engine [turn its propeller blade edges to the wind] or it will catch fire.' Skipper put the nose down and I literally rose into the air and floated in the bomb bay. Took me 30 secs to get from bomb bay back to my chair – instruments and maps all over the place – flung on floor – hell of a job finding them. (Speedo touched 370 mph.) Cecil Watkins wireless operator/air gunner had similar experience down near the flare chute. He also floated in mid-air and was flung all over the place. He was hanging on like grim death, with his legs trailing out in the air behind him. That is a hell of a job.

Levelled out over the south-west suburbs of Hamburg at 50 ft, and thus lost searchlights. Set course 252 degrees Compass and battled along just above the ground. Then altered course 304 degrees Compass to hit the coast, still at zero ft. It was too low to map read, so I just told the skipper to make straight for the coast and we would sort ourselves out later. Shot at by every gun from Hamburg to coast – tracer coming up, not up, but across at us. [Stirling's] gunners had the time of their lives. Everyone but the engineer and I did, in fact. The captain was shouting like a boy, and the gunners were having competitions. Shot up gunposts and one's first burst went ahead of us and that was the only one he fired, because we accounted for the gun crew. We were so close at such point-blank range that in the moonlight we saw the gun crew, hit by our guns, stagger and fall as we shot. Opened up at every searchlight we saw, both in outskirts of Hamburg and across Germany – gunners put out 15 between them – shot up a village and passed a train. Unfortunately, gunners had stoppages, so could not deal with it. They fired until their guns would not fire any more.

We came out down the mouth of the Elbe, which is positively the worst place in Germany to cross the coast. Hit the coast in Elbe estuary. Searchlights were playing on the water in an effort to pick us up. In the light of one of the searchlights we saw shells skipping along the water. They were being fired from Cuxhaven. We were so low at one stage that rear gunner called out, 'eh, Skip, if you go any lower I'll get my feet wet!' Every island had a gun or a searchlight – some both – and they gave us all they had. More islands should be marked on the map, and then we would know when we're past the last of them. They kept looming up every few minutes, one after the other.

The islands once past, the question was whether our juice would allow us to go out to sea and then fly west, or whether we should turn west at once and skirt the Frisians [chain of islands off the north Dutch coast], chancing the fighters – and us with no guns. They all had stoppages. The rear gunner fired 3000 rounds, the front gunner 2750 and the mid-upper 2000 rounds. What a night!

I decided that even if we had to ditch the kite near the English coast, it would be wise to go out to sea, we did for 20 mins. Ground speed 147 mph. Then we went 270 degrees and Cecil tried to get some loops [radio position signals] – not much joy. Then I worked out roughly how far we had to go to get clear of the Frisians and gave a course for home. Could not use the Gee [navigation device], and loops not much good; too low probably, 1500 ft. Finally, got a loop that put us 57 miles from the coast and on track. Had no track of ground speed, however, and did not know how long that would take. Think the fix put us too near, in any case.

Engineer gave warning about juice, so when we saw the coast coming up, even though we knew where we were (Haisborough Light), we got a QDM [a magnetic bearing]. I was unwilling but had to admit that the procedure was wise. Found we were nearly on track. Just stooged on waiting for the beacon. It came – and all was well. The engineer told the captain that he must on no account make more than one circuit of the aerodrome before landing because the tanks were nearly dry. We had just enough to get down and no more. It was no more than the truth, because just as we landed, the starboard inner died on us. The point is that we had been hit in the tanks and three engines use more juice than four, strange as it may sound.

Supposed to be a big do, but all except No.3 group scrubbed – only some 100 got to target. Had 13 mins petrol left when landed. It subsequently transpired that 64 actually got to target. Our losses were 34.[1]

The final near miss Col recalls in his diary occurred two-thirds of the way through his first tour of operations, on the way back from bombing Mainz on 12–13 August 1942.

Mainz is a cathedral town, the seat of Catholic authority in Germany, one of a string of Catholic Cathedral cities along the Rhine's west bank and known to the German pilots as the Pfaffengasse – Priests' Alley. I visited Mainz and these other cities several times for their beauty and historical significance. One of Mainz's main attractions is the sublime stained glass windows created in 1977 in St Stephan's Church as a symbol of post-war reconciliation, by the French-based Jewish artist and Russian émigré, Marc Chagall. These windows line the transept and chancel, enclosing the altar, and depict scenes from the Old Testament. By day, they bathe the church's interior in blue light, as if suspended in the waters of a tropical reef. This masterpiece replaced the windows blasted out during three bombing raids on Mainz, between 12 August 1942 and February 1945, the first of which Col took part in. Although neither this church nor several others were spared in those raids, Col thought he and his crew had been saved by divine intervention that night when OJ-'A'Apple came under attack, with Jock Watt once again in command of their Stirling.

Went to Mainz like a bird – good navigation – 8-9/10ths cloud but dropped a flare and pinpointed the island in the plan. Saw it through a hole in the cloud. But, damn it, by the time the skipper, good old Jock Watt (what a man!), turned the kite we had lost it. Got there at 01.43 and did not set course [for home] until 02.23 – 40 mins and we never saw the target again. Started off at 11,000 ft and went down to 7,000 ft to try to get below the cloud. No joy, but had icing even at that height. Decided to return home.

It was not until we were about halfway back that things started to happen. We had been stooging along at 11,000 ft not far above the cloud layer gently weaving as was Jock Watt's invariable custom when over enemy territory. I remember that there was no cloud but bright starlight. It all happened at once. A bang and a clatter, and the smooth, horrible sound of ripping silk and many snakes of fire. The ME110 came so suddenly out of the cloud underneath, to fire one long, raking burst that we had time only to identify it before it had gone as suddenly as it came. It did not return and why, no one will ever know. Perhaps it was Jock Watt who said it was the mercy of God, but it was more, and that is why I have called this story the Mercy of God – and Jock Watt.

Watt's account of the episode is contained in a combat report completed soon afterwards at Lakenheath. It includes the following:

The E/A [enemy aircraft] was commencing its attack when first seen firing an approx. 10 seconds burst of cannon and m/g [machine-gun] fire. As it closed in from port quarter our rear gunner, Sgt Hughes, fired two short bursts at a range of 750 feet and E/A broke away sharply to port when about 300 feet away. Again our rear gunner fired two short bursts at this range, aiming at the cabin of the E/A, which was clearly outlined and in a steep bank. No strikes were observed on the E/A, but Stirling was damaged, the port fuel system being hit, causing petrol to escape and for a short time black smoke and flames were observed coming from the region of the port inner engine and also from near the W/Op's [wireless operator's] position. In addition, both M/U [mid-upper] and front turrets were rendered inoperative, and the power operation of the undercarriage put out of action. The flames died down quickly as Stirling took evasive action by making a steep diving turn to port and E/A was not seen again as cloud cover was entered immediately after.[2]

Col's diary describes this sequence in richer detail:

The plane was shot to pieces – our ME110 had seen to that; we knew we had no guns; we knew the controls had been damaged; we knew we did not have enough petrol to make base. But it was not until the engines began to cut one by one as we tried to get the undercarriage down to land at that welcome strange 'drome that we knew things were grim.

I think Jock Watt had known all the time, as very little about a kite and her engines ever escaped his notice. That was why he was so brusque when things were going well, but became 'so gentle' and 'so kind' – I think he thought it was likely to be the last of so many ops flown together. It nearly was – but that is the story as well as being the reason for its heading – that was the Mercy of

God. What followed was Jock Watt's part in it. The fighter stayed for only one burst, but that was enough. The front and rear turret were put out of action and the turret jammed with the guns facing the opposite way from that in which the fighter had struck. The hydraulics of the mid-upper were shot away and the guns would not fire.

A fire broke out in the port inner [engine] and another inside the machine itself. We knew that the tanks had been badly holed, because over all was the overpowering smell of vaporising benzene. We did not know at the time that the entire petrol system had been disorganized; the engineer did though, and his work in coping won him the DFM. Nor did we know that the oxygen system had been destroyed – which was just as well, because when we smelt the vaporising petrol, we breathed the more deeply into our oxygen masks as we flew on, or rather staggered through the air like a woman with a middle-aged spread. We became increasingly aware of a heaviness in the head. But we did not know we had no oxygen.

The ME110 attacked from not more than 100 ft, so it could scarcely miss. It must have been led by some means right on to us. When we had recovered from the first stunning shock – I don't know how long that took for, at times like that, time means nothing – there was a rush to do something. The front gunner who, irony of all ironies, had come from Training Command to get experience, yelled to us to get him out of his turret. The wireless operator struggled with the fire; the engineer juggled in a frenzy with his petrol controls; the mid-upper cursed his gun audibly over the intercom.

I have forgotten exactly what Jock Watt said, but quite calmly, quite quietly, he called to us that there was no need to worry; we were still flying; we were coping. He told the front gunner who, as I have said, was not in our crew, not to fret. He would soon be out of his turret; and he ordered me to go and let him out. I did so. Then Jock set about trying to make 'A' Apple fly. The wireless operator for his part, having coped with the fire, set about trying to cope with the jigsaw ruin that was his set. The old 'A' Apple staggered about all over the sky, doing its own evasive action. We tried getting down into the cloud but conditions were dreadfully bumpy, with the worst icing I have ever seen, which made the machine all the more hard to control.

Jock did not say much after his first encouragement, and what little he did say was to the engineer, Eddie Owen. Eddie worked in silent grim desperation struggling with fast ebbing petrol. He shared with the skipper a knowledge of how bad things were. No-one else said anything at all. What was there to say? God knows how many times he changed tanks, with the situation worsening all the time; but of that period, my lasting impression is the kindness of Jock's voice – he was usually impatient of engineers and their instructions – and the calmness of Eddie's.

We staggered on. The coast, I knew, ought to be near, but I had no navigational means of discovering how near. The fighter damaged more than the petrol tanks. The cloud was 10/10ths below us and with slowness, but a dreadful inevitability, we were losing, ever losing, height. We did not know then, but we must have passed over Dunkirk at 4000 ft – in a plane barely able to fly, let alone weave. We limped on and on, making for that part of the coast that was nearest England. The cloud was still 10/10ths and the first absolutely certain knowledge we had that we had crossed the coast was the sight far ahead of a beacon. I identified it as Manston and set course from there to Oxford Ness and base. Even then we were afraid to hope, thinking we might be mistaken. But before many minutes the unmistakable North Zeeland loomed up and we knew that we could at least hope again.

Jock Watt thought at first that we could make base, but remembering that the undercart might not come down, he turned and made for a 'drome [Manston] near the Thames estuary that is known through the RAF as the 'haven for lame ducks.' We called up the ground, letting them know we were in trouble and were coming in to land. The skipper went to put the undercart down at that stage – but, no joy. The controls had been damaged by the fighter. 'OK 'Apple' crash land on left of the flare path.'

'Trouble with undercarriage, will call again.' Had to wind it down by hand.

Port undercarriage down and starboard nearly but not quite. By that time, the fuel question was urgent. Just as soon as the green [warning] lights showed, the starboard outer cut. Then flying at 600 ft [altitude]. Turned cross wind when [outer] port engine cut. Turned away from flare path, but could not maintain height on two motors; losing height down to 150 ft. All balance cocks were then turned on and they picked up again. When all four came on again and aircraft returned to flare path we managed to get to 400 ft in direction of flare path. Then with Manston funnel coming up, both inner engines cut, down to 30 ft having just cleared a wood, then up again when all four cut.

'We're for it blokes, hang tight.' She hung for a second, then she hit, rolled on and crossed a road, struck a ditch, took off for 90 yards, landed again, passed between two telegraph poles taking the wire with it, crossed several gardens, slewed to starboard and came to rest with the front turret concertinaed against the back wall of a house – unoccupied, but those on either side were occupied. The port undercart collapsed. Thought the skipper was badly hurt because his face was covered in blood. He yelled out 'all out. Hurry!' There was a small fire in the starboard inner, so I hopped up with the extinguisher. Fortunately, it went out by itself. Then we all went and had copious cups of tea in one of the houses.

I forgot to say that the collapsed undercart and the wing came to rest over an Anderson shelter in which were two small children. We got them out uninjured and the first thing the little boy said was 'coo, what sort of machine was it?' They were in the shelter because an air raid warning was on. Went to Manston, had some food, had a sleep and came back to base about 11 am. Interrogated – lunch and breakfast together – bacon and egg first and then roast beef after – and now I am going to bed.

This episode produced a couple of exciting finds during my search. One was Watt's combat report, which I obtained from the National Archive in London; the other was a photo of their Stirling crashed into the row of houses, sent to me from the United States by the author of a book on the history of 149 Squadron. For Col, this episode and his earlier ditching in the English Channel won him the Distinguished Flying Cross, which he received from King George VI at Buckingham Palace in February 1943. The citation noted:

Pilot Officer Frank Colwyn JONES, Royal New Zealand Air Force, No. 149 Squadron, has participated, as navigator, in attacks on many of the enemy's most important targets. During a sortie over Essen, in June 1942, his aircraft was badly holed by fire from ground defences; later it was attacked by an enemy fighter. The aircraft was so badly damaged that it was necessary to alight in the sea but Pilot Officer Jones, whilst in the dinghy, maintained an accurate plot of its position until the crew were rescued. During another sortie, in August, 1942, his accurate navigation was responsible for the safe return of his aircraft which had been seriously damaged by an enemy fighter. Pilot Officer Jones has displayed high courage and extreme devotion to duty.[3]

Col was by then all too familiar with the destructive power of the Luftwaffe's night fighters – but also with the RAF's capacity to hit back. A little over two weeks after Col's crash landing in Kent, Otto had his first brush with the enemy – and with the 'wingtips of lady eternity' – which resulted in his being shot down by a Stirling's rear gunner. Like Col, Otto defied death many times: forced to bale out four times, attacked by a British night fighter while landing once and suffering wounds significant enough to be decorated twice for them. But by a series of miracles he and Fred ended the war with their health – if little else – intact. Now I felt the lucky one as the 90-year-old professor told me his story. With remarkable immediacy and detail, Otto-Heinrich Fries brought back to life the perils of night combat over Germany from the perspective of one of the men trying to kill my great-uncle.

CHAPTER 9

INTERCEPTOR

DURING THE MASSIVE RAIDS on Cologne and Hamburg, Otto Fries flew in hopeless confusion. His job was to intercept and snuff out the arsonists, whose bombs were engulfing the homes and factories below in a sea of flames. But despite the hundreds of bombers churning the air about him over Cologne in May 1942 and Hamburg in July 1943, he failed to attack a single aircraft. Even by the latter raid, Otto had yet to claim his first kill. But his despair on both occasions went much deeper: he shared the German defenders' sense of powerlessness at the overwhelming scale of the fury being unleashed by Bomber Command. 'I saw all of Germany's cities in flames, but that [Cologne] was the first city I saw *really* in flames. The sight was entsetzlich, shocking. We saw the city burning, we knew there were thousands of people in cellars down below and we were hanging up there able to do absolutely nothing to stop it.'

The night fighter pilots were used to Raumjagd – being guided one by one to a particular bomber, by ground controllers responsible for a specific zone. 'Raumjagd was a reasonably comfortable affair, but suddenly we were faced with a completely new tactic from the British. That night over Cologne the bombers came in masses. For the first time we were given clearance to free-hunt – the so-called wilde Sau, the 'wild boar' approach – but there were too many machines, we couldn't settle on one. I couldn't get behind a bomber, they were racing about from all directions, and the Lichtenstein [on-board radar] had so many squiggles on its screens it was going crazy.' After Cologne, the Luftwaffe changed its tactics fundamentally, sending up more fighters and giving them greater scope to free-hunt. Not until more than a year later did Otto Fries shoot down his first bomber, but from then on success came steadily, adding to the staggering scale of losses German night fighters began inflicting on Bomber Command from late 1943 onwards.

Cologne had been a deeply demoralising experience for Otto, but he felt an even greater sense of powerless rage as he flew above the blazing city of Hamburg in July 1943. The Gomorrah raids were the first time Bomber Command spread radar-jamming metallised strips from aircraft to overwhelm German radar with a blizzard of decoys. Called 'window' by the RAF and Düppel by the Luftwaffe, it literally foiled the German defences and forced the night fighters to rely largely on the naked eye. In the months that followed Gomorrah the Luftwaffe success rate dropped: their radar completely blinded by window, the night fighters felt they were reduced to chasing ghosts across the sky. Otto knew of at least one senior Luftwaffe pilot over Hamburg during Gomorrah who simply returned to base, such was the confusion created by the strips: 'I was fassungslos – struck dumb. I had such a rage in my belly that I couldn't do anything – I wanted to bale out of the aircraft, I felt so helpless.'

Otto struck back a month later, in August 1943, shooting down his first bomber as described in Chapter 5. On 22 October 1943 Otto shot down his second bomber in conditions that were almost hauntingly surreal, showing how weather could both enchant and imperil aircrew. Otto and Fred were by then also carrying a rear gunner, Konrad Deubzer, to keep an eye out for prowling RAF night fighters so that Fred could concentrate on radio communications and radar. Soon after taking off at 7 p.m. to intercept bombers heading for the central city of Kassel, they found themselves blinded twice over: first by radio distortion and second by the weather. The ground to air radio guidance to their targets was being blocked by bombers equipped with special radar-jamming devices, so all Fred could hear was a signal that alternated between a sound like an electric drill in masonry and a continuous succession of claxon-like blasts they named 'the bagpipes'. Lacking help from the 'eyes on the ground', Otto climbed to 6000 metres and flew towards where he estimated the bomber stream would pass. That was when the second 'blinding' began: as he climbed higher a dense wall of cloud gathered ominously, and soon he was flying 'as if swimming in a milky brew', with only his instruments to determine the ME110's position relative to the horizon and the ground.

On nights when nimbus thundercloud brewed over Europe, it held aloft ice particles and conjured a magical play of electricity about Otto's Messerschmitt ME110. Flickering small blue flames – St Elmo's fire – danced from the antler-like radar antennae and appeared as a wave of cool, blue foam on the leading edges of wings and in phosphorescent circles around the twin propellers. Beneath the Messerschmitt's long canopy, sitting in the darkness, Otto and his two crew were enchanted by the electrical display. What appeared as miniature storms of forked lightning danced on the armour-plated glass windscreen and when Otto ran his flying gloves along the plexiglass beside him it crackled and spat small charges from the glass surface. Otto joked: 'We're being stalked by a ghost and it's nowhere near midnight yet. I wonder what sort of fantastic ghost story Edgar Allen Poe or E.T.A. Hoffmann would make out of this!' Fred shot back: 'That explains why my radio is completely dead, although it's in perfect working order and I've got everything switched on. Let's quit this magic show and turn around. In this crap we're not only blind, but deaf and dumb as well. Even if a Tommy [Englishman] flew straight past he'd be able to tickle our wings without us seeing him.'

Otto turned the plane back on its course and nosed it down to 4500 metres. As he did so the electricity dancing on the leading surfaces diminished and before long they emerged from the mist and Otto could soon pick out the horizon below the thick cloak of cloud. The radio distortion did not abate, however, so Fred left the R/T on 'receive' and Otto began searching for targets by sweeping the nose back and forth in a snaking motion, trying with the help of Fred and the on-board radar to 'sniff out' any bomber unlucky enough to find itself in the 45-degree wedge in front of their ME110. Nothing.

Then a brief burst from the ground control: 'Eagle 98 from Kingfisher [ground control's call-sign for that night]. Adjust 300 degrees to your present course. Courier approaching you at 40 to 45 degrees...' Then static. Otto banked sharply to port. Fred reported he was still picking up nothing on the three radar circles, which indicated the altitude, distance and position to port or starboard of a target. Then a smudge: 'I've got something – but it seems to be just Düppel'. No sooner had Fred dismissed it as a target than Otto saw a large, dark shadow pass quickly underneath, heading the way they had just come.

As Otto swung the ME110 again steeply to port he calculated in his head the compass fix needed to set him on the bomber's tail. When the needle came around to 120 degrees he levelled the aircraft on its course – but there was no sign yet of the bomber on Fred's radar screens. 'Take off after him, we've got some catching up to do,' Fred said. Otto opened the throttle and the ME110's speed picked up to 430 kilometres per hour. 'The stupid mutt!' said Fred suddenly. 'Classic case – he's had the bright idea a nasty night fighter may pop up in the vicinity and he has to hide himself, so he's chucking out a bundle of Düppel every few seconds and spreading out a lovely welcome mat for us to follow. He's just two Kah-Ems [kilometres] ahead of us.'

Otto switched his guns from safety and levered up his seat to bring his line of vision level with the reflector-gunsight, then he adjusted the light on the sights – bright enough to see the markings but not so bright as to spoil his night vision. Fred counted down the distance and when the ME110 was a kilometre behind the bomber Otto throttled back to avoid overtaking it. Fred guided him in: 'Distance 500 metres – a bit higher, left slightly...Distance 300, a bit higher, right slightly.' Then Otto saw the shadow, just above the horizon and silhouetted clearly against the night sky. 'I see him, you can switch the radar off.'

He flicked the safety cover forward from the top of the control stem so that his thumb was on the firing button for the two 20-millimetre cannons mounted under the nose, and made ready to squeeze the control stem trigger for the four machine guns. An accurate burst of just a few seconds was usually enough proof of the devastating combination of this firepower. Otto drew closer, positioning his ME110 behind and to port, so the bomber remained silhouetted just above the horizon. 'It's a Short Stirling,' the Bordfunker and gunner said in unison over the intercom. Otto snapped back: 'Shut up, will you? You're putting me off with your blabber.'

Otto crept closer to what was, in fact, a Lancaster – EM-'R' Roger of 207 Squadron, based at Spilsby, near the Lincolnshire coast. Unusually, she carried a crew of eight that night, instead of seven. The pilot, Squadron Leader Alexander Lyons McDowell, was a married man from Vancouver, one of four Canadians on board, including the rear gunner. 'Hurry up and shoot before he sees us,' urged Fred.

'Quiet, quiet – just a little bit closer...'

Suddenly the rear end of the Lancaster blazed into action. Lines of tracer fire shot past the ME110, then there was a hard, sharp crack and Otto felt a stab of pain in his left calf muscle. 'He's got me in the left leg!' Instinctively he darted the ME110 to the right in a mid-air sidestep, then tugged lightly at the control stem to bring the bomber's rear gunner into his sights, blasting him with a short machine-gun burst. Otto Fries said this was the only time he intentionally shot to kill. The rear gunner, curled behind a thin skin bubble of plexiglass and the rack of machine guns, stood no chance under a hail of nearly 100 bullets a second.

Swinging the fighter back to port, Otto unleashed a second burst into the Lancaster's left wing, this time also using his twin cannons. Despite the blinding effect of the muzzle flashes from his own nose guns, he saw the explosions as the cannon shells struck. Suddenly the plane reared up and the damaged wing simply snapped off – Otto even heard the sharp crack. With its remaining wing leading the stricken bomber in an horrific dance, the dismembered Lancaster spiralled to the ground. Otto lost sight of it, until a few seconds later he saw a massive impact explosion, which shot out several lightning-like cascades. The detached wing, freed of its body, spun like a flaming sycamore seed to the ground, striking a minute after the main wreckage and in a similar but smaller fireball. Fred noted the time – 8.35 p.m. – and radioed ground control: 'Kingfisher from Eagle 98 – Sieg Heil – request location'.

'Viktor, understood – congratulations – stand by.'

Ground control radioed co-ordinates showing the Lancaster had come down south-east of Aachen, near the town of Nettersheim in the Eifel hills, south of Cologne. Nettersheim's mayor later informed Otto that he had watched the exchange of fire from the ground and had cycled to the crash site – a crater 8 metres deep and 25 metres across. Nothing remained of the Lancaster apart from fragments spread over a wide area. Its eight crew lie today in the Rheinberg War Cemetery, just inside the German border with the Netherlands city of Nijmegen.[1] Otto was uninjured. The stabbing pain in his leg had been caused by a ricocheting bullet that had struck a parachute flare strapped to his flying boot but had not ignited it.

By Otto's fourth kill – a Stirling with 75 (NZ) Squadron he shot down on 19 November south-west of Brussels – he was becoming practised at attacking from below and behind, then ducking off to the side to avoid answering fire. What makes this encounter stand out, however, is that three of the crew survived to describe in detail what it was like to be on the receiving end of Otto's guns. The Australian pilot and English navigator evaded capture and were able to debrief RAF investigators two months after the episode, once they had made it back to England. The third survivor – bomb aimer Jack Hyde, RNZAF – wrote from Christchurch more than 40 years later a brief account of how the bomber exploded just as he was jumping out. Hyde concluded that the blast had opened his parachute, since he regained consciousness only after hitting the ground, breaking his pelvis and spitting out two teeth as he came to. He spent the next year in German military hospitals before being interned in a prisoner of war camp. Of the seven crew, four were killed, including the 23-year-old wireless operator, Pilot Officer Bill Kell, of Dannevirke. The RAF loss report noted what the pilot, Flight Sergeant Noel Parker, and navigator Sergeant Robert

Griffith remembered of what happened:

The rear gunner reported having sighted the fighter and instructed the Pilot to prepare to 'corkscrew' and then gave the order to 'corkscrew starboard.' As the Stirling dived, the pilot saw cannon shells passing to port. (This and the subsequent attacks were marked by approximately 3-second bursts from the fighter.) The rear gunner did not fire, and the Stirling climbed to port. As the bomber dived again the fighter made a second and equally unsuccessful attack, to which the rear gunner replied with a half-second burst. He did not fire again, nor did he give any further instructions to the pilot. Nevertheless the pilot continued to corkscrew and a third long burst of cannon shells also missed the Stirling, but the rear turret became unserviceable after this attack, possibly due to damage by machine gun bullets.

Finally, when the pilot had begun to think that the fighter's ammunition was spent, a fourth attack was made as the Stirling was at the 'top' of the corkscrew. (No warning was given by the gunners.) The pilot heard two explosions in the starboard wing, but saw no shells go past. No further attack was made and the pilot heard nothing more of the fighter.

Almost directly after the last attack, the wireless operator told the pilot he could smell petrol, and the mid upper gunner reported a fire in the starboard wing. The pilot tried 'side-slipping' in the hope that this might extinguish the fire, but when he looked out he saw a blaze of light coming from the fuselage, which he first thought must be caused by petrol from a starboard tank. He immediately ordered the crew to abandon the aircraft, height then being about 8000 to 9000 ft....

A controlled fighter heard operating in the St Trond area from 1943 to 2000 hours claimed a victory at 2000 hours. He was informed by his base that his 'Sieg Heil' was south of Brussels. The fighter was operating at 12,000 ft, which agrees with the Stirling's height at the time of the attack....

The pilot believed that 'corkscrew' manoeuvres properly directed make it nearly impossible for the fighter to score hits on the bomber. Although he received no instructions from his gunners after the first attack, and the fighter met practically no opposition from the Stirling's guns, the fighter was able to score hits only on the fourth attempt.

Otto Fries's next experience of aerial combat six weeks later was so intense it could not have brought him much closer to his quarry without collision. His clash with a Lancaster from Col's 115 Squadron returning from bombing Berlin on 29 December 1943 was a display verging on stunt flying that belied the bulk of the four-engined bomber and strained Otto's every sinew. It all started unpromisingly when he took off in foul weather and was deployed well away from the estimated track of the bomber stream, far to the north of St Trond. His fighter was one of only two in his squadron to take off, while the group positioned in the bombers' path was grounded by the weather. With ground temperature at freezing point and cloud below 80 metres, the prospects for success looked as poor as the visibility as he cleared the runway at 8.42 p.m. Added to that, a heavy pea soup for lunch and an evening meal full of onions had brewed up to make Otto acutely uncomfortable in his strapped-in confinement.

At exactly 10 p.m. he heard the distraction he needed – a bearing from ground control guiding him onto an approaching bomber. Otto swung the Messerschmitt around to stalk the bomber from astern. Fred quickly picked up the Zacken – squiggles – in his radar windows, indicating a target 3 kilometres ahead and flying at the unusually high altitude of 6000 metres – at least a kilometre higher than normal for a bomber. When Otto was 700 metres behind the position indicated on the radar he slowed his approach. Only a thin layer of mist, as indistinct as a silvery fold in dark velvet, delineated the horizon from the star canopy that enclosed him. At a distance of 300 metres he could just pick out the barely perceptible rear profile of a Lancaster's wings, with its fuselage and four engines, which emitted a crimson glow from their exhausts. At 10.05 p.m. he closed to 150 metres for the kill.

Just as Otto was about to attack, the bomber flipped off to starboard, crossing through the Messerschmitt's gunsight as it did so. Otto fired on reflex and, as he did so, the rear gunner shot a stream of fire laced with tracer back in his direction. Because of the evasive action of the Lancaster, however, this answering fire arced harmlessly into the darkness like an uncontrolled garden hose spraying droplets of light. Otto reported the contact to ground control. 'Barabbas from Eagle 98 – Pauke – we're staying on the ball.'

'Viktor, understood.'

Otto wrenched the throttle levers back to reduce revs as he plunged the Messerschmitt to starboard to follow the Lancaster's steep dive.

'Keep an eye on the speedo, Fred, and let me know if we start to red-line. I have to keep my eyes glued to the lad in front.'

The Lancaster began 'corkscrewing' – weaving and see-sawing – trying to shake off its pursuer as it plunged towards the cloud cover. Otto, determined to follow the bomber's every move, flung the Messerschmitt with complete disregard for his Bordfunker and gunner behind him in the long cockpit. He was oblivious to their shrieks as the gunner, perched on a flip-down seat without a harness, floated up against the perspex canopy, his ammunition belts snaking weightless about him, then was rammed back against the floor as Otto pulled out sharply to follow the bomber upwards again. In a desperate save-or-lose-all manoeuvre, the bomber pilot broke from the corkscrewing action and suddenly tipped into a vertical dive to reach the cloud cover. Otto stuck to him, provoking a note of panic in Fred's response. 'Are you mad? You're pushing it past 700 Kah-Ems!' The speedo was already well beyond the red-line reading that showed dangerous strain was being exerted on the wings.

No sooner had the Lancaster dived straight down than it arrested its fall and roller-coasted back into an almost vertical climb. Otto rode the course like a bronco, but the audacity of the bomber's manoeuvre so threw him that his reaction brought the two aircraft almost to a collision, the bomber sliding only metres above him as Otto continued on his downward trajectory, then sought to fasten the Messerschmitt back onto the bomber's course. The bomber pilot had the advantage of surprise, but Otto's aircraft was faster and more agile – though not enough to allow him a clear shot. Otto could think of only one way to seize the initiative: to anticipate the very instant the bomber teetered in its turn and to fire at that point. Otto attuned himself to the bomber's rhythm, hung back to head off the next scything turn, then let loose a burst into its port wing – a hit, but no flames and the rear gunner answered with a salvo, again thrown wide by his aircraft's careering movement.

The seven minutes this uneven duel lasted left Otto exhausted and boiling in his flying suit. But the Lancaster pilot continued to throw the larger craft around the sky like a toy, though the low cloud cover that had kept so much of the night fighter force grounded now also meant the bomber had some distance still to dive before finding sanctuary. Otto unleashed a third burst, this time into the starboard wing and causing the inner engine immediately to glow with flame and to trail a thick train of smoke. '22.14 hours – altitude 3300 metres – you've got your teeth into him now!' said Fred. The bomber at this point stopped weaving and made for the clouds below. Otto closed the distance until he was so close he could feel from his own vibrating wings that he was in the Lancaster's slipstream. He fired a short burst into the starboard wing, between the engines, and saw the detonations explode into flame: he had probably ignited the fuel tanks. Otto tipped the Messerschmitt off to port and watched the stricken bomber cartwheel over its starboard wing and comet until swallowed by the cloud. Shortly afterwards the cloud layer pulsed with a sudden brightness as the bomber exploded. Fred intoned the official rites – 'For the report, altitude 2800 metres, time 22.16 hours. Congratulations' – and added, 'But that was one tough nut!'

As Otto went through the formalities with ground control, he noticed for the first time that his arms and legs were shaking and he was drenched in sweat. He had never before witnessed such masterful acrobatics from such a large aircraft. The conditions for landing were no better than when he had taken off, so he had to rely purely on instruments, touching down perfectly as if on the calmest and clearest of days. It was 10.55 p.m. He had been locked in an intense struggle with the Lancaster for 11 minutes and it had taken a further 24 minutes to return to this point. When he climbed out of the cockpit Otto could hardly stand because his knees were trembling so violently.

The Lancaster pilot and two crewmen survived, one making it back to England; the remaining four on board died and lie buried in a churchyard near where the Netherlands, Belgium and Germany come together.[2] Otto Fries seldom learned the fate of the airmen he shot down. When I provided him with the details of several of the kills credited to him and Fred Staffa, he was particularly keen to learn how many of their crew had escaped. By the time that encounter took place in December 1943, Otto had already survived being shot down once, and was to have his life saved by parachute three more times, as the tables were turned against the Luftwaffe.

CHAPTER 10

THE HUNTER AS TARGET

THE RAF LED THE COUNTER-CHARGE against the German night fighters in a superb, wooden warhorse – the twin-engined Mosquito fighter-bomber. Otto fell prey twice, possibly three times, to attacks by Mosquitoes. The first such encounter, in May 1944, left him badly injured. His squadron had just taken delivery of the revolutionary Heinkel HE219 Uhu, or owl, the best night fighter Germany produced. Otto had recently been appointed technical officer responsible for ensuring the squadron remained in good flying order, so was given the job of testing the new plane. By then thoroughly attuned to the ME110, he did not take immediately to the new HE219. One of the first aircraft to sit forward on a nose wheel, the Heinkel made Otto feel he was pitched forward, almost off balance. Instead of stepping up onto the wing and pulling himself into the cockpit, he scaled a tall ladder that had to be flipped end-over itself, to get into the Heinkel. Once inside, the two crew settled themselves into the world's first ejector seats, needed to fire the pilot and Bordfunker well clear if baling out, so they would not risk jumping straight into the propellers on the wings mounted high and behind the cabin.

On that first trial flight on 19 May 1944, Otto had put the new plane through its paces in the early hours of the morning, running through the instrumentation routines and, most important, testing how the more sluggish aircraft reacted when thrown about the sky as if during combat. He had just settled on a leisurely course back for base when suddenly crashing and splintering rent the night and the port motor erupted in flames.

'Enemy night fighter!' Fred yelled. On reflex, Otto speared the Heinkel steeply down to starboard and shut off the fuel cocks for the burning port engine, hoping to starve the flames of fuel. Despite his efforts to feather, then shut down, the burning engine, it continued to sputter like a giant sparkler. Then the flames swelled more brightly to blaze with the intensity of a rocket's after-burner. The safety of cloud cover lay well below, seemingly beyond reach as a potential refuge. But, puzzlingly, the unseen enemy night fighter – was it a Mosquito? – had not followed through on the attack.

Otto told Fred he was going to try to make it back to base, but would jettison the canopy in case they had to crash land and make a hurried exit. Otto tried to release the front half of the canopy, expecting it to flip up back on its hinge like a Messerschmitt's and to be torn free by the slipstream. Instead, it telescoped back on the rear section, but with such suddenness that Otto, his seat raised to allow him to test the gunsight, took a tremendous blow to the forehead, which knocked him senseless and opened up a gushing cut along his hairline. He slumped forward, pushing the Y-shaped yoke forward and sending the Heinkel into a steep dive. Fred, seated back to back with the pilot, yelled in alarm and glanced back in horror to see his skipper obliviously steering them to their destruction. In the panicked few seconds in which Fred's shouting failed to rouse his long-time pilot and friend, the Bordfunker concluded the only option was to catapult himself from the plummeting Heinkel. He lifted the safety flap on the seat release and pushed the button to fire the high-pressure ejector canisters. In the panic and confusion, however, Fred opened his parachute before releasing his seat harness, so that the parachute stays bound him to the seat base. He floated upside down to strike the ground headfirst at a speed of 5 metres a second.

Otto, meanwhile, was becoming groggily aware that he urgently needed to arrest the plane's headlong plunge, which had now reached a speed that threatened to tear the wings off. He hooked a forearm under each horn of the yoke and pulled back with all his strength. The Heinkel responded, scooping out of its dive and re-emerging above the cloud layer. Otto almost blacked out again as the centrifugal forces drained the blood from his head. His returning senses registered blood dripping from his nose and chin. He shouted to Fred, then realised the Bordfunker's compartment was empty. He could hardly see, let alone clear his head enough to attempt an emergency landing. But how to get out? With a mixture of instinct, terror and anger at what a stupid way this would be to die, Otto groped around in the blackness of the cabin. He was aware the instrumentation differed from the Messerschmitt's, but had no grasp of what he needed to do to save himself. He tried one button, but this merely slid the armour-plated windscreen cover into place; another lowered the undercarriage, then the flaps, causing the plane to slow and jump up, as if it had plunged into a wool bale.

Desperation battled with a determination to keep a cool head, though his forehead was on fire. With great effort he mastered his panic, and remembered a torch on a lanyard around his neck. Wiping the blood from his eyes again and probing the torch's beam around the cabin, he took in, on his right console, the safety flap covering the release rod for his ejector seat. Otto hinged it back and thumped the activation rod with all the strength he could muster. A bursting sound accompanied the snapping of his chin onto his chest as the pressure canisters blasted him into the night air. He unclasped his harness and shed the seat, but continued to free-fall until he felt the moisture of the cloud layer pressing on his hands and face, a sign he was low enough to breathe without oxygen. His brain was still spinning inside his burning skull, and as he pulled his rip-cord and started to pendulate back and forth under his parachute canopy he suddenly threw up violently into the dark void below. He could see nothing in the blackness beneath him. He remembered the flare pistol strapped firmly to his right leg, the cartridges in a left pocket of his flying trousers. He loaded and fired three flares in quick succession, lighting up the scene below. As he repeatedly wiped the blood from his eyes he could make out a road winding through a small village surrounded by paddocks. A light wind pushed him closer to them as he floated earthwards.

The soft earth of the paddock partially cushioned the shock of hitting the ground, but the parachute canopy engulfed him, and he had to struggle to free himself from the cloying net of silk and tangled guy lines. Once he had fought his way out, Otto gave thanks for small mercies as he saw he had come down right next to a huge cow pat. His forehead burned with a hellish intensity, and the blood from the wound continued to run off his nose, chin and earlobes. His collar had become a sticky swab. Dizzy, feeling wretched, he tried to stand, but fell several times before he succeeded, with a profound effort, in regaining his feet. Otto gathered his parachute and set off in search of help, clasping the unruly bundle before him. He staggered across the paddocks, tripping over fences and stumbling once into a shallow, water-filled ditch. He had to overcome an urge just to pillow himself in the parachute and sleep. Finally Otto reached the fence to a farmhouse. He groped his way along the wire until he found an opening, then staggered through an open yard between woodpiles till he came up against a shoulder-high wall, beyond which ran the village road. He threw his bunched-up parachute over onto the road and tried to climb over, but lost his balance and tumbled headfirst to the ground, the parachute cushioning his fall.

He scraped up the bundle and staggered along the road, crying for help. No signs of life. He made his way to a church, pushed open the door and succumbed to an overwhelming need to rest. Under a ghostly light hovering through the stained glass windows beyond the altar he curled up in his parachute on a pew and fell asleep. The pain of his wound woke him. He saw his continued bleeding had run down to leave a slick on the pew, then pooled on the floor. Some habitual sense of decorum prompted him to try to wipe up the mess with the parachute, but this just smeared it over a wider area. He left the church and continued down the street, bleating for help. A recurring blackness before his eyes caused him to fall, but his thinking remained clear enough to know his need of medical treatment was becoming more urgent the more blood he lost.

A large, affluent-looking house lay ahead. Surely it would have a telephone. Otto made his way to the door and rapped on the knocker. Nothing stirred. In growing frustration he pummelled the door with both fists, but to no avail. He remembered his pistol and drew it from its holster, grasped the barrel and hammered on the door with its grip. Still not so much as a shuffle could be heard inside. In sudden rage he shouted, 'Damn you, I need a telephone!' He released the pistol's safety catch, cocked the weapon and was about to fire at the lock to blast it open when a sound froze him – the 'ting-ting-ting' of a railway crossing. With a renewed fierceness of purpose he struggled towards the bells and, with any luck, a stationmaster's hut. A train rushed past and he saw in the stillness of its wake a hut beyond the tracks – now just a few more steps. He swayed in the open doorway and registered the shock on the face of the Dutch stationmaster as he took in Otto's bloody mess of a face and the streaking from his soaking collar. 'I'm a German pilot – shot down – I need a doctor.' Otto slumped to the ground unconscious.

The rhythmic jolting of being carried on a stretcher revived Otto and he learned he was in a military hospital in the Netherlands, between Utrecht and Eindhoven. As medical orderlies lifted him onto a gurney, another rolled past. On it lay Fred, deathly white, his eyes rolling and the top of his head looking strangely distorted. 'Fred! What's happened to you?' No answer.

'What's happened to my Bordfunker? When will he be able to fly again?'

The doctor shook his head: 'Think about yourself first and when *you'll* be able to fly again.'

'What's he lost? What happened to his head?'

'He slammed headfirst into a paddock and that has caused extensive bleeding around the top of his skull. We just have to hope he hasn't fractured his skull. We'll find out soon from the x-rays.'

'He's got a thick, Bohemian skull. It'll take more than that to put a dent in it!'

'Let's hope you're right!'

As the anaesthetic took effect Otto slipped back into oblivion while the doctor set to work stitching the gash to his forehead.

For three days Otto drifted in and out of consciousness, his mind replaying like a loop tape a scene in which he was being shot down in flames, the vision each time interspersed with white angels drifting noiselessly past. Otto *knew* he was dead. Then, on the third day, the rasping sound of curtains being drawn back cut through the miasma. The sun poured in, illuminating his bed and Fred asleep in the one beside it. He became aware of the glowing crown of a chestnut tree heavy with blossom, a gentle breeze and the sound of bells from the clock tower of the nearby town hall, telling him he was safe.

Otto was given extended leave to recuperate at his home village, while Fred Staffa recovered at his home in the Sudetenland. The only men of fighting age Otto saw while he was home were wounded, like him – some much more badly. During this time he learned the Allies had landed at Normandy. After four weeks convalescing at their homes, Otto and Fred returned to a new airbase at Venlo, in the Netherlands. Recurring headaches kept Otto grounded, but when the medical officer refused to declare him fit to resume flying, he travelled to Amsterdam to get a second opinion. A Luftwaffe doctor there gave him the approval he wanted: 'If you're crazy enough to want to get back in the air, I'm not going to stop you.' By the end of July Otto and Fred were flying together again.

By December 1944, six months after the Allies' successful landings on France's Normandy coast, the advancing front revealed itself to the Luftwaffe not only in frequent attacks on their new airbase in north-west Germany at Münster-Handorf and any other key military targets, but also in the deteriorating state of their ground facilities and aircraft. Otto's Heinkel HE 219 was relatively new but regular attacks on the base's hangars had forced the squadron to disperse the fighters under outlying canvas shelters. The aircraft were suffering the effects of exposure to mid-winter weather, compounded by the disruption to supplies of replacement parts needed to keep them in good working order. In the preceding few weeks Otto had already had a number of frights. Stalking a Lancaster, he had pressed the fire button, only to turn on his port landing lights instead. On another occasion his six cannons had started firing uncontrollably just after take-off. With RAF Mosquito fighter-bombers prowling constantly in the vicinity, such equipment failures were potentially fatal and at best deeply unnerving. Now, on 5 December 1944, as the crew bus took them to their aircraft, Otto grumbled to Fred about whether the latest piece of equipment to play up – their radio – would choose to work that night.

Just after 7.30 p.m. Otto taxied through a lingering mist to await the green signal light for take-off. Fresh in his mind was the weather forecaster's advice to return to base before an expected thick ground fog gathered. Upward-pointing spotlights cross-stitched the landscape in distinctive patterns to help night fighters orient themselves to their own base – or to others should they need to land in an emergency. This orientation matrix also offered the Mosquitoes a dazzling invitation to prey on German aircraft as they took off or landed. For this reason, Otto hugged the ground after take-off until well beyond the airstrip, then doubled back parallel before ascending through the 'Mosquito infestation zone' of 2000–5000 metres to reach his own 'hunting' altitude of 8000 metres.

Otto had adopted this approach after an experience one night, when he had climbed to 4500 metres, the altitude of the approaching bomber stream en route to Berlin. He had soon found himself engaged in an hour-long duel of pursuit and evasion with a Mosquito, as each tried to manoeuvre the other into its sights, then found repeatedly that his opponent had looped back to turn the tables. From that point on, Otto chose to climb steeply and drop into the bomber stream like a bell curve, in order to avoid the attentions of the British night fighters.

Now on 5 December, Otto had just retracted the undercarriage and the flaps following take-off when Fred sputtered a curse into the intercom. 'Damn! Both radios are out – short- and long-wave. They were working fine when we were getting ready for take-off. Now they've both cut out at the same time. What should we do – go back or carry on?'

Otto weighed up the options. The sensible thing would be to return to base, since they could not communicate with the ground either for guidance to target or to gain landing clearance. On the other hand, the weather was forecast to remain clear for a few hours

– time enough to inflict some damage on the enemy. Fred could meanwhile stay tuned to the radio traffic of others in the fighter group, and follow the guidance they received on the expected course of the bomber stream. Otto felt he could land with the help of his airbase homing beacon, so long as he was careful, since the emergency landing strip running alongside the main runway had been hit by two bombs that afternoon.

He checked with Fred: 'You're sure your radios are both okay to receive, or have they given up the ghost too?'

'Not yet, but I can't guarantee they'll stay that way.'

'All right, we'll give it a go then. The weather looks to be okay for a while. If the weather frog is right, we should be able to make it home – as long as there's no fog. Stay tuned to the Y-frequency and follow the instructions Willi gets. He's Eagle 94. He took off just before us, so if we piggy-back on his instructions we should stay pretty much on the right course. Fingers crossed!'

After ground control tried several times in vain to elicit a response from Otto's Eagle 98, it switched its attention to Eagle 94, keeping up the string of instructions Otto had been relying on. Having reached 8000 metres, he levelled out, slipstreamed on Eagle 94's guided approach to the bomber stream and instructed Fred to tune into the Luftwaffe's general instructions on the whereabouts of the stream. To no avail: the RAF was jamming these signals with the characteristic distortion the Luftwaffe airmen called 'soul borer' and 'bagpipes'.

Otto swept the night sky for any sign of activity. Suddenly a lightning-like flash lit up the sky across to starboard, then cascaded down in the green and red flares of target markers. Far below the darkness sprang into life as the jarring whiteness of the magnesium-fed fires spread out to engulf a surrounding area in a flaming pond splashed with the reds of the first bomb explosions. Otto tipped over his starboard wing and accelerated in a steep dive towards the flames. His wings started to vibrate as the speedometer edged beyond 600 kilometres per hour. Fred, monitoring German fighter command radio, reported to Otto that Soest, in the eastern Ruhr district, was under attack – but also that their own radar had now cut out. Otto closed the distance quickly, dropping 3000 metres by the time he was over the now giant lake of flame. Against this hellish backdrop Otto saw the silhouettes of a group of Lancasters passing to port a few hundred metres below his Heinkel. With no help from his own radar, Otto sought to position himself below the vulnerable underbelly of a Lancaster, but each time he dropped to a lower altitude he lost its silhouette. Stark against the fiery backdrop below, but melting into the darkness, the bomber rose in the horizon of his vision.

With impotent fury he watched explosion after explosion ripple the flaming city. Glancing above him he saw with a cramp of terror that another wave of Lancasters was on its bombing run in a head-on course to his and, in the same instant, he both saw and felt a pummelling of the air as bombs fell around his aircraft. Then no more explosions; the attackers had turned for home. Fred fiddled with his radio tuner until he grabbed a snatch of instructions giving the bombers' course back to England. Otto fastened onto the course co-ordinates and set his altitude to that of the bomber stream.

The radar remained useless, so Otto swept his nose back and forth like a dog trying to pick up a scent. Nothing, not even the turbulence he would normally expect from the slipstream of so many powerful engines threshing the air ahead in unison. All the way west to the Maas River in Holland, Otto followed a target that never solidified beyond his mind's eye. Then he gave up the futile chase and turned east again for his own base, dropping to 2000 metres, where he felt he would be safe from both Mosquitoes and trigger-happy German flak crews. With some relief he locked on to Münster-Handorf's homing beacon and readied himself to land.

But then Fred snorted into the intercom. 'Rotten luck – the Dortmund group is coming in to land because their base is completely fogged in. Our radio transmitter is still dead, I can't get landing clearance from ground control, so you'll just have to make your own judgement when it's safe to land. Plus ground control keeps repeating a warning to look out for competition – so the Mosquitoes are on the prowl. Good luck, Otakar!'

Otto knew the machines circling to land were separated in altitude by only 100 metres, and would drop down to fill the slot below as each landed one by one. This left no gap for an unannounced aircraft to slip in. Also, mere seconds separated the time a landed plane taxied off the runway from the next clearance to land, since each was assisted by landing lights switched on and off in an instant, to provide as little inducement as possible for the Mosquitoes to swoop down and attack. The risk of collision was increased because none of the aircraft used landing lights, for fear of becoming an easy target.

With some 20 night fighters lining up to land and the ground fog starting to roll in, Fred could only monitor the hectic radio traffic in the full knowledge their time would run out before they could get into the queue. Otto assessed the options as he circled 500 metres above the airfield: the ground fog building from the west was accentuated by the upward spotlights, while in the east – his preferred approach route – Mosquitoes were ready to pounce the moment they saw a German fighter slowing to land. Otto knew how to foil these attacks: approach in a low, tight curve and begin the landing procedure while still turning; extend the flaps only halfway until the very last moment before the wheels touched, so that the sudden drop in speed when the flaps were fully extended almost coincided with the increased security of being on terra firma.

Otto tried to make out the bomb craters on the emergency strip, just in case, but the gathering ground fog obscured any distinguishing features, quickening the urgency to land before the fog veiled the whole airbase. He told Fred they had no choice but to risk landing immediately.

'Would you rather land on the grass?' asked Fred.

'Too risky. If we hit one of those craters we'll break up. Okay, here's what we'll do. Load a red flare. I'll make a wider curve and let you know when I'm on approach. Then fire the flare behind us. With luck they'll see we're in strife and let us come straight in. But watch out that we're not attacked from behind.'

At 140 metres altitude Otto lowered his undercarriage and approached the strip at 200 kilometres per hour, then applied full flap. Suddenly a deafening crash and splintering sound erupted with a blinding flash in the cabin, stunning him just as a sharp blow yanked his feet from the rudder pedals. Otto's first thought was that Fred had accidentally discharged the flare pistol in the cabin, but almost immediately his Bordfunker's panicked yell brought him back into focus. 'Enemy night fighter! I think the tank's on fire!'

Otto instinctively pulled the lever to jettison the cockpit canopy and roared: 'Get out! Then drop your seat straight away and open your chute!' Without the canopy the rush of air almost tore off his flying helmet. He swiftly unclasped his harness and groped for the ejector-seat rod to his right. He hinged back the safety cover and prepared to thump the rod to fire him free of the stricken machine. He waited an instant to hear the crash of Fred's seat being fired free of the aircraft – but nothing came. 'Get out, get out!' Otto yelled again.

'I can't – my catapult's kaput!'

Otto's heart leapt. 'All right, belt up again – we'll slide this crate in somehow!'

The engines continued to hum as if nothing had happened. Gradually Otto's sight returned and with huge relief he saw they were not on fire. The explosions behind the cockpit had been cannon shells striking the aircraft. Their flashes had temporarily blinded Fred, making him think the fuel tanks had ignited. Otto could see the wings behind the engines were peppered with bullet holes, but the aircraft continued to fly unaffected. He made a snap decision to risk a belly landing.

He gently increased throttle for more speed, then flicked up the switch to raise the undercarriage. As he tried to bank to starboard onto final approach, he noticed with another stab of alarm that the rudder controls were useless. He tried to compensate by increasing the power in his port engine and, using the right aileron, managed to line up with the emergency strip and set up for a shallow approach, easing the throttles to reduce speed. Now on short finals, he closed both throttles and killed the magnetos to reduce the risk of fire on landing. The aircraft continued to float as Otto edged it lower, then drew the Y-shaped yoke sharply into his chest to raise the Heinkel's nose as its wings were poised to embrace the ground – gently, Otto hoped.

As he noticed the runway edge racing past, he was suddenly aware that he had no time, or spare hands, to refasten his harness, still undone after aborting plans to eject. Instead, he anchored his feet firmly in the rudder pedals and braced himself for impact: nothing else would stop him being thrown forward onto the sharp instrument panel. He readied himself to cradle his face in his arms the moment he was able to let go of the yoke.

With a lurch he realised the plane was hopping in a roll over the uneven surface of the grass emergency strip – not sliding or scraping to a standstill. That meant the wheels were still down – the Mosquito must have shot away the hydraulics. Now he was racing towards the bomb craters, with every chance at least one wheel would plunge into a trough and bring the aircraft careening over onto itself, like a steeplechase horse breaking a leg as it misjudged a jump.

In a flicker that was more reflex than realisation, he took in the dim shape of the edge of the first crater, the second a little further on to its left. Instinctively, he thrust his right foot with full force on to the right brake, slewing the plane around to the right, just missing the crater. But he was still too fast – no control. His heart, throat – every muscle – contracted in one terrific spasm of concentration and effort. He tried to brake again, but the pedal was slack to the push; all the fluid had squirted from wrecked pipes in his first, life-saving wheelie. Friction had him in its grasp, however, and he felt the aircraft level, then slow. It rolled to a stop just short of the end of the runway. They were down safely.

Together they walked in wonderment around the Heinkel. The rear of the fuselage, the cross tailpiece and twin 'fins' were riddled with holes, and fuel dripped from the punctured fuselage tanks. On inspecting the plane closely a few days later and writing it off, mechanics found an unexploded cannon shell from the Mosquito lodged in one of the fuel tanks.

Otto and Fred had scarcely recovered from this close escape when they were shot down again by another Mosquito. Unusually, the story can be told from both sides. The 'Intruder Personal Combat Report', written by Flight Lieutenant Vaughan of 85 Squadron, which Otto later obtained, makes short work of a long and frightening night:

> We had completed uneventful patrol east of Frankfurt supporting raid on Zeitz and set course for base at 21.40 hrs. At 21.45 hrs on vector 290 degrees navigator reported contact 3½ miles ranging crossing starboard to port. We closed in on target, losing height to 10,000 ft, indicated air speed 260. At 4,000 ft range two pairs of brilliant white exhausts could be seen. We closed in to 150 ft below and astern and identified target as HE 219 by twin fins and rudders, narrow wings with marked taper on trailing edge outboard of engines, long nose and those brilliant exhausts. Confirmation was obtained as to target's identity from my navigator using night glasses.
>
> I dropped back to 600 ft range astern and fired a 2-second burst between the pairs of exhausts but no strikes were seen. Closed in to 400 ft range and fired another 2-second burst and immediately a large explosion occurred in the port engine and we pulled to starboard to avoid debris which was coming back to us. And passed over enemy aircraft which went down to port with port engine on fire. We did a quick starboard orbit and saw burning fragments of aircraft falling and small fires starting on ground suggesting it had disintegrated in the air. Mosquito landed base 23.45 hrs.
>
> Ammunition expended:
>
> SAPI [semi armour-piercing incendiary] 62;
>
> HEI [high explosive incendiary] 56. Total 118 rounds.
>
> Claim: 1 HE 219 destroyed.

On that snowy January night Otto and Fred were among eight crews scrambled at 7 p.m. from Münster-Handorf to intercept approaching bombers. The technical failures Otto had experienced when they had crash-landed the previous month continued to dog him. This particular night the glitch turned out to be the oxygen feed, which forced Otto to return immediately to a lower altitude where they could breathe freely. But Otto knew he was now in the Mosquitoes' preferred hunting band so, hoping to avoid being tracked and stalked, he changed course every three minutes, all the time straining to make out ground control's radio signals amid the jamming noises transmitted by the RAF. It was towards the end of one of these tacks that Otto was abruptly brought up short by a cracking and splintering sound, his control column was wrenched from his hands and the intercom went dead. Despite this, he could make out Fred's alarmed shout over the noise of his engines: 'Enemy night fighter!'

In the same instant, Otto saw the Mosquito slide over his plane and he made to position himself to attack the British aircraft from behind. He armed the weapons, hearing the gun covers slide back, then as he cocked his right index finger over the firing button he drew back the yoke to bring the Heinkel's nose upward to bear on the Mosquito ahead. But it came back lifeless; the Mosquito must have shot through the cabling for the elevators. He still had the use of his rudders and the ailerons, which controlled roll, but Otto knew he had no prospect of landing, let alone of pursuing the Mosquito.

The Heinkel began to roller-coast, losing speed each time it climbed, then accelerating with each dive. Otto tried to compensate by trimming the tail elevators and throttling back each time it flew downwards, knowing that maintaining altitude was crucial to getting close to base before baling out. When the Heinkel was down to 1000 metres, Otto wrenched back the throttles and in the comparative silence of the lower engine revs he shouted to Fred to bale out. Then he thrust the throttles forward to bring the nose of the aircraft up again and levered open the safety strip for the ejector seat. Otto discarded the cockpit canopy and waited for the percussive roar of Fred's ejector seat being fired clear of the aircraft, then he thumped his own ejector-seat rod and felt himself being propelled into the night. The slipstream immediately caught him and flipped him round. Otto unfastened the harness, then jettisoned the seat itself. He counted a few seconds before pulling the rectangular handgrip on his parachute ripcord. As he swung there, he felt the cold pressing damply on his face and he could make out snow shimmering below. Otto took the flare pistol from the right pocket of his flying trousers, loaded a cartridge and fired a magnesium flare downwards. He could see in its light Fred's parachute floating earthwards to his left. Otto fired two more flares, to illuminate the landing zone.

He saw that he and Fred were coming down in a heavily wooded area, with only a small clearing, in which he could make out a cluster of village buildings. On one side of the village, tall pine trees rose up in a dense wall; on the other, an area of deciduous trees presented a physically less hostile prospect for landing. Otto pulled on the left stay of his parachute harness and felt himself slide towards his left. Too far – he would sail clean over the village and was now heading straight for the deciduous trees. He let the tension off the left parachute stays and felt his course correct itself. But too late: he felt a splintering of branches.

Otto found himself cradled in the top of a large oak, and seconds later the parachute canopy settled silently and gently over its broad crown like a bird net. Awkwardly he swung downwards, pawing the air with his boot for a solid footing. Once he had found a reliable foothold among the springy outer branches, he released his parachute harness, twisting the safety clasp like a jar lid, then springing it loose with a thump. Otto fumbled in the darkness for his flare pistol and shot another magnesium flare upwards, to show the lie of the land. The oak in which he was perched stood on the edge of a steep bank, above a small valley through which a narrow road ran alongside a stream. A small bridge spanned the stream, the road leading on towards the village. Fred had landed in the village, and shouted to Otto the moment the flare shot skywards. 'Otakar! Come down to the village, but watch out for the stream!'

As he clambered down through the dim body of the oak, branch by branch, Otto winced, aware he had given his right knee a heavy whack. He could not remember this happening, but now he felt the knee swelling painfully inside his flying suit. He reached the bottom branch and surveyed the snow-covered ground below with a mixture of irritation and concern. He had no option but to try to shimmy down the tall oak's thick trunk. Otto knew his injured knee and thick flying suit would not make things any easier, but two things might help: his thick gloves and the inflatable dinghy on his back, which could serve as a cushion to break a fall. He fired the compressed air bottle, let the dinghy inflate and then fall like an oversized doughnut to the snow.

Now he began the descent, using his acutely painful knee as a brake. Too late he registered the hindrance of his life vest bunching between him and the tree trunk. Its inflation bottle was fixed to his left thigh and he felt it dragging against the rough bark as he slid downwards. Then, with an affronted hiss, it burst into life as the friction activated the compressed air release. The chest panels of the vest flared out like a bullfrog's jowl and bounced him out from the tree trunk. Struck by the comic stupidity of his fall from grace, Otto closed the distance to the ground in a soundless instant, the inflatable dinghy receiving him like a catcher's mitt.

Now he scrambled down the steep bank, floundering in the deep snow. Fred met him at the bridge over the stream and led him towards a tavern. They knocked on the door, which opened to reveal a nervous publican, who told them they had come down in a small village north of Frankfurt. The whole village had taken shelter when they heard the screaming of aircraft engines and the impact of the Heinkel, thinking it was an enemy bomber that might crash into their houses. With great relief, the tavern owner phoned Otto's and Fred's airbase to report them safe. Then he opened the bar and treated them like kings. Otto's knee had swelled up so much his flying dungarees had to be cut from him. But that did not dampen the celebrations that awaited him and Fred once they made it back to their mess. As Otto recalled, 'We poured oil on the flames that night!'

But home base did not necessarily mean home safe. Otto Fries told me that despite his narrow escapes in the air, he had felt most terrified – and certain he was about to die – two months before this baling out over the small village. The experience was the one time he was caught in a bombing raid, and came relatively late in the war, in November 1944. By this stage, following the D-Day landings in Normandy in June, the Allied advance had increased the pressure on the German air defence. Otto's squadron had been moved from Belgium to the Netherlands, then on to Münster-Handorf in Germany's north-west.

Because of the frequency of attacks on their airbase, the squadron had moved into living quarters away from that target, and were accommodated in a convent nearby.

That November morning Otto had returned from night operations relatively late, turning in at 6 a.m. and sliding into sleep with some difficulty. He dreamed fitfully of making an emergency landing and standing alone on the runway under a thundercloud. He woke to the realisation the cloud was the crashing of flak guns, accompanied by the wailing of the hand-sirens being cranked by nuns running along the corridors. He tore open the blackout curtains to see about three dozen US Flying Fortress bombers approaching through the brown smoke clumps of flak explosions. Knowing the convent lay directly on the bombers' approach path to the airbase some 3 kilometres beyond, Otto sprang into action, alerting his room mate, Paul Stieghorst, who simply snuffled and turned over.

Otto, by contrast, watched with mounting panic as the bomber formation drew nearer, then the lead aircraft dropped his smoke marker to signal the start of bombing – not with the airfield in range, but rather the convent. 'Paul! The smoke signal has us marked. Get out!' Otto dragged his heavy, flying dungarees over his pyjamas, stabbed his feet into slippers and grabbed his cap and gloves as he took off along the corridor and drummed down the wooden stairs for the exit. Already he could hear bombs whistling downwards close by.

Trenches that had been dug into the grass in front of the convent for shelter seemed too far away, so he sprinted for the beech forest instead and threw himself to the ground as the first crunching explosions shook themselves into him through the earth. The explosions and the droning of 140 engines combined as a sickening thunder, interspersed with the shrill splintering of glass and trees. As the sound became deafening he thought he was about to die: 'It felt like someone was running a steel brush down my spine, from my neck to my tailbone. It was the most terrifying experience of the war for me – far worse than being shot down, because I was so helpless.'

Suddenly, total silence returned, itself an assault on the senses. A whistle sounded the all-clear – punctuated by five distant explosions of bombs falling beyond the convent. Otto took in the shattered woods, cloaked in acrid smoke. As he shook off the dirt, he saw the edge of the nearest bomb crater only three steps to his left. Some distance beyond that he noticed the trench shelters had been obliterated by two direct hits. Grit, fragments of masonry and splintered beech wood littered the ground between the craters and the convent in which he had been sleeping just minutes before.

The building itself stood undamaged apart from its windows, all of which had been blasted out, some of them spilling tattered blackout curtains from their frames. Still dazed, Otto skirted the crater-pocked stretch of ground to reach the building. One door had been blown away completely; the other swung precariously on a broken hinge. As Otto crunched his way up the stairs over glass splinters he saw, framed in the doorway at the top, his room-mate, Paul Stieghorst, standing barefoot and in his pyjamas. 'Man! How did you get here – from the cellar?' Otto asked in astonishment.

'Hardly! I couldn't jump into the cellar with the nuns in this get-up! This is as far as I got, and I've been tucked in the corner behind the door the whole time. A swinging door missed ripping my nose off by just a few centimetres! Can you get me my slippers? I can't move here for all the glass on the floor.'

Otto carried on up the stairs, found Paul's sports shoes, shook the glass splinters from them and threw them down the stairs.

It was just after ten in the morning. At first glance, their room looked just as they had left it, except for the crystal shower of glass everywhere. The blackout curtains were shredded. Otto and Paul raked the glass splinters from their beds, fixed blankets around the empty window frames and went back to sleep. At midday, an orderly woke them for lunch and they made their way to the canteen. As Otto spooned soup into his mouth he overheard a nun say to his commander, 'God has held his hand over our convent!' Paul grinned and elbowed Otto in the ribs, spilling his soup. 'See, we're in the wrong job – we should be nuns!'

Just four weeks later Paul Stieghorst and his Bordfunker were blasted from the sky south of Bremen by flak from their own side. Otto was sent to break the news to Paul's father. By then, December 1944, Germany had clearly lost the war.

Part Three

RECKONING

CHAPTER 11

COPING WITH LOSS

Cast a cold eye
On life, on death.
Horseman, pass by!
Epitaph on the headstone of Irish 'war poet' W.B. Yeats

BY THE END OF 1942 the mounting death toll among Col's friends was affecting him in ways he only hints at it in his letters home, but it clearly influenced his decision to return to operations. By the time he completed his first tour and left Lakenheath just before Christmas 1942, a huge swathe had been cut through 149 Squadron and others to which some of his friends had been posted. But for Col the biggest blow had yet to come: on 2 February 1943 his closest wartime friend, Barry Martin of Christchurch, died in the wreckage of a 7 Squadron Stirling shot down near Rotterdam on the way back from a raid on Cologne. On board was the first H2S radar unit captured by the Germans, a find that proved so important in the 'stealth race' against Bomber Command described in Chapter 6.

Many firm friendships were cut short by death, so Col's and Barry's had flourished against the odds. It continued after Barry completed his first tour in July 1942 then volunteered for a second tour, with 7 Squadron at Oakington, just north of Cambridge and

west of the cathedral town of Ely. Col followed his dead friend's
path to Oakington in January 1944, but was himself killed a few
weeks later on his first op of his second tour. With this knowledge
weighing on me, I sought out Oakington in the summer of 2007. I
approached through the town of Histon, along narrow corkscrew
lanes with thatched cottages on the rise and old stone walls setting
off the colour of hollyhocks, poppies and hydrangeas. It was
obvious, as I had been told, that Oakington's heyday as one of the
RAF's premier stations was long past. Once a base for one of the
finest bomber squadrons of the war, now only a small cluster of
buildings breathed any life at all, and these as a refugee settlement
centre. The hedgerows pressed close to the road verge, preventing
me from gaining any perspective on the former airfield itself and
foiling my sense of direction.

Neatly manicured Oakington-Westwick village appears to be a
recent retirement housing estate. A stencil-like iron 'welcome' sign
at the village entrance features a Lancaster bomber soaring over a
country church and an ox ploughing a field – a reminder of both its
origins and its glory days. After parking on a rough verge, I walked
up a metal access road until I reached two galvanised, farm-style
gates sporting faded signs saying 'Defence Property Keep Out.' I
climbed over and found myself on the scaly remains of what had once
been Oakington's perimeter track. Here the lumbering 'heavies' – the
Stirlings and Lancasters – had taxied to the start of the runway and
taken off into the night. A square hay bale lay where it had been
thrown from a vehicle and a few small, self-sown oaks brushed the
edge of the carriageway. The broken asphalt gave off a tremor of
heat and memory. Here you were, Col, for the last time.

This had also been Barry's last point of departure. Col first learned
of his friend's fate when he phoned Oakington in early February
1943 to invite Barry to his investiture at Buckingham Palace, only
to be told he had just been reported missing in action. Col was to
receive the Distinguished Flying Cross from King George VI, but
now his proudest moment of the war was overshadowed by anxiety
over whether he would ever see his close friend again. Barry
was also awarded the DFC, gazetted only after his death. And I

later discovered the two shared another honour, this one relating specifically to their time at Oakington.

I drove along a lush country lane into the village of Longstanton. St Michael's Church sat atop a rise, ringed with old headstones and set back from a large chestnut tree that shaded both a corner gate and an ancient well. It was a timeless scene, where I was as likely to have seen the vicar riding past in a horse and trap as met the gardener on a ride-on mower. Driving through the village's main intersection towards a soulless new housing estate clustered down the hill, I passed another old church, this one sturdier-looking and with a significance I learned of only later. All Saints' Church contains the Roll of Honour listing those killed flying with 7 Squadron, including Col Jones and Barry Martin. I discovered this when going through the squadron's archives at the RAF Museum in Hendon, west London, where a facsimile is held. I was sad not to have seen inside the church, but I regretted more that Col, during his brief tenure at Oakington at the coldest point of winter, never had the chance to cycle through these lanes when they were green and speckled with bright flowers as they were on the day I visited.

I had another visit to make. It took me back to Mildenhall a few months later, and to the bungalow of 92-year-old Fred Coney, the president of the association for 149 Squadron and three others that operated from that airbase during the war. Coney, a lanky figure with a lively sense of humour, eased himself into my rental car and chatted while we drove the short distance to St John's Church at Holywell Row and the Beck Row War Cemetery beside it. Using his walking stick, Coney picked his way carefully across the lumpy grass, around the back of the stone church to a section neatly demarcated from the other headstones and containing the graves of 78 Commonwealth servicemen who died during the war. A US F-15 fighter-bomber from Lakenheath thundered overhead as we surveyed the rows of uniform white headstones. Most buried at Beck Row died while flying from Mildenhall, Lakenheath or other airbases nearby. The most famous grave is that of an Australian pilot, Rawdon Hume 'Ron' Middleton, who earned the Victoria Cross for a breathtaking act of self-sacrifice in November 1942. In a letter to his mother on 2 February 1943, Col wrote of these deeds, and of his regard for Middleton:

We heard the other day that one of the chaps from the squadron, Flight Sergeant Ron Middleton, has been awarded a posthumous Victoria Cross. You will probably have read about it in the paper. He was a great friend of mine and a fine chap. His exploit, in the official citation for his award, was 'unsurpassed in the annals of the RAF.' He was badly wounded over Turin, losing one eye, having his face torn open, and also being wounded in the body. They flew at 5000 ft through a pass in the Alps, and when they got to the English coast he told the rest of the crew to bale out. He did not leave the machine. Perhaps he was too weak. In any case, it had no automatic pilot, so had he left the controls, it would have crashed and perhaps killed someone on English ground. So he flew out to sea and went down with it. Two of the crew baled out over the sea and were drowned. The rest were saved. The deed caused a tremendous wave of emotion right throughout this country. There are a number of ex-149 Squadron chaps here, so we sent his mother a cable, each signing it. I have written a letter which we are all going to sign and post it to her. He was a fine chap. Then in today's paper I read that they had found his body. It was washed ashore on the south coast. It was the death of a brave man. He was an Australian, the best they send out.

I had wanted to visit Beck Row Cemetery because Col had been a pallbearer at the burial there of another 149 Squadron friend and colleague. Eric Wynn, a Canadian pilot, and his entire crew died when their Stirling caught fire and crashed shortly after take-off on 24 August 1942. They were among 8000 airmen to die in crashes over Britain, more than one in seven of all the Bomber Command aircrew killed during the war. Col described the ceremony in his diary four days later:

Was a pallbearer at Eric Wynn's funeral which was held at 11.30 am at St John's Church, Mildenhall. Don't like funerals – burial service at open grave – coffin draped with Union Jack and vivid with flowers – earth drab by comparison. Burial service solemn but lovely – same impression as Handel's Funeral March. Guard of Honour fired a salute over the yawning grave. Then the Wing/Co.

stepped forward and saluted and each in his turn, we followed him. It was the last tribute.

This was death, the death of an officer and a gentleman, and all about the day was vividly alive with sunlight and flowers. And so he joins the growing company of plain little white crosses. Good old Barry [Martin] was there, cut up and his funny red face all solemn for once. Thank God that Barry has finished. We are on ops tonight – if the skipper can get his crew together in the kite.

Wynn had been Col's friend and Barry's pilot on many ops, and the Canadian was among the very few friends they had seen buried in English soil. Most Bomber Command airmen either came down and were buried in German-held territory or were lost without trace.

How did the airmen cope with the loss of friends and comrades, and on such a stunning scale? A few years after the war the *Auckland Star*, Col's old paper, reported some key findings of a study published in the British *Journal of Mental Science*, written by a doctor who had served for four years as medical officer on a wartime bomber station.[1] In 'Morale and Flying Experience', Dr D. Stafford-Clark wrote of the pent-up stresses of flying at night, enduring many hours of danger, noise and discomfort, knowing the chances of surviving 30 ops were less than even and to do so unscathed were about one in five:

> There was no single moment of security from take-off to touch-down, but often the sight of other aircraft hit by flak and exploding in the air, or plummeting down blazing to strike the ground an incandescent wreck....
>
> Their attitude to losses and death of friends was particularly striking. It was one of supreme realism, of matter of fact acceptance of what everyone knew perfectly well was inevitable. They did not plunge into outspoken expression of their feelings, nor did they display any compromise with conventional reticence about the fact of violent death. They said 'too bad…sorry about old so-and-so…rotten luck.' Their regret was deep and sincere, but not much displayed or long endured. They were apt and able to talk of dead and missing friends, before mentioning their fate, just as they talked of anyone else or of themselves.

It took the loss of particular friends or leaders, flight commanders or squadron commanders, to produce a marked reaction among a squadron. Then they might feel collectively distressed, have a few drinks because of that, go on a party and feel better. But they made no effort to escape the reality of the situation, nor was there any of the drinking to forget, referred to in accounts of flying in the last war. They were young; they were resilient; they lived until they died.

Col's earlier letters reflect a keen awareness of the effect his own death might have on his mother, to whom he downplayed the dangers while urging his sisters to shield her from some of the more alarming experiences. But not even the more candid comments in his letters and diary reveal how he truly felt about losing his friends. His close brushes with death are related more as adventures. There are, however, glimpses of the camaraderie he enjoyed with his fellow aircrew – an indication of how big a blow their deaths must have been to him. On 15 September 1942, two weeks after Eric Wynn's funeral and after Col had already completed his tour of 30 operations, he took off with his regular crew, skippered by his Canadian friend, 'Al' Greenslade. His diary records how he felt flying with this crew for the last time – and then of learning what happened to them two weeks later.

Last trip to the mouth of the Gironde mine-laying 6 hrs 50 mins long and an uneventful stooge, during which the whole crew combined to pull my leg. Every five minutes someone asked me where we were; what the [signal] colours of the day were; whether the course was right; what the ETA base was; what was the nearest big town; what the lights were on the starboard; what the ETA French coast was; I said we had 11 mins to run and the skipper said it was coming up there and then. It was a bloody cloud, which he knew full well. Finally hit the coast about 4 miles to port – good pin point and came home thereafter like a bird. Up the Channel, the skipper persisted in seeing land ahead where no land was; and then laughed like hell when I told him he was nuts. Banged my head and scratched my hand ripping up to see his damn land, which did not improve things. Finally, got browned off and that made them laugh even more. Everyone but me had an uproariously funny trip. So ended my last op. Glad and sorry to finish – leaves an emptiness as well as a relief. Absolutely first class crew and skipper – would go anywhere with them. Well, what next?

Friday 2 October 1942

Leave 18/9/42 – 2/10/42 – London – Devon Kelly House, Clifton – London. Had a wonderful shikker [night on the town] with Jack Ekelund, Barry and Mac McGieger in London. Came home about 9 pm on 2nd to find that my crew had gone to Krefeld. Never saw them again because they did not come back. Al Greenslade, Bill Hughes, Bill Orange, Les Moore, Smithy, Goldsmith – missing, the only Stirling not to return. Worst thing in the war to me. They were grand chaps and all day 3rd I could hear their voices. Hated it all. Report that a crew was seen baling out over the target. Also that a Stirling was seen fairly low being fired at, but with no answering fire. I wonder…. Fine chaps.

None of the crew survived. Col had flown his first op with Al Greenslade to Hamburg in July 1942, when they had been 'coned' by searchlights and had shot their way along the Elbe estuary to the coast at rooftop level. For the last third of Col's tour Greenslade replaced Jock Watt as his regular skipper and their crew flew 10 ops together. Some of that crew appear in Col's photo album, fooling around together on and off their base. Wireless operator Sergeant Bill Hughes, a 21-year-old Londoner; another Briton, air gunner Flight Sergeant Bill Orange; Sergeant Les Moore, a 20-year-old air gunner from Leicester; and Sergeant Marshal Smith, a 21-year-old flight engineer from Cambridge. Another Canadian, Flight Sergeant Robert McIntyre from Vancouver, joined Greenslade on the fatal trip that night, filling Col's job as observer. The last member of the crew, Flight Sergeant Benjamin Goldsmith, a 22-year-old air gunner from Lancashire, had shared Col's luck the night in early June when they had both been shot down returning from Essen and Col had ditched in the Channel. Goldsmith was one of only two crew to make it clear of their 149 Squadron Stirling, landing by parachute in a German flak battery in Belgium. Although wounded, he had 'jumped the wire' and evaded capture, making his way back to Britain with help from the Comete Line escape route.

Col's sense of loss at their deaths comes through in his most revealing letter to his mother, later that month.

I am now back at the squadron [from leave in London], messing about doing odd jobs here, before being posted to my next job, which will probably be some sort of ground work. I expect to spend some weeks on this squadron, however, doing one or two jobs which the Wing Commander here has in mind.

I had my fair share of narrow escapes while I was doing my operations, so I think that perhaps your prayers for me may have had something to do with getting me through safely. Still, I suppose mothers pray for sons who don't come back, so where are we?

The personnel on the station has changed very greatly since I came here. I scarcely know a soul, where once I knew nearly everyone – that is, among the flying crews. A good many have gone missing; more have finished their operations and have been posted away elsewhere, new crews coming to take their places. I am the very last of the flying crowd who were here when I came. Now I have finished, and in a little while I shall be going. You know, it seems queer for me to be watching others preparing to fly, and telling them what to do, while I stay on the ground. For 11 months I was flying; and now I am not. It seems as though one part of my life has suddenly come to a full stop. It will take some little time to adjust myself.

Rather a sad thing happened. When I came back from leave, I asked where my skipper was, that is the captain of my old crew. I was told that he was flying that night, so I thought that it did not matter much as I would see him in the morning. Do you know, I never saw him, for he never came back. He and his crew – my old crew – just went missing. It is possible they are safe, of course, but only time will show that. He was a Squadron Leader, A. Greenslade AFC, DFC, a Canadian and a very fine chap. His crew thought the world of him. I was with him on the trip for which he got his DFC. It was over Hamburg. We came out on three engines over the outskirts of Hamburg at 50 feet, and we flew over Germany to the coast at that height. It was an exciting trip. The skipper's handling of the machine was masterly. He brought us back. The two gunners were great friends of mine, dam' good chaps. It is hard to realise they are not here. For several days afterwards, I kept on hearing their voice. Still, that's the way things go. I met the skipper's wife in London. She is a nice girl. I had lunch with them, and we had a great yarn. It is so hard on her.

Tomorrow will be exactly a year since I came to this squadron. It has been an eventful year, but a very happy one for me. I have seen a good many chaps go missing. I have seen a good many finish their ops, as I have done. I have seen three married and been best man for two of them. You know, one forms friends when one flies with men; and some of the chaps I have met here I shall not forget. I have flown with two Wing Commanders (both of them now dead), a Flight Lieutenant (also dead) and two Squadron Leaders (one missing). Each of them we called 'Skip,' short for skipper, and no-one cared a damn. I think that the crew of an aeroplane is the best example of democracy one could find. You get to know each other so well when you fly together. You learn what a man is like when things are sticky. That is when you appreciate his worth. We had a grand crew, simply grand. We would have gone anywhere with our skipper. Now it is that skipper, that great chap, and those gunners, who are missing. I do take that to heart.

One Wing Commander was named Knocker. Both he and his wife were New Zealanders [In fact, only the wife was]. He was a fine man, one of the most popular officers on the squadron. Everyone liked him; and he was grand to fly with. I did two trips with him, but was not in his regular crew. He was posted to another squadron – and went missing. So did the Flight Lieutenant, whose name was Turtle. I flew with him while his usual navigator was ill. He went on his 54th trip.

I have just heard the boys take off on another trip. They won't be back for some time. I always wish them good hunting to myself. A kite always looks so lonely, as it nips smart off in the darkness; but the kite and the crew don't feel lonely. They have the warmest sense of companionship. Often when we are well away from danger and out to sea coming home, we have a good chat and laugh over the inter-com. We all sling off at each other, tell yarns and hand round the thermos flask of tea. Everyone curses the navigator because he tells them they will have to wait a long time before getting to base; but it's then that the sense of companionship is greatest. At the same time, if I ever have to look back through the astrodome, I see the mid-upper gunner ceaselessly turning his turret from one side to the other, while the rear gunner is doing the same. They never relax their vigilance against fighters.

Finally someone says 'coast coming up' and everyone takes a new lease of life. Base is not far away now. The navigator nips up beside the pilot to have a look-see what part of the coast it is, and then later we see the aerodrome ahead of us. That's a thrill. I begin to pack up all my gear and put away my maps and get ready to get out of the kite as soon as it has landed and taxis back to where it stays when not flying – its 'dispersal point,' as it is called. Out comes a lorry or wagon of some sort to meet us, we all pile in and the first thing after taking off our flying clothes is a cup of tea. Boy! How we have longed for that. But as soon as we land, and get out of the kite, out come the cigarettes. No matter if I haven't any, I still get one. No matter if some other chap hasn't one. We all smoke someone's. Another trip over. Though there were times when I thought that base was far too far away, I have had a good time.

I went to NZ House when I was in London last to enquire about some of the boys in the army. Ken Turtill is a prisoner of war, at present in Italy. That means he will be all right, at any rate. Cam is all right, and as far as I could find out so are Jock Cairns and Jack Walton. They were chaps I knew at 'Varsity. The casualty lists have been pretty staggering, though, I am afraid.

On 17 March 1943 he wrote to his mother about the loss of Barry Martin.

Perhaps you may have heard me speak of Barry Martin, with whom I roomed from the day I joined the squadron until he was posted after having finished his first tour. He managed to get back to another squadron to start his second tour. I rang him up to ask him to come to Buckingham Palace with me. They told me that he was missing. Then just the other day the adjutant at that squadron rang to say that news had been received that he and four other members of the crew had been killed. It was a bitter blow; we had been together so long. I knew him better than anyone else in the RAF. I have seen so many go. The tragedy of it was that two days later his award of the DFC was announced. He never knew that he had won it. His father was killed in the last war when he was a baby. His mother married again after some years, and then some few months ago Barry's half-brother was killed in a flying accident in NZ. God, what a load his mother has to bear.

After Barry's death Col wrote to his friend's mother, Guin Heaps of Christchurch. She replied:

Dear Colwyn

Your air mail letter took three months to come out. Oh lad thank you; you don't know what it meant to me to get a lovely letter like that from one who loved my Barry and understood him so. From a once rather delicate boy he has always been stubborn, moody, unselfish, thoughtful and straight as a die. He often wrote of going off on leave with Colwyn and especially the time you went to Clifton College and the four or five nights in London after which you had stayed up and retired in the early hours. How thankful I am for his little sprees and that he'd always tell me, his mother, knowing I'd understand and [knowing] my love for him: He knew I'd understand his enlisting in that dangerous RAF but at the time of his death I did not even know of his [return to] flying. Did he tell you I lost his step-brother, Brian Heaps, 21, in March last year on his last hour of flying [training]?

Don't agitate too much to get back to flying Colwyn, you are helping there anyway and have done so much. And have you a mother or sweetheart? You'll think I'm an old fool but I want to save others as much as I can.

When a bomber went down, it usually meant the deaths of seven or eight men. On the German side, the chances of surviving a shooting down were greater but often ended in the death of the two, sometimes three, airmen. The Luftwaffe losses continued to mount, accounting for one in three who flew night fighter operations during the war. The pilot who shot down Barry Martin's Stirling, Oberleutnant Hans-Dieter Frank, was himself killed in combat in September that year, with 55 'kills' to his credit, among them also Al Greenslade's Stirling. The German losses, though fewer than Bomber Command's, had a similar psychological effect. Luftwaffe airmen regarded death with the same, almost perfunctory, realism as the RAF crews: it was part of the job and the death of a comrade in arms was a sad, but unavoidable, consequence of war.

'If we had spent too much time thinking about the comrades who died, we wouldn't have been able to do our job,' Professor Fries told me. But at his first operational base, St Trond, a cemetery for fallen RAF airmen grew steadily along the airfield perimeter, as did the rows of German crosses in the Luftwaffe cemetery in the grounds of the nearby palace. The casualty rate among Luftwaffe crews was lower than for the RAF mainly because they were not ranging as far from home base and because they did not routinely fly over the sea, so that if they had to bale out they generally did so over territory under German control.

In our discussions about the loss of his comrades, Otto Fries maintained a quiet reserve for nine months. It was only one night, after a discussion about the devastating costs of the war to Germany, and to so many of his family, friends and former colleagues, that he wavered for a moment. There were two close friends in particular, both former room mates, whose deaths shook him. Both had a bemused inability to take seriously any form of authority and, because they flouted it with such good humour, they got away with it. 'Nachtjagd Tony' Flegel, 19, shared a room and many a laugh with his fellow Leutnant, 'Otakar' Fries. Tony died in June 1944, when he lost control of his plane while attempting to land on a runway blocked by a crashed fighter. He and Otto had once been shot down on the same night. Otto made it back to his barracks after Tony, whom he found regarding himself with concern in the full-length mirror. Asked why, Tony, a real ladies' man, complained that the impact of his heavy landing by parachute had lessened his sex appeal by making his legs even bandier.

But it was the death of Oberleutnant Paul Stieghorst that hit Otto hardest. When he learned that Paul had been shot down and killed by German flak near Bremen, the news shook him deeply. 'With Paul I had a special relationship,' Professor Fries began. 'He was so happy and so clever.' It is a humbling experience when a distinguished 90-year-old former professor breaks down in tears over events more than 60 years in the past. His face glistening, Fries explained how he volunteered to travel from his base to deliver the news of his good friend's death to Paul's family in Westfalia, in Germany's north-west. This was customary among officers, to spare the family the impersonal blow of a telegram. Otto was greeted by Paul's father, a Protestant minister, whose face betrayed no emotion as Otto imparted the news and then broke down 'howling'. Pastor Stieghorst was completely still for a moment, withdrawn deep into himself, then he said quietly: 'Gott will, dass ich auch in dieser

Hinsicht meine Gemeinde vorangehe – It is God's will that, in this regard too, I serve as an example to my parish.' He offered neither words nor gestures of comfort and Otto left feeling desolate and rather embarrassed.

The attrition rate among the night fighters rose steeply as the war entered its last two years. The increasing scarcity of fuel for training and the pressure on the Luftwaffe to replenish squadrons depleted by losses led to condensed instruction programmes for newer pilots that, almost literally, became crash courses for many. Increasingly, too, the German Nachtjagdgeschwadergruppen – night fighter groups – were finding themselves outgunned: under attack from RAF Mosquitoes by night, and confronting an increasingly dense swarm of Thunderbolt and Mustang single-engined fighters escorting the US heavy bombers by day.

After the D-Day landings in June 1944 the Allies were able to fly fighter escorts from bases on the continent. As they advanced beyond the belt of coastal radar stations they deprived the Germans of much of their means of detecting bombers approaching across the water from Britain. Outgunned and partially blindfold, the German air defence was completely overwhelmed. Some former German daytime fighter pilots belonging to the Berlin Jägerkreis of former Luftwaffe airmen told me that by late 1944 they were routinely outnumbered 10 to one by US fighters when attempting to attack bombers in daylight, and if they shot down a US fighter it was 'pure luck'.

The night fighters were not as routinely exposed as their daytime colleagues, but their losses also climbed steeply as the war turned against Germany. For each of the five months to October 1944, the Luftwaffe lost an average of 2600 aircrew, more than treble the monthly average of 775 killed during the previous three and a half years.[2] The younger crews, with less experience and shorter training, had the poorest life expectancy. Professor Fries recalled the arrival at his squadron in October 1944 of 10 new crew pairings. By Christmas that year all 20 young men were dead.

That Christmas of 1944 Otto could find little to ease his despondency over Germany's deteriorating fortunes. He had spent every

Christmas so far with his family in the Pfalz, the Rhineland Palatinate region bordering France and Luxembourg, but now the war had drawn too close. Paris had fallen to the Allies in August, though not everything was going the Allies' way. In Holland in September, the Germans had repulsed the biggest airborne assault in history, when 40,000 Allied troops attempted to capture the Rhine bridges around Arnhem. Then, in December, Germany had unleashed half a million men and 500 tanks in the Battle of the Bulge in the Ardennes, along the Luxembourg–Belgium border, thrusting deep into US positions and shattering the Allies' belief they would be in Berlin by Christmas. Despite these demonstrations of continued German tenacity, however, Otto and his companions knew the war was lost.

One Bavarian in Otto's squadron had used most of his 10 days' recent leave trying to return from his home, a journey disrupted frequently by bomb damage to railway lines. With the Allied advance on the ground in Europe, Otto's squadron had been relocated further east into Germany itself, to Münsterland, near the Dutch border. Even though this airbase was much closer to his home than the Bavarian's, he opted that Christmas to remain at his barracks in the convent. As dusk gathered he sat in the elegant chamber he had shared with Paul Stieghorst, killed just a few days before. Otto stared forlornly at a festive arrangement his mechanic, a gardener in civilian life, had fashioned for him from the branches of a fir tree. Shimmering with candles, the arrangement became a shrine to his close friend. Otto thought of the joyous anticipation experienced on Christmas Eve during his childhood and wondered what had become of 'peace on earth, good will to all men'.

Earlier that day, just after lunch in the canteen, the nuns had tried to lift the men's spirits by singing Christmas carols – in the full knowledge that once darkness fell, they would prepare to take off against the enemy. As dusk fell, Otto and his fellow aircrew drove gloomily to their readiness room on the edge of the airfield. The waning moon had disappeared from sight, but the weather forecast this frost-hard night promised it would be starry and clear above a layer of mist. The bus pressed on through a fog that was expected to produce a heavy frost in the early hours of Christmas Day.

The only concession to the season in the readiness room was a Christmas fir tree, but there on the wall was Adolf Hitler's photo, and instead of tinsel or streamers the familiar models of RAF bombers hung from the ceiling like decoy ducks in flight. The crews lounged disconsolately in armchairs or dabbled at chess. No one could be bothered playing skat, usually their favourite card game. A few drank coffee – never Otto, as it kept him awake well after he had landed and was safely back in bed.

After they had been waiting about two hours, the alarm sounded, sending them all scrabbling into their lockers for life jackets, flying gloves, flare cartridges, radio and navigation booklets. Once the crew bus reached the tarmac, Otto and his mechanic had an exchange of forced joviality, then Otto and Fred climbed the flip-ladder into their respective ends of the bubble cockpit, which the mechanic closed over them. As Otto went through the routines of checking his switches and equipment, his sense of isolation was made worse by the condensation freezing on every surface of cabin glass. He grew warm rubbing vigorously with his flying glove to clear his windows. Otto could see the mechanic turning to a totem pole in the freezing cold outside while he waited for the green light for engine ignition.

The light came, the engines burst into motion and the mechanic pulled the cords to free the wheel chocks. As the Heinkel taxied towards its starting position on the runway, Fred exchanged passwords with the control tower, which gave the all-clear to take off. Once again, Otto went through the intensive ritual of checking all instrumentation, surrendering his instincts to its myriad readings, then took off north into the void of darkness and mist. The ground control instructed him to turn 180 degrees towards the enemy, flying at 5000 metres.

Climbing through 4000 metres and donning his oxygen mask, Otto saw they had left the mist below and were once again in the company of the moon, its weak light shimmering in reflection on the plane's wings. He levelled off at 8000 metres and drew back the engine throttles to reduce the power he had needed for the ascent. The instructions from the ground were so disparate Otto felt they were like clues in a scavenger hunt. Then, suddenly, orders came for all night fighters in the region to head for a point south-west of Otto's current position.

But they were too late. Already Otto could see the target-marking coloured parachute flares they all called 'Christmas trees' – for once, the term seemed perversely apt, though with tidings of hellfire. The darkness below was already flashing with explosions, which quickly seemed to flow into one, like a lake of molten lava. Otto thrust forward the throttle levers, arrowing the Heinkel down at more than 700 kilometres per hour towards where he judged the bombers would be crossing above the target. By the time he had the flames beneath him, however, the attack had finished, leaving no sign of the bombers but just a blizzard of distortion on Fred's tracking radar.

The ground control directed them into a three-quarter turn and reported bombers spread between 3500 metres and 5000 metres. Otto turned the Heinkel into the moon's face, which transformed the mist below him into a milky pond, while behind him in the east the red flames of the burning target spread a glimmering band, like an inverted sunset. He knew the bombers must be ahead somewhere, but Fred's radar screens were still snowed. 'Fred, turn that piece of junk off and help me look,' Otto said as he began snake-nosing the Heinkel back and forth in search of prey.

Suddenly, twin lines of tracer-laced fire crossed from left and right simultaneously in front of them, like Christmas fairy lights, as the trigger-happy gunners of two bombers mistook each other for a night fighter. Otto dipped the Heinkel under the archway of the tracer streams. The darkness swallowed their sources as suddenly as they had appeared and for half an hour Otto searched in vain for at least one of these bombers, before he gave up the ghostly pursuit and turned for home, landing in thick mist.

Two hours later, just before midnight and Christmas Day, and after the mist had fallen, Otto stepped out into the night silence and was spellbound by a star canopy clearer and brighter than he could remember ever having seen it. The mist had come down to earth this Christmas, seemingly drawing the heavens closer. All around lay a frost already crisp and even. He yearned for peace.

Otto had nothing to celebrate that Christmas. When he did have an occasion to mark, it was rarely with wine, despite his origins and his regular trips to his vineyard home. He often brought a bottle or two back with him from leave, but he never stocked up for a regular tipple. With the possibility of the RAF attacking on any given night, the crews knew a clear head was part of the formula not just for success but also for survival. If they were grounded by the weather, the non-commissioned crews always headed off to the pub or the soldiers' mess and drank either beer or liqueur, rather than wine. Only the officers habitually drank wine, but not Otto, even after he was promoted to Leutnant. One who tasted Otto's offering enjoyed it so much that he asked for a case to be sent north. He was killed in action that night. Then another fellow officer said he would take over the wine order in his dead comrade's place – but he, too, was killed the following night. The case of wine never left Otto's home cellars.

Nor were more senior veteran crews immune. Unlike the RAF, the Luftwaffe did not screen, or ground, crews after a set number of operations, so the policy of 'fly until you die' also claimed many of the most seasoned pilots by the war's end. Among the most distinguished Luftwaffe aces to die late in the war were the commander of Fries' 1st Night Fighter Group, Major Walter Ehle, and the commander of 3rd Night Fighter Group, Colonel Helmut Lent. Both had been awarded the Knight's Cross with Oak Leaves for their staggering tally of bombers shot down: 38 and 110 aircraft, respectively. Lent received the ultimate garnishing of swords and diamonds to his oak leaves, Germany's highest military honour at the time. Both died in accidents, Lent when an engine cut out while he was attempting to land at an airfield in north-western Germany, in October 1944, and Ehle when he crashed into trees beyond his airstrip at St Trond in November 1943, killing himself and his two crew. Even the war's end did not spare another St Trond ace and Germany's top-scoring night fighter, Heinz-Wolfgang Schnaufer. He downed 121 bombers during the war, including seven Lancasters in one 14-minute killing spree on 21 February 1945. Then in 1950, having survived the war, he was killed near Bordeaux when his open-topped sports car crashed into a truck, bringing its load of metal gas cylinders down on top of him.

By the winter of 1943–4 Otto Fries and his colleagues were attending a funeral ceremony for comrades every week to 10 days. But the death of Walter Ehle was different. He was a veteran of the Spanish Civil War, though still only in his late twenties. Ehle was aloof in the Prussian military tradition and all the pilots looked up to him, Otto included. 'I was shocked. He was an exceptional pilot. He was my boss – my Gruppenkommandeur. We couldn't come to terms with the fact he had crashed on landing; we couldn't understand how this could have happened.' Otto had grown accustomed to losing comrades, but with Ehle's death he saw it could happen to any one of them. Though the youngest Leutnant on the squadron, Otto was asked to carry the Ordenkissen, the cushion on which all Ehle's medals were displayed at the funeral, to be buried with the ace.

The opposing airmen were jousting on a tightrope, with often the slightest turn of luck determining who would prevail and who would become yet another casualty. The evening of the day Col helped to bury Eric Wynn beside Mildenhall airbase in August 1942, he flew off to bomb Nuremberg, where Otto tilled the darkness in his Messerschmitt without reward, before being shot down himself – on his mother's birthday. For Otto's colleagues, however, this was among the most successful night's hunting of the war so far, accounting for one in seven of the 160 aircraft dispatched to Nuremberg – among them the Stirling of Wing Commander Cecil Charlton-Jones, who had flown Col and his crew back to base after their rescue from the English Channel a few months before.

CHAPTER 12

ABOARD THE 'FLYING COFFIN'

THE WINTER OF 1943–4 was a bleak time for Bomber Command, a war of attrition in the air that killed Col and many thousands of others on both sides. Col began his second tour in February 1944 in a bomber the Luftwaffe night fighter pilots nicknamed the 'flying coffin' – the Avro Lancaster. Harris called it his 'shining sword… the greatest single factor in winning the war'.[1] Although undoubtedly the finest RAF bomber of the war, it could also be a death trap when shot down, and the glee of many of the Luftwaffe night fighters responsible for this destruction was tempered with sympathy as they watched their quarry plunge earthwards, knowing the crews inside had little hope of escaping.

Did the Lancaster deserve the name the Germans gave it, and did Col and the tens of thousands of others who flew in this famous aircraft during the war feel it reduced their odds of survival? What must it have been like to be confined in this tube of explosives for up to eight hours at a time in the darkness? And then to be swatted about the sky, as Germans flung burning metal all around and the desperate pilot bent and buckled the rules of gravity to throw his huge craft into any available hole in the blackness? I hoped that finding answers to these questions would help me to understand better how Col experienced the last hour of his life.

I had other questions too. How could RAF bomber crew losses

have climbed to such a staggering rate at exactly the time this legendary aircraft was becoming the mainstay of Bomber Command? And why was Col, who had completed his first tour in 1942, so determined to rejoin the fight late the following year, when the chances of surviving were getting worse? Part of the answer to both questions was a belief, that winter, that Germany would be defeated, and the Allied high command seemed intent on pushing its advantage, whatever the cost. Indeed, the tide of war began to turn against Germany soon after Col stopped flying operations from Lakenheath in October 1942. Col shared this growing optimism, and he wanted to ride this tide to victory in a bomber, not watch from the ground.

After failing to destroy its air defences in the Battle of Britain in summer 1940, Germany had abandoned its plans to invade Britain, but the steady change in Germany's fortunes began two years later, with the defeat of Germany's most famous Field Marshal, Erwin Rommel, at El Alamein in November 1942. This began the retreat from North Africa and the Mediterranean, while the German surrender at Stalingrad in February 1943 quickened the ebb-flow on the eastern front. At sea, the once-mighty surface fleet of the German Kriegsmarine had been either sunk or driven to find sanctuary in coastal waters, so that the U-boat 'wolf packs' remained the last serious threat to Britain's maritime supply lines.

Col's letters home reflect the firming conviction in Britain that the Allies were on the road to victory – and his belief that bombing Germans out of their homes was a fully justified means of ruining their appetite for war and punishing them for the destruction and misery they had unleashed across Europe. By the time Col wrote home at Christmas 1942, he believed the Germans had put themselves so far beyond any notions of human decency that they deserved no mercy:

Europe will be over before the war in the East. Some think here that Turkey will come in on the Allies' side finally. That may be; but Hitler is doomed – and damned. There was a remarkable demonstration in the House [of Commons] the other day. All the members stood for a moment to express their horror at the Nazi atrocities on the Jews. God help the Nazis when the war goes against them, for no-one else will be able to. I have seen documented photographs from Russia of what the Germans have done. It makes you sick to look at some of them.

Two months later, in February 1943, Col forecast that Bomber Command was winding up to deliver the knock-out blow to Germany:

I think that the war in Europe is taking a definite turn for the better. The RAF is giving Germany sheer hell in the air. The newspapers here recently published an aerial photograph of Düsseldorf. The place is a shambles, literally. We are systematically doing to the Ruhr what the Nazis boasted they did to Warsaw, Rotterdam and tried to do to London. They are in for terrible things as the summer and the autumn come on. Every night we hear the continual drone as hordes of heavy aircraft pass over on their way out. Larger numbers go now than when I was flying, and larger numbers will go all the time. We are losing more aircraft, but the proportion of losses to numbers is hardly any higher. Jerry is doing his best to reinforce the crumbling defences of the Ruhr, but whatever he does, the boys still get through.

By late 1943 Bomber Command was growing in strength by the day – and showing what this meant by night. Yet the air over Europe remained one of the deadliest places to wage war, and as the methods of killing became more sophisticated and the resources devoted to this task increased, the casualty rate among airmen on both sides and the toll of civilian dead in German cities climbed. Churchill, knowing an assault by land on German-held territory would be suicidal at that point, argued to Stalin that the nightly aerial onslaught by Bomber Command represented the second front the Soviet leader was urging. The bombing was clearly drawing off pressure from the beleaguered Soviet Union, as more and more German men and firepower were being transferred from the eastern front to the west to help staunch the waves of RAF bombers by night and the US attacks by day. By the end of 1943 the Luftwaffe had become primarily a defensive element in the air war in the west, deploying some two million personnel to defend against bombers taking off from England.

But this extensive German aerial minefield of radar, searchlights, flak guns and night fighters was inflicting enormous losses on the bomber force. After a massive build-up of men and machines through the first half of 1943, Bomber Command was equipped to carry out large raids on Germany on a consistent basis through the winter of 1943–4. But in this show of strength, Bomber Command was not alone; the Luftwaffe night fighters also reached their peak strength and effectiveness during this period. In just one example of the terrible consequences for the RAF, more airmen were killed in the 95 bombers downed during one night operation to Nuremberg in March 1944 than died serving with Fighter Command during the entire Battle of Britain in 1940.

This was the climate of escalating losses in which Col began his second tour of operations in February 1944. He had taken part in only one previous op in a Lancaster: the first of the firestorm raids against Hamburg, in July 1943. The night he died was just the second time, and I wondered whether the aircraft's design might have helped to seal his fate. To begin to answer that, I needed to get a feel for the inside of a Lancaster. This is what took me to Lincolnshire in May 2008, to visit the base of the only aircraft of its type still flying in Britain. The Lancaster's home, RAF Coningsby airbase, is just down the road from the wartime base of the legendary 617 'Dambusters' Squadron, whose billet, the Tudor-style Petwood Hotel, was also my lodgings for the night. I had driven there from the 149 Squadron reunion at Mildenhall and arrived to find the hotel still in a flurry after the Dambusters' reunion festivities the previous evening.

At Coningsby next morning I entered a spacious hangar, as clean as a sports hall despite the array of wartime aircraft that operates from it. At the far end, the Lancaster's condor-like, rising outer wings reached from wall to wall, its sleek lines no less impressive than in its heyday. A mechanic seemed as small as a doll up beside the bomber's bulbous nose, as he restored the gleam to its perspex windows after its weekend of flying as star turn for the reunion.

My guide asked me first to turn out my pockets of anything – coins, keys – that could fall into crevices and gum up the works, then ushered me inside its lichen-green fuselage through the main hatch, which is just forward of the tail's starboard cross-piece.

Crews praised the Lancaster's speed and its ability to climb high and perform acrobatic manoeuvres that belied its size – as so many night fighters like Otto Fries also discovered the hard way. Its chances of evading danger were thus better, and it ended the war with a lower casualty rate than either of the RAF's other two four-engined 'heavies', the Stirling and the Halifax. But the Lancaster was much harder to escape from once it was mortally damaged, and in that sense its designers sacrificed crew safety for aircraft performance.[2] This much was obvious the moment I stepped inside. The fuselage is an obstacle course, even when the aircraft is stationary and has light infiltrating through its windows. First comes the bell-housing of the dorsal gun turret, followed by the step up to the raised floor covering the bomb bay, which runs to just short of the nose; then the real trap – the main wing spar, which anchors the wings across the fuselage. This obstacle is as tall as the space remaining to climb over it – a large, flattened semi-circular opening arching to the height of a car wheel. Add to these obstructions the challenge of struggling free wearing a full flying suit and bulky sheepskin bomber jacket, and of being pinned by the centrifugal forces of a craft spinning out of control, possibly filled with flames and smoke. For me it was a sobering shuffle through a potentially deadly maze.

Whatever bomber an airman flew in, his chances of making it through the war unscathed were slim. When Col finally persuaded his superiors in January 1944 to allow him to return to operations, he worsened his survival odds by volunteering for one of the most dangerous jobs in Bomber Command. His closest wartime friend, Barry Martin, had joined 7 Squadron of the Pathfinder Force (PFF) immediately after finishing his first tour in 1942, and was killed within a few months. Col joined this same squadron – one of the original four pathfinder squadrons – nearly a year later. The PFF was made up of crews chosen for their proven ability to find and hit a target under the most challenging circumstances. 'Bomber'

Harris had opposed the formation of a pathfinder force, concerned that cherry-picking the best crews would strip regular squadrons of experience and leadership and perhaps lower both their morale and their effectiveness. After an intense debate, however, Harris had been overruled by *his* boss, Air Chief Marshal Sir Charles Portal. By February 1944 the pathfinders were proving their worth by enabling the bomber stream to identify the target quickly, release its bombs accurately and get out without perilous delay.

This contribution to improved performance came at a price. Pathfinders had to arrive ahead of the bomber stream, thus attracting the undivided attention of the prowling night fighters and the fresh fury of the searchlights and flak batteries. They generally added to their aerial flare marking with normal incendiary and blast bombs to highlight the target on the ground. After the initial pathfinders had departed from the scene, others known as 'backers-up' followed with fresh flares, to replace the earlier markers carried off course by wind and natural drift. The remarking was important to reduce the incidence of the bomber stream dropping its load in the wrong place, and to correct the 'creep-back' effect as nervy bomb aimers pressed the release 'tit' too soon in their eagerness to high-tail it away from the target.

As bomb aimer, dropping target markers was Col's job the night he died. Berlin lay obscured below unbroken cloud, forcing the pathfinder aircraft to use sky markers – parachute flares above the clouds – for the waves of bombers in their wake to 'blind bomb'. The Germans called the green, red, yellow and white flares 'Christmas trees', and did their utmost to prevent these grim tidings from concentrating the deadly effect of the following main force.

Otto Fries was always particularly pleased to shoot down a pathfinder. A 7 Squadron pathfinder aircraft lost during a raid on Brunswick (Braunschweig) on 14 January 1944 was probably one of three Lancasters he shot down that night. It seems unlikely Col had a chance to do his job over Berlin a month later before his Lancaster, too, attracted the attention of one of Otto's colleagues – though the outcome of that duel was far from certain.

That night, 15–16 February 1944, Col's Lancaster was among

43 bombers lost on this single raid – four of them from his own 7 Squadron, which suffered the highest losses that night. Among the other casualties in the squadron was the oldest New Zealand pilot to die with Bomber Command, 39-year-old Squadron Leader John Hegman DSO, DFC, of Auckland, who lies with his crew near Col in the Berlin War Cemetery at Heerstrasse. His photo was published in the *Weekly News* beside Col's on a page of New Zealand casualties some weeks later. Only three men survived among the four 7 Squadron crews shot down. A store of experience and skill was lost on this single raid – a wing commander, flying as second pilot to Hegman, and two squadron leaders were among the dead. The medal count of those four crews included two Distinguished Service Orders, one Conspicuous Gallantry Medal, eight DFCs, seven DFMs and one OBE.[3] In the course of almost seven months, as the Battle of Berlin raged in the skies, Lancasters of 7 Squadron took off 353 times. In all, 26 of its aircraft failed to return during the campaign, leaving 146 men dead and 39 in prisoner of war camps. As on the night Col and John Hegman died, 7 Squadron suffered the highest loss rate of any squadron during the Berlin campaign.[4] These were some of Bomber Command's best crews, men who were on at least their second tour and who had therefore beaten the odds many times until then.

7 Squadron's losses, though extreme, were not unique among pathfinder squadrons, and by early 1944 the chances of getting shot down were increasing. From late summer 1943, German night fighters introduced a new attacking technique using upward-firing cannons, mounted rear of the cockpit and angled forward at 70 degrees. This enabled them to approach a bomber undetected and to open fire from beneath its undefended belly. Otto frequently used this so-called schräge Musik – slang for jazz – and said it made shooting down a bomber 'almost routine'. This new technique meant night fighters could attack with virtual impunity – so long as they avoided firing on the bomb bays, which would risk detonating the load and bringing hellfire and destruction down on their own heads. Few bomber crews were warned of this unseen danger and many of them died without knowing what had hit them.[5]

The dense cloud over Berlin did not spare it from misery on that February night. The 891 four-engined aircraft dispatched to attack the city made up the biggest bomber force Harris had sent against Germany since the Hamburg firestorm raids of the previous July and August, when Col had flown his previous op. The Berlin force carried 2600 tonnes of bombs, nearly twice the 1430 tonnes dropped by 1000 bombers during the Operation Millennium attack on Cologne in May 1942.[6] The Battle of Berlin, from late August 1943 to March 1944, thus neared its end with a bigger bang than its previous 17 raids. That single raid destroyed more than 1000 residential buildings, as well as some important factories in the Siemens industrial district, near present-day Tegel Airport. At least 320 people died on the ground in Berlin and a further 59 in outlying areas hit by stray bombs.

Harris had promised Churchill at the outset of the Battle of Berlin: 'It will cost us between 400 to 500 aircraft. It will cost Germany the war.' He was half right: it cost Bomber Command 492 aircraft – and more than 3000 crew – but it failed to pound the Germans into submission. The capital held out to the end, finally defeated only in the desperate street-by-street fighting against the Red Army in April and May 1945 – the Battle of Berlin on the ground.

As the nights shortened and attacking such distant targets thus became even more dangerous, Harris turned his attention away from Berlin in late March 1944. The war lasted another 14 months. The 55,500 aircrew killed by its end made up nearly half of the 125,000 men who flew with Bomber Command during the war.[7] Every one of them was a volunteer and almost every one an officer or a non-commissioned officer (NCO). In addition, nearly 10,000 had become prisoners of war and 8400 more had been wounded. On the basis of sheer numbers mustered, most were Britons, but New Zealand suffered disproportionately for a small country: with a wartime population of just under 1.5 million people, it lost 1850 of the 6000 men who left its shores to serve in Bomber Command.[8] By comparison, Australia lost more than 4000 of the 10,000 men who flew operations with Bomber Command and Canada nearly 10,000 aircrew. US aircrew, who flew daylight raids, fared no better than those in Bomber Command, with almost half killed among the 80,000 who flew with the 8th and 9th Army Air Forces from bases in Britain.

The New Zealand fatality rate of nearly one in three well overshadows that of one in ten of the 15,000 New Zealand Division troops who fought in the 1916 Battle of the Somme in northern France, during which overall New Zealand casualties reached 40 per cent. In that campaign Australia suffered some 25,000 casualties, a third of whom died, while Canada sustained 24,000 killed or wounded.[9] The scale of bloodshed in the trenches has come to symbolise the profligate waste of human life in wartime. Yet in the war that followed, the proportionately far greater losses suffered by Bomber Command are not nearly as widely known. On a purely statistical basis, stripping away skill and luck, an individual's chances of surviving a tour of 30 operations were less than even once the proportion of aircraft lost topped 2.3 per cent.[10] Well above this figure, the actual loss rate was often much worse: during that bitter winter it frequently exceeded one-tenth of the aircraft dispatched on a given night and sometimes was more that one in eight, as the German defences reached the peak of their effectiveness in the early months of 1944.

Generally, aircrew who survived their first tour were put on ground duties for six months, then required to return to operations. Col was unusual in that his superiors were trying their best to *prevent* him from flying again because, it seems, as navigation officer for 115 Squadron he was doing a particularly good job of training navigators. Col finally got his way, but at a point when volunteering to return to ops was akin to playing Russian roulette with more chambers loaded than empty. Why Col did so is a question that becomes harder, not easier, to answer with the distance of years. He knew that even if he did not die on this raid, he had volunteered to keep flying until his number would almost inevitably come up. I could not fathom this apparent will to self-sacrifice, what pushed him to this decision, but I hoped at the very least to find out what really happened to him the night his Lancaster, MG-'W' William, met its end.

Skipper Jock Watt, whom Col admired so much, at the
controls of their Stirling in 1942. *(Collection Col Jones)*

The 'flying wedding' party at Church Stretton, Shropshire, about
which Col (sitting at right) wrote in May 1942. Al Shoreman
is standing at left next to Jock Watt. *(Collection Col Jones)*

Leutnant Fries bearing the medals of his commanding officer, Walter Ehle, buried along with his crew at St Trond in November 1943. *(Collection O-H Fries)*

Otto (far left) and Fred Staffa (3rd from right) play skat while waiting for combat orders in the readiness room at St Trond airbase, Belgium, in 1943. *(Collection O-H Fries)*

Fries's Messerschmitt ME110 at St Trond, Belgium, 1943. *(Collection O-H Fries)*

A Heinkel HE219 after the German surrender, showing the SN2 radar 'antlers'. *(Collection O-H Fries)*

Paul Zorner after being awarded the Oak Leaves to the Knight's Cross in September 1944. By now he had shot down 58 RAF bombers. *(Collection Paul Zorner)*

St Trond's - and Germany's - most successful night fighter, Heinz-Wolfgang Schnaufer, displaying 'kills' on his ME110 tailplane in 1943. Schnaufer's total for the war was 121 bombers. One of his tailplanes is on display at the Australian War Memorial in Canberra, the other at the Imperial War Museum in London. *(Collection O-H Fries)*

A Luftwaffe padre at the grave of RAF airmen shot down during the first 'thousand bomber' raid, against Cologne in May 1942. They are being buried beside Otto's airfield at St Trond, Belgium. *(Collection O-H Fries)*

A flak tower, 40 metres high, in Hamburg, similar to those built in many major German cities during the war. *(Paul Grant)*

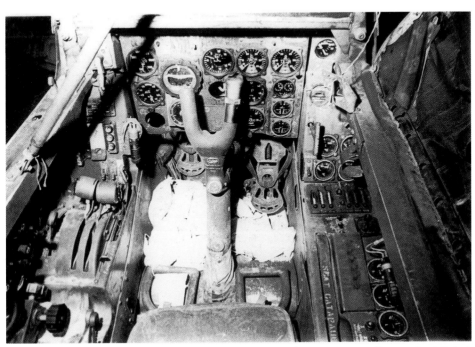

Cockpit of a Heinkel HE219. *(Collection O-H Fries)*

Kurt Köhn in February 2008, at the site of Col's bomb crater near Penzlin. He is pointing towards Berlin and the approach path of the stricken Lancaster. *(Stephen Harris)*

Col Jones's headstone at the Heerstrasse Cemetery. *(Stephen Harris)*

Professor Fries at his Berlin home in 2008. *(Stephen Harris)*

Paul Zorner, 88, in 2007 at his managed care home in Homburg-Saar, south-west Germany. *(Stephen Harris)*

The memorial at the centre of Hamburg's Ohlsdorf mass grave depicts Charon, 'death's boatman' of Greek mythology, ferrying souls across the River Styx to the afterlife. *(Stephen Harris)*

Fred Coney in 2007, between the graves of 'Ron' Middleton VC (left) and Eric Wynn (right of picture), at Beck Row Cemetery, Mildenhall. *(Stephen Harris)*

Berlin Commonwealth War Cemetery, Heerstrasse, on Remembrance Day 2004. *(Stephen Harris)*

CHAPTER 13

THE LAST NIGHT

WHEN I SET OUT to find answers, the destruction of 'W' William had been a mystery for more than 60 years. The New Zealand Air Department had written to Col's mother, Emma Jones, shortly after the war, but its brief account struck me as not only incomplete but also possibly misleading. I knew from this official version roughly when and where the Lancaster had come down, but little more than that. Living in Berlin, I was now close enough to return to the area as often as it took to put together a fuller picture – or so I hoped. The place where Col died lay in the former Russian zone, which had become the German Democratic Republic (GDR) after the war. The GDR was neither democratic nor was it honest about wartime experiences in its part of Germany, which the Soviets had occupied in 1945 and set up as a puppet state. The victors had rewritten the history of this part of Germany to suit their own political ends, and I knew that even if I could overcome the gaps or distortions in the official record, I would need a stroke of luck to find a firm path back to February 1944.

Luck seemed already in short supply for the crew of 'W' William as the seven men clambered on board for their final operation. This had come as an unwelcome surprise to them; they had been expecting two weeks' leave – or so the mother of one wrote to Emma Jones after their sons' deaths. Another mother wrote that her son had invited Col to spend the leave with them in Scotland. But that would have to wait, and they soon found out why they had been added to the battle order for that night: 'Bomber' Harris had big plans, requiring all available aircraft. He wanted to round off the seven-month concentrated bombing campaign against Berlin with a show of force that would deal 'the Big City' a final blow. Col – 'Jonah' to the established crew he had joined only that month – had spent just 80 minutes in the air with them, including a short test flight that very morning, Tuesday 15 February 1944. He knew he was in good company – a close-knit crew with whom he had quickly formed a bond: fellow Flight Lieutenant Roy Barnes DFC, pilot; Sergeant John Dalziel, aged 20, flight engineer from Northumberland; Pilot Officer Jim McLachlan DFC, 28, navigator from West Lothian in Scotland; Pilot Officer Raymond Bett, 23, wireless operator, from Stafford; Flight Sergeant 'Eddie' Marshall, 20, mid-upper gunner from Sheffield; and Flight Sergeant Edward Campbell, rear gunner. 'W' William had been in the thick of the Battle of Berlin, taking its crews safely to Germany's capital and back nine times since it had arrived at 7 Squadron the previous September. Roy Barnes, Col and the other crew took it up at 11 a.m. on 15 February for a 45-minute test flight. Then at 5.09 p.m. – 6.09 p.m. in Berlin – they took off into the thickening darkness. Col's job as bomb aimer was to light up this flat, sprawling city, which offered little by way of helpful feedback to the ground-scanning H2S navigation and target-finding radar.

What happened during the next three hours will never be known for sure, but I was able to track down a few people who remember that night and who have thrown new light on the version of events given to our family soon after the war. What we knew was limited to the sparsely worded description in a letter sent to Col's mother – my great-grandmother – in January 1948 by the New Zealand Air Department, quoting the report of the post-war investigation into the loss of the aircraft.

On the night of the 15th/16th February, 1944, a four-engined aircraft approached the village of Marihn from the direction of Berlin at about 11 pm. The aircraft was hit by fire from night fighters and exploded in the air. Police from Penzlin, the neighbouring town, were responsible for the burial of the crew, which took place on 17th February, 1944.

This, the official word on Col's death, though brief was also wrong. I began to suspect a mistake as soon as I started gathering information from elsewhere. The first path of inquiry took me to the man I initially thought might have shot down 'W' William, Paul Zorner, who was in the air that night in a Messerschmitt ME110. Refreshed after two weeks' leave during the full-moon period when the RAF flew no major attacks, Zorner took off through dense ground fog from his airbase at Lüneburg, just south of Hamburg, then climbed through thick cloud to 6500 metres and headed north, hoping to intercept the bomber stream. He skirted the Hamburg flak defences and flew into deteriorating weather over Schleswig-Holstein, bordering Denmark. As he tracked back east towards Kiel the weather improved and he quickened his approach when he saw the trail of a bomber going down in flames.

Just after 8 p.m. Zorner's Bordfunker, Heinz Wilke, picked up squiggles on his radar, indicating an aircraft 300 metres above them. The 15 Squadron Lancaster, 'LS-O', had taken off from Mildenhall about 20 minutes after Col's had cleared the runway at Oakington, further west. In the pilot's seat was a 23-year-old from Alexandra in Central Otago, Flight Lieutenant Willis Mark Harris. Zorner drifted up and fired from behind and slightly below into the Lancaster's starboard wing, then he immediately had to jink off to starboard to avoid the answering fire of the bomber's rear gunner. But the Lancaster's wing was already well aflame, so Zorner hung off to the side of the bomber and waited for its death throes. The stricken bomber began to descend in a wide spiral, which became steeper the lower it fell. Then, at exactly 8.22 p.m., it simply tipped into a vertical dive and struck the Baltic, north of the city of Stralsund. Harris's body washed ashore at Hiddensee three months later, the only crew member recovered. He is buried in the Berlin War Cemetery at Heerstrasse, his grave not far from Col's.

In a book on his experiences published in 2007, Zorner reflects on what it felt like to destroy an enemy bomber, and usually all on board.

It is impossible to describe the feelings that come over you in the face of the death struggle of such an aircraft. As an airman you shudder at the prospect of what your weapons have wrought just seconds before, and you hope your opponents emerge alive. As someone fighting for the safety of defenceless people, you observe the tragedy unfolding in the night sky with utterly cold satisfaction. As a soldier you have an almost scientific, mechanical view of the scene, since you're a tradesman qualified in the destruction of the enemy's attacking capacity. You want to see what effect you have had and would like to remain in the vicinity as long as it takes to be able to report the 'kill'.[1]

Some 40 minutes after Harris's Lancaster plunged into the Baltic, Wilke picked up a new 'squiggle' and Zorner intercepted another Lancaster before it could release its bomb load on Berlin, shooting it down in a fashion almost identical to the first and again ducking away from answering fire. This Lancaster crashed at Neuruppin, north of Berlin, at 9.11 p.m. and as I matched up the details I wondered whether this could be my great-uncle's plane. It is an eerie feeling thinking you may come face to face, more than six decades later, with the killer of a family member – even one working to the impersonal imperatives of combat. I knew from my research that Zorner had shot down 59 bombers, killing around 400 RAF airmen. The need to find out if one of these might have been my great-uncle mingled with a deep apprehension that Paul Zorner might be Col's killer. Of course, curiosity had the upper hand.

I visited Neuruppin and Marihn, both north of Berlin and about 70 kilometres apart, a distance that a Lancaster would take about 10 minutes to cover flying at top speed. I wondered, therefore, whether there could have been a mix-up between two separate incidents of broken, black shapes falling to earth on a moonless night. After all, the report mentioned night *fighters*, plural, and I knew they usually hunted alone. I also wondered whether the time of Zorner's second shooting down that night, 9.11 p.m., and that reported to my great-grandmother of nearly two hours later, could have become confused in the four years between his death and the letter conveying that brief crash report. I later received a copy of another report, from the exhumation team sent to Penzlin in 1947. This more extensive report was the first to mention a crash time: 9 p.m., according to local reports. For some reason this was changed in subsequent references to 11 p.m., which I thought unlikely, since this was some two hours after the Lancaster would have reached Berlin.

I had tucked away in my mind from earlier research the unusual name of Zorner, one of 23 pilots who shared in the 35 'kills' officially attributed to particular Luftwaffe night fighters that night, so when I learned that a Paul Zorner had just published a book recounting his experiences, I wondered whether I had stumbled on a welcome coincidence. I phoned and emailed the book's publisher, asking for Zorner's contact details, and was told the former pilot now lived in a managed-care home for the elderly. The publisher gave me Zorner's number, which I phoned. I was struck by the strong, authoritative voice, not unfriendly but without any obvious warmth either – possibly a little wary. I outlined the background to my search. Then I sent him a letter, asking whether he might be the pilot who had shot down Col Jones's plane. I enclosed a detailed map showing the respective locations of the crash sites. A few days later a copy of Zorner's book arrived from the publisher and I quickly established that the plane he had shot down over Neuruppin was not Col's, since Zorner himself had identified it as another aircraft.

I later visited Zorner in Homburg-Saar, in Germany's south-west, and found him surprisingly congenial, relieved to take off his tie when I arrived not wearing one. During a three-hour conversation, he explained the simple logic that drove him during the war: 'When we experienced what your namesake, Harris – supported by the Americans – carried out with his bombing of German cities, that really made me angry. I said once to my Bordfunker that the only way we could fulfil our duty to our homeland was to drive the losses of the Royal Air Force so high that they would just say: "The successes don't justify the losses; we'll call a stop to it." ' Of the night Col died, Zorner remembered only the shooting down of the two Lancasters, as described above. These kills contributed to his tally of 33 bombers in just five months that winter, and of 59 by the end of the war.

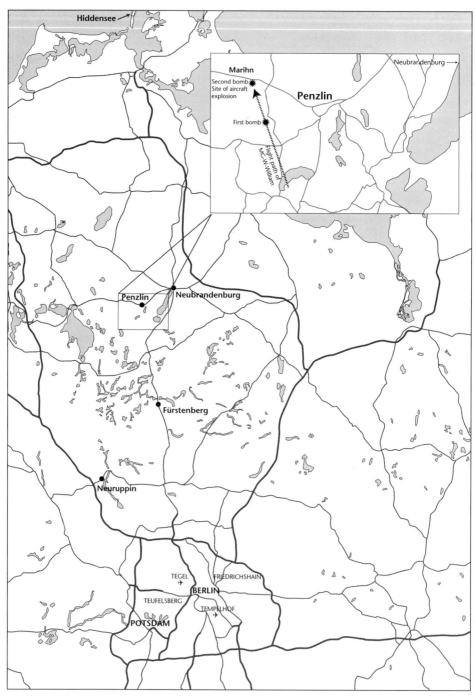

Map 3: *The last night — where events unfolded*

My attempts to find out more about the events of 15 February 1944 took me several times to Marihn and Penzlin, the two towns mentioned in the 1947 crash reports. Not until my third visit did I glean what I was looking for. One morning 64 years after Col died, my children and I drove north from Berlin along a straight road lined with mature trees. The scrawny pine forests and sandy soil around Berlin soon give way to the richer agricultural land of Brandenburg. As we progressed north the sun filtered weakly through a thickening February fog, which had closed in by the time we drove through Fürstenberg, about 90 minutes north of Berlin, to obscure the turn-off to the former women's concentration camp at Ravensbrück, where many of the inmates had been used for medical experiments.

I wanted to see what Penzlin looked like in mid-February, the time Col and his crew met their end there. The conditions certainly lent an atmosphere of reflection, if not foreboding. I had arranged an 11.30 a.m. meeting with the Lutheran pastor of the Marienkirche, the old brick church on the crown of the town. Over the phone I had explained briefly the background to my visit. To my surprise we were met at the church entrance by not only the pastor, Hartmuth Reincke, but also an older man. Kurt Köhn was dressed plainly and wore large plastic-framed glasses. Born in 1930, he had lived in Penzlin all his 77 years and in that time had seen the Nazis, the Russians and the nation of East Germany come and go.

The reason for his unexpected presence became clear at the outset: Köhn was a 13-year-old schoolboy when, on 16 February 1944, he heard the news that was spreading rapidly through this quiet rural town. A British bomber had exploded over the outskirts of the town during the night, injuring old farmer Karl Boldt, badly damaging his farmhouse and disintegrating in countless pieces over his fields. When Köhn got back on the train from his classes in the nearby town of Neubrandenburg at lunchtime, he jumped straight onto his bike and joined the steady trail of townsfolk on the 6-kilometre road to the Boldt farmstead.

He found a scene of devastation beyond his imagination. For Köhn and most other natives of Penzlin, this was the first, shocking visitation of a war that, even by early 1944, had taken its sons away but had left the town itself untouched. A bomb crater some 7 metres wide and 4 metres deep had been torn in the yard just south of the farmhouse, which had collapsed inwards with the blast. The explosion had evidently triggered a larger one on board the Lancaster, which accounted for the hail of debris and body parts strewn over 500 metres. A crowd, already large and still growing, was now busying itself gathering up pieces of the aircraft, as much for souvenirs as to help the police. Köhn came across no body parts himself, nor could he remember seeing engines, wheels, or any of the larger pieces usually found in the wreckage of a large bomber, but he and his friends quickly gathered up bits of clear perspex from the cockpit canopy and gun turrets, because this material burned like fireworks.

Köhn and Reincke drove with us to the farm, where we were met by Ingeburg Barz, Karl Boldt's granddaughter, who had lived there all her life. On the night of the explosion Frau Barz had been away at Neubrandenburg, half an hour's drive east, celebrating her sixth birthday. Sixty-four years later, as we stood where the crater had been – 20 metres from her house – she recounted what her grandfather had told her. Boldt had arrived injured in the larger town nearby, Penzlin, late the previous night, to report what had happened and to seek help. He told police and friends that at the time of the explosion he had just returned from collecting his wife in a horse-drawn cart from the railway station in Marihn, the small village closest to his farm. Boldt had resumed the running of the farm while his son was away serving in the German army, the Wehrmacht. A French forced labourer assigned to help him on the farm was unharnessing the horse in the yard in front of the stables when they heard a heavy bomber under attack and approaching from the direction of Berlin to the south. The aircraft sounded damaged and was flying very low, apparently in an attempt to shake off the attacking night fighter.

They watched in horror as the bomber, heading straight for them, jettisoned a large bomb – the one that left the crater. A split second later the explosion appeared to tear the Lancaster apart in mid-air. It seems probable, from the wide dispersal and minute fragmentation of the debris, that the upblast detonated what was left in the bomb bay. The force of the explosion blew the Frenchman through the gap between the stables and the farmhouse. He landed on his head in a paddock 50 metres away, stunned but otherwise uninjured. Boldt was still gripping the handle of the farmhouse front door when the blast tore it open with such force it broke his arm. His wife, standing next to him, was unscathed. And there was another compensating mercy that night: young Ingeburg's absence meant she was not asleep in her bedroom, which bore the brunt of the explosion. The blast collapsed the entire side of the house and also wrecked the stables and barn, killing several animals.

The size of the explosion was a clear sign the Lancaster had not been destroyed purely by enemy gunfire, but by an explosion of bombs still on board, possibly a full load. This did not match up with the New Zealand Air Department's reported crash time of 11 p.m., which would have been about two hours after 'W' William would have reached Berlin, because by then Col's Lancaster would already have dropped its target-marking flares, incendiaries and any high-explosive blast bombs it had taken off with and it would never have remained in the vicinity for another two hours. With a near-empty bomb bay, a low-flying bomber would have created a point of impact on crashing, even if it exploded before hitting the ground. Clarifying the timing was therefore important to establishing what actually happened.

Ingeburg Barz confirmed my doubts, saying her grandfather told her the explosion occurred two hours earlier, just after 9 p.m. Further evidence came when I received Col's personnel file from the New Zealand Defence Force archives. The documents, which the family had not seen, included several relating to the RAF investigation into the crash and the recovery of the human remains. The earliest of these, dated 25 September 1947, cites German records giving the explosion time as 9 p.m. – two hours earlier than our family had been told.[2] This would have been about three hours after the Lancaster left Oakington and would be consistent with an arrival time over Berlin to light up the target about 15 minutes ahead of the main bomber stream. If so, Col's Lancaster could easily have been picked up as a lonely signal by the radar, a night fighter directed onto it, and been chased north. It seems likely either that the Lancaster had been mortally damaged by this stage or that the pilot was hugging the ground so its defenceless belly would not be exposed and so that the mid-upper and rear gunners could maximise their fire, with the fighter more visible against the sky.

I later found out that 'W' William had first jettisoned another bomb a kilometre to the south of the farm, near the small town of Mollensdorf. This suggested to me that Col, as bomb aimer, had not yet had time to drop his explosive cargo and was frantically trying to do so, either in the knowledge a crash-landing was imminent or to enable the Lancaster to gain speed and height to make good its escape. Instead, it seems the upblast of the second bomb detonated what was still in the bomb bay. This would have produced an explosion big enough to atomise the bomber in mid-air and, even at that low altitude, to strew its fragments over half a kilometre without leaving a single, main point of impact.

The Lancaster had somehow blown itself up, pursued but not shot down by a night fighter. Whether a fighter crew claimed a 'kill' is not known, but both Col's Lancaster and the one flown by his 7 Squadron colleague and fellow Aucklander, John Hegman, were among only eight of the 43 aircraft Bomber Command lost on this raid for which no Luftwaffe pilot was given the credit. The result was the same, but I felt a sense of triumph the Lancaster had not been shot out of the sky by the enemy but had fought to the last. More powerful than that feeling, however, was a sense of closure. Our family now knew in all probability what had really happened. I felt I had at least been able to pay the crew that tribute – and at the place where they had risked all and lost.

The men would not have suffered. Col, and no doubt all the crew, knew the risk of dropping bombs so far below their safety height – he had commented on this in his diary at least twice. The bombs would have been switched to safety but these often exploded anyway, just as primed bombs sometimes did not go off. It seems that in the desperation of trying to evade a heavily armed, faster and more agile pursuer, Col and the skipper must have decided the risk was worth it. The body of the skipper, Flight Lieutenant Roy Barnes DFC, came to rest in what was left of the Boldt farm stables and was able to be identified by a shattered fragment of his dog-tag. Two other bodies were recognisable as human forms but not identifiable, and were buried in separate coffins alongside Barnes at nearby Marihn cemetery.

In many similar cases of RAF crew buried in the Soviet occupation zone, the Russian authorities would not allow the British to recover the remains, but the families of Col's crew were more fortunate. The RAF's Missing Research and Enquiry Unit (MREU) exhumed the bodies in 1947 for reburial in Berlin. Its investigation report records that there was also a fourth coffin, which 'contained one small, confused, heap of unidentifiable remains'. That left three crew unaccounted for, and the investigating officer suggested they might have either tried to bale out and died away from the crash scene or were discovered later and buried elsewhere.[3] That seems unlikely, particularly in the light of something Frau Barz told me: a few years after the war – she could not remember exactly when – a friend's dog started pulling an airman's glove from under the rubble of the farmhouse. When the dog's owner looked more closely she found it was on the hand of an intact skeleton. By then the war had brought much suffering to that part of Germany and this was not the only body making its way to the surface. I wondered what became of this skeleton. For years afterwards, once a small barracks built by the army on the site of the destroyed farmhouse had itself been removed, Frau Barz's farmer husband turned up pieces of human bone while tilling his vegetable garden near the crater. The grave of Flight Lieutenant Barnes, DFC, has its own plot in the Berlin War Cemetery at Heerstrasse. Alongside it are six headstones laid closely side by side – the collective grave for Col and his five other fellow crew members.

Metal fragments from the aircraft – mainly bullets – occasionally worked their way to the surface of the surrounding fields. Herr Barz gave me one such fragment: a piece of aluminium body panelling, part of Col's plane, a tangible link to the past that I shall treasure.

The tiki given to Col by Princess Te Puea may lie out there still. It may even be found one day. I described this to Frau and Herr Barz and explained its significance, just in case it might one day be returned to the Tainui tribe.

A week before his death, Col wrote a last letter to his mother. Though he typed it on Oakington Airbase Officers' Mess letterhead paper, he was careful not to mention he was going back on operations.

Dear Little Mother,

Pay no heed to the printed address at the head of this page. It is just Air Force paper which I happen to be using for this purpose.

Well it is half past six on one of the coldest days we have had this winter. We actually had snow, and there was a bitterly cold wind blowing. It still is, in fact. The winter has not been particularly cold, but today has made up for a lot. To make matters worse, the fire is sulky, and I am tired of poking it – remember at home how I always poked the fire? – in case it gives up the ghost altogether.

I found myself mentioned in dispatches the other day.[4] That is a minor sort of an honour, not very important. It is not a medal, but a sort of a minor pat on the back. I don't know why it happened. It just did. It was not worth sending you a cable about, and it is not worth making a song about at all, so please don't mention it to anyone, or anyone who knew anything about the RAF would smile. I just tell you because I know you will be pleased.

I received a parcel from you the other day. Thanks ever so much. The contents arrived in good order and condition, and we have the odd late supper in my billet. I also got a letter from Lass the day before yesterday, giving me all the news. I do hope, dear, that you are keeping well and fit, and that you are happy. Do look after yourself, little lady. I think about you a lot, and wonder if you are well and not too lonely. The war is progressing favourably. It may not be long now.

CHAPTER 14

DEATH ACROSS DISTANCE

THE TELEGRAM, when it came, was completely unexpected:

> Regret to inform you that your son Acting Flight Lieutenant Frank Colwyn Jones DFC has been reported missing on air operations on the night of 15/16 February 1944. The Prime Minister desires me to convey to you on behalf of the Government his deep sympathy with you in your great anxiety. Letter following.

The telegram carried the signature of another Frank Jones, Minister of Defence. My great-grandmother received the news in her one-room flat in Parnell, Auckland, not from an anonymous telegram courier, but from her two daughters, Florence 'Lass' Exton and Gwen Restall. Col himself had seen to that, putting Lass's name as next of kin in place of his mother's, and writing to his sister in August 1942:

If bad news should come concerning me, it would be a terrible shock to Mother to open an envelope and read a bald, cabled statement. I thought that if you received the news, you could break it to her more gently. Tell her I have done so. Another thing – and this is most important. Should you ever receive a cable saying that I am missing, don't tell her anything for 24 hours, because in that time some good news concerning me may be heard. I have known that to happen. By this time I suppose you will have received my letter telling how we went down in the North Sea off the Dutch coast. Well, when we got back to England, I just managed to get a cable stopped then. What a frightful shock it would have been to little Mother especially, and all so needlessly. Mind you, I don't anticipate that anything bad is going to happen to me. All this seems to me to be making a mountain out of a molehill rather, but it is better to be prepared.

Lass took her nine-year-old daughter, Judy, with her that day in February 1944. Judy recalls how devastated her grandmother was by the news. But they hung onto the hope Col had been captured or was making his way back to Britain with help from the Resistance. Then, in November 1944, the Air Department notified Col's mother that he was now officially presumed dead. His personal effects arrived from England in June 1945, along with an inventory, touching in its small details, and a request to donate his uniform for use by someone else.

New Zealand, along with so much of the rest of the world, was sifting painfully through the detritus of war. Col was just one of the many New Zealand airmen who would not come home to share in the elixir of victory. Yet the tributes sent to his mother show that his loss, even among millions, deeply touched some of the people he had met while overseas. Nothing in Col's letters indicates he had a serious romance while he was in Britain, though he had broken off a relationship with a woman in Auckland before leaving for the war. He spent some of his leaves, however, with the sister of an English friend killed early in the war and he met another woman, Mary Whitfield, when he and Barry Martin went on leave together to Bude, on the Cornwall coast. Mary Whitfield wrote to Col's mother two months after he was lost on operations:

Dear Mrs Jones

You have by now received the official news that Colwyn is missing and I know from how he spoke of you it must be a great blow. I am writing as I felt a more personal letter might be appreciated, knowing how formal and inadequate these notifications seem to be.

Colwyn may or may not have mentioned me but I have known him nearly three years now – in fact since his first leave from operations when he came to Bude and stayed at Clifton College with Barry Martin. I was a secretary there at the time and joined the WAAF [Women's Auxiliary Air Force] six months later, since when we have met periodically and I came to know him very well.

He changed a good deal in those three years. When they came to Bude they were young and full of optimism. Barry's death upset him terribly. And then one by one the others with whom he came over were missing or killed until he eventually came to believe he had to go too. It seemed to me to be a wrong ideal to have and I tried to reason with him but as you probably know nothing would change his view once his mind was made up. During the year he was instructing, the C.O. [Commanding Officer] did everything to prevent him from flying. He was an excellent teacher, the best they had had at Waterbeach [Airbase], and I remember meeting with him a crew which he had trained and during the evening every one of them bothered to tell me aside what a wonderful help he had been. He not only did his own job but all the others too and his interest in them was such a personal thing. They owed everything to him. You can imagine I felt very proud to be a friend of his.

I saw him last for a few days in January when he told me he had volunteered for pathfinding as it was the only way they would let him fly. It was a shock to me. I had hoped the 'powers that be' would win in the end as they always seem to do over things I've wanted since I've been in the Service. Though it is the most dangerous job in Bomber Command he was quite set and sure. His whole attitude was much happier and when we did discuss the matter it is obvious he had no illusions about it – the chances were a hundred to one that he would not get through his second tour but he said he had no ties – when he left you he said goodbye and whatever happened you would understand.

His last letter to me was postmarked Feb.15th in which he had done no flying to date. It was that evening according to his C.O. that they set out for Germany. It must have been his first operational flight and I can imagine with what excitement he must have taken off after so many months of being grounded. He has told me of the nervous strain the men feel when setting out and then the thrill and the horror of being over the target with flak and searchlights surrounding them. And in spite of my feeling what a complete waste of opportunity for someone with such intelligence, understanding and character, I know he would not have had it otherwise.

On re-reading this letter it seems totally inadequate as to what I feel and want to express but maybe it will be some consolation to you to know how everyone from his C.O. to the merest child put their trust in him and were never disappointed. That reminds me of a small incident that happened when he and Barry were staying at Bude. We walked one afternoon intent on taking a photograph of the church and I turned to find Colwyn sitting on a stone bench with half a dozen small children around him. I came to discover it was typical of his interest in everyone with whom he came into contact.

And so I'll finish hoping yet that he is safe and well somewhere and that we shall hear news soon.

Yours very sincerely

Mary Whitfield

Col's mother received no letters from her son's former fellow aircrew, of the type he had written to Barry Martin's mother. Most of Col's friends had been killed over the two years since he had flown his first operation. Several mothers of the crew who died with him wrote, with pain, pride and even hope in their words. Millicent Bett, mother of the wireless operator, Raymond, took the initiative nine days after the Lancaster went missing: 'I am writing to the other boys' mothers, as I think it will be nice for us all to get in touch with each other just to cheer each other up in the long days of waiting for news. I don't know if Jonah [Col's sometime nickname] is your only son, but Raymond is all I have. My husband died 14 years ago and I have seen many dark days trying to hold up for his sake. He is 23 and we were such pals and I am very proud of him. May God give us courage to carry on.' Raymond Bett's headstone in the Berlin Commonwealth War Cemetery bears the inscription: 'God gives us love. Someone to love he lends. His loving mother.'

The mothers of some of the other crew wrote to Col's mother in the weeks following the loss, but if those in Britain remained in touch with each other, their contact with Emma Jones did not long survive the distance separating them on opposite sides of the world. So many people were mourning. While Col had been alive, he had helped the closest relatives of some of his friends to prevent their death from hardening into the finality of a diminishing past. From Kent, the mother of Peter Paine, one of Col's earliest room mates in the sergeants' quarters at Mildenhall, wrote to Emma Jones in April 1944, shortly after Col was reported missing on operations.

Dear Mrs Jones

I expect that Colwyn will have told you about me, and the many times that he has spent his leaves with us. I promised him that should anything happen to him that I would write to you. He was here on his last leave at the end of January and he told me then that he was not going to tell you that he was going back into operations, as he did not want you worrying over him.

I think that the raid on Berlin in which he had been reported missing must have been almost his first trip, as I had heard from him only a few days before that he was about to join his new squadron. I have been to the New Zealand Air Force Headquarters to see if there was any further information, but they told me last week that they would not expect any news for at least another month. I see from the report in *The Times* of the raid that many men were seen to bale out, so we must hope that Colwyn has landed safely somewhere. I shall be informed if he is a prisoner, and will see that he has letters and parcels and what I know he will most want – books.

Colwyn first came here with my son, they were in the same squadron and became friends, and after I lost my son I begged Colwyn to come just the same. We liked him so much, and I know that he was very happy with us. He just made himself thoroughly at home, in fact he once said to me that he followed me around just like he did his own Mother, and I tried to do for him what I thought you would have done. I feel so very sad for you all those many miles away, it must be so much harder to bear than for we Mothers here in England, who at least have the memories of many happy leave times, but I can assure you that Colwyn was very happy, he loved England, and enjoyed visiting different parts of the country and seeing all the old places.

It was entirely his own wish to go back on operational work, he was doing a very important navigational [training] job, but he told me he could not bear to see the boys going out any longer, and he simply had to go with them again. I think you can be very proud of him, and I do most sincerely trust that he is alive and safe somewhere and you will see him again one day. If I can do anything for you over here please tell me, and believe me that my husband and myself feel very deeply for you in your trouble, we know too well what you must be suffering.

Very sincerely yours

Winifred Paine

Emma Jones also exchanged letters with Winifred Paine's daughter-in-law, Peter's widow, Ruth. One of these letters came after the body of Col's skipper, Flight Lieutenant Barnes, had been positively identified. In a letter written from her home in Shortlands, Kent, in August 1944, Ruth Paine compared the uncertainty about Col's fate to that of her husband, Peter, killed in March 1942:

I know how hard it must have been for you to get the information about F/Lt Barnes being killed – I have had equally indefinite information about Peter, in that a cap marked 'Paine' was found near a destroyed Wellington but the Air Ministry don't accept these things as proof and I have been told that a very high percentage of missing airmen are probably still alive, although it won't be known until after the war. I am <u>determined</u> not to give up hope and it may well be that both of them will return.

Colwyn was one of the most cheerful and entertaining people I have ever met. I remember so well what fun he was during the last leave Peter and I had together when he was staying with us in Highgate. Going into town with the two of them was like taking a couple of schoolboys out for the day and I remember how much we teased him about his enthusiasm over everything and his expression 'I nipped smartly up the road…' etc! On the last evening of the leave Peter and his parents and I returned from a theatre, all of us, I think, feeling a little depressed at the thought of Peter going back on 'ops' the next day – and found that Colwyn had arrived unexpectedly from his visit to Surrey and his very amusing account of his visit and the journey back made us laugh so much that we decided we might have saved the money for the theatre tickets and stayed at home listening to him instead!

I was glad to find that he was just the same when I saw him again nearly two years later. I was particularly glad too that he was able to get down to see our son, Crispin. As I told him, I had intended to ask him to be godfather but as I had no answer to my letter – it was delayed I think while he was being posted to a new squadron – I assumed he must have gone east and I asked someone else.

You must have been terribly proud when he won the DFC. He wrote such a typically modest and understanding letter in answer to my congratulations. His letters gave me so much pleasure as he was the only one of Peter's RAF friends I really knew well. When Peter's personal effects were sent home I gave his RAF ties to Colwyn and I think it was typical of his sympathy and understanding that he said he would wear them on 'ops' and on the Christmas card he sent he added 'I wore Peter's tie to Hamburg, Ruth.'

Crispin and I will be leaving here in September and I shall not be able to return home until the flying bomb menace is finished, as Shortlands has been very badly damaged, but I am giving you that address as I don't know yet where we shall be for the next few months. I feel the war really can't go on for very much longer now.

Yours very sincerely

Ruth Paine

Emma Jones continued to receive a steady stream of tributes, in which disbelief was initially mixed with a forced optimism that Col might be posted among the prisoners of war. On 14 February 1945, one day short of a year after Col died, the chief sub-editor at the *Auckland Star*, Ralph Kenner, wrote:

It was not until I read the official announcement that I could bring myself even to think of Col as no longer with us in the flesh: the lamp of hope still burnt strongly. Now, they tell us he has gone. But you know and I know that Life cannot end, for it is eternal. Therefore, the individual expression of Life that is Col continues on even though undiscerned by the physical senses. There are times when I actually feel his presence – that glowing smile, those friendly thoughts, the tender solicitude for you and all that you hold dear. The real Col changes not; he has merely gone on to new experiences.

Your son was one of those rare friends with whom one could converse on the deepest topics in the most natural and friendly way. On occasion he would come into my room and within two minutes of 'squatting' on the edge of the desk he would be launched into the most intimate talk on some deep yet fascinating problem of living. And we both knew that what was being said was sacred to the innermost thoughts of each other. Col was a straight shooter; he hated pretence or humbug. He did not pretend to be any better than he thought he was and yet I thought I discerned in him one of the gentlest, rarest natures it has been my privilege to encounter.

Like so many others of our fine young men, Col saw there was a job to be done for the Empire – and humanity at large – and he set off deliberately to do that job, knowing that in a human sense the chances were that he would not return. He told me that a few days before his departure. I, of course, expressed the opposite view, but he quietly indicated that he knew what he was doing, that it was well worth while and that he was fully prepared to pay the cost....

We are all proud of his grand record of service, proud to be his friends. And so, when you sometimes feel specially kind thoughts around you it may be that Col's friends are joining with you in gratefully saluting his splendid memory.

With kindest thoughts to you all whom Col holds dear,

Sincerely

R. Aulben Kenner

My great-grandmother never recovered from the loss of her son; Anzac Day ceremonies were particularly painful for her. She died nine years later, in 1953, just after learning a young New Zealand beekeeper had become the first person to scale the summit of Mount Everest. Her daughter, Gwen – Col's younger sister and my grandmother – died aged 95 on 10 January 2008, the day before Sir Edmund Hillary passed away.

At the time, I was back in Auckland going through Col's remaining effects – a life reduced to fit into an old suitcase of documents, letters and photos: primary school reports, job applications and references, degree certificates, yellowed clippings of newspaper articles by him and about him, his photo album sent back from Britain, the unpublished manuscript of the planned book about the building of the centennial Maori waka. These remained of Col – forever a young man whose restless sense of adventure was fit for a young country, but who died answering the distant call of a people to whom he felt a tribal sense of belonging.

CHAPTER 15

GROUND ZERO, YEAR ZERO

BY THE TIME Col's bomber exploded nearby, Penzlin had lost many of its young men on various fronts, and from the early 1940s had taken in a steady influx of refugees, mainly women and children, from the bombed cities to the west, including those of the Ruhr, the Rhineland, and Hamburg. Despite these casualties of the war, it still felt remote to young Kurt Köhn in 1944. His father was at the front, but had not married his mother, so the family unit was unchanged. Even when Penzlin sounded its own air-raid siren, it seemed merely an occasion for the boy to swing into action with his Hitler Youth troop, which acted as pedestrian marshals, ushering people briskly but jauntily into the town's air-raid shelter. 'We thought of this as fun – as sport.'

The real fear, when it came, rolled in from the east. As 1944 tipped into 1945 and the realisation of inevitable defeat solidified, a new type of refugee began arriving in Penzlin, bringing horror stories of what the Russians were doing to German civilians, particularly women, as they advanced westwards through the Baltic coastal region of East Prussia. The nearest the actual fighting came to Penzlin was the shelling of Neubrandenburg, the larger town where Köhn went to school, and where a defensive line had been established beyond its medieval walls. Köhn's Hitler Youth troop had helped to dig anti-tank trenches east of Penzlin. But the only serious defences were those at Neubrandenburg, their real purpose to slow the Russian advance and thus buy time for the German troops to withdraw westwards and surrender to the British or Americans. Penzlin lies 130 kilometres north of Berlin, far enough away for its boys and older men to escape being sucked into the suicidal defence of the capital ordered by Hitler. Penzlin's boys were trained to fire rifles and the Panzerfaust anti-tank grenade launchers, but the weapons remained firmly locked away in the town hall. When the rumble of Russian artillery could be heard in Penzlin, the Wehrmacht officers guarding its small arsenal told the boys, 'Go home to your Mummies.'

By the time the first wave of Russian troops reached Penzlin on 29 April 1945, nine days before the German capitulation, Köhn and most other townsfolk had melted into the surrounding country-side, finding refuge with friends and families at isolated farms. The Russians found the town deserted. The next day – the day Hitler committed suicide in his Berlin bunker – the Red Army began putting Penzlin to the torch. The soldiers spared the 11th-century Marienkirche, but razed the town hall next to it, destroying seven centuries of public records and igniting the small arsenal's ammunition, which boomed and crackled in accompaniment to the mayhem. One elderly woman remained in her home, rather than flee the arsonists, and burned to death. As I drove out of the town to the site of the Lancaster bomb crater with Köhn and Pastor Reincke, they gave me a commentary on the destruction that April night: 'This was the main street and that's where the town hall stood.... All the houses along here were burnt down.... This grassed area had shops on it....' Penzlin is a smallish town, its population in 2008 just 2500, but the roll-call of that 1945 destruction took a dispiritingly long time to run through.

News of this destruction was carried out to the dispersed townsfolk on a column of smoke. Four neighbouring towns were also set alight – 'pure retribution', Köhn said, for what the Germans had done on the march to the gates of Moscow. None of these towns had provoked its fate by offering any resistance to the Russians. The first wave of Russians had been combat soldiers who, after destroying the town, moved on quickly, intent on staking the Soviet territorial tide-marker as far west as possible. It was the second echelon – the supply companies and the 'politicals' – who meted out vengeance against the people, not just their buildings. With what struck Köhn as a practised savagery, they set about raping the women and pillaging everything still standing. Fear and despair turned to desperation. In his office beside the Marienkirche, Pastor Reincke leafed through page after page of the church register, the columns that record the deaths of April and May 1945. The many entered as 'name unknown' reflect both the number of refugees by then in the town and also the fact so many died violently, often by their own hand. Köhn estimated that the Russians murdered only a small minority – about 20 – while most victims killed themselves rather than submit to what they thought lay in store. The mayor shot himself, as did several other prominent Nazi Party members, but many more drowned themselves in the deep lake nearby.

The Russians remained fearful of the prospect of attacks by the so-called 'Werewolf' partisans – die-hard Nazis who continued guerrilla attacks in areas already captured by Soviet troops. According to Köhn, this fear was unfounded around Penzlin, but it provided a useful pretext for the harsh measures against the civilian population. By mid-May, the occupying soldiers had set up an administrative command centre amid the smouldering ruins of the town. This restored some control, including over their own men in uniform. The Russians also set about arresting anyone who had exercised authority under the Nazi regime. Leading Nazi Party figures were sent to Neubrandenburg, where they were interned with thousands of others awaiting their fate. The leader of Köhn's Hitler Youth brigade received an 18-year sentence – the term of his natural life thus far – and was deported east. A friend of Köhn's, slightly older than him, was also interned, returning to Penzlin only in 1954.

The end of the war also meant the end of Köhn's schooling at the age of 14. He could not travel to school in Neubrandenburg because the Russians had commandeered all the railways and restricted their use. He remained at home with his mother and worked on the Boldt farm, turning peat, close to where the Lancaster had come down. Penzlin's school reopened three months after the war's end. In 1951 Köhn returned to this school, but as a music teacher and choirmaster. Ingeburg Barz's father returned from Russian captivity in 1946 to the home left in ruins by Col's bomb and resumed farming. He was among the few soldiers from the village to survive the eastern front.

The undamaged Marienkirche became the centrepiece of Penzlin's regeneration. A new town hall was built down the road and the site of the old one now serves as a car park. The destruction of the historical archives left a gap that can never be filled. Compounding this, however, was what Köhn described as the deliberate effort by the authorities of the post-war East German regime to suppress living memory as well. How else could such wanton, vengeful destruction be recast as a 'liberation' on which the future brotherhood under socialism could be built? The regime frowned on Köhn's efforts to collate some of the town's history. Little wonder he and Pastor Reincke are among a handful now trying to make up for lost time.

Leutnant Otto Fries ended the war with his life but almost nothing else to make a new start. It felt like Year Zero – no country, no future. 'We were shattered. I reflected on how many comrades I had lost – young, intelligent men – all for nothing. I cried real tears. We realise now that a German victory would have been a terrible thing for Europe, but at the time we felt we had lost everything.' Stationed in Germany's far north at Westerland-Sylt, Otto joined all his comrades in surrendering to the British. Their 'prison' was a school at Mildstedt, beside the town of Husum, described by its most famous son, author Theodor Storm, as 'the grey town on the grey sea'. Soon afterwards they were transferred to a larger camp close by in Schleswig-Holstein, near the Danish border. Then, in late July 1945, all airmen whose homes lay south of the Main River, which runs through Frankfurt, were transferred to another holding camp in preparation for release.

As part of the pre-release formalities a British soldier called the airmen one by one to a barrier. He instructed Otto to turn out his pockets and, curious, asked him to explain what all his medals had been awarded for. The soldier's eye fastened, magpie-like, on the German Cross in Gold, a glittering decoration awarded to Otto for completing 100 operations against the enemy, and which his comrades called the 'fried egg'. Would Leutnant Fries sell it? 'No, take it – you're the victors.' 'I'll pay you for it – money? Coffee?' But Otto would not yield: 'That's a badge of honour. I won't sell it. You'll have to take it from me.' The soldier smiled and shook his head. 'British politeness,' Professor Fries chuckled, recalling the episode as he showed me the medal.

His other medals were among the few things Otto Fries retained from the war. He kept three parachute grips from all but one of the times he was forced to bale out, a small piece of Heinkel from one of those occasions – complete with a Mosquito bullet hole – and his flyer's watch and Knemeier wind direction calculator. When defeat was imminent he left his logbook with the father of one of his squadron colleagues, whose home was near their last base. Otto had planned to collect it on his release from internment, but the father burned it, fearing the British would punish him if he was found with evidence of such extensive combat against them.

The British sent Otto home, but that was literally a bridge too far. The French controlled the few remaining Rhine crossings to his home in the south-west and he had been warned they ripped up the release papers presented by any German trying to make it across to the western bank. This put his own home out of bounds to him. Otto's Bordfunker, Fred Staffa, could not go home after the war either. He came from the Sudetenland, the German-speaking territory of today's Czech Republic that had been ceded to Germany as a result of the 'appeasement' of Hitler by Neville Chamberlain and France's Premier Edouard Daladier at Munich in 1938. The Czechs expelled the German majority from the Sudetenland immediately after the war.

Otto went instead to his old university town, Heidelberg. When he presented his ration card for the first time, the German distributing the food – a communist, Otto later learned – looked at his Luftwaffe uniform and snatched his card with the denunciation: 'War criminal!'

Some were clearly already constructing the 'new Germany' by purging the memory of the old. Germany's communists were among the few groups to resist Hitler, and most paid with their lives. Little wonder those who survived felt justified by history, and believed that strong measures would sometimes be needed to snuff out the embers of any of the 'anti-proletarian' tendencies they blamed for giving rise to Nazism. The communists' perverted ideals, however, dealt Otto a serious blow a few years later.

It happened after he had made his home in the part of Berlin that belonged to the new 'workers' state' of East Germany. Immediately after the war the occupation authorities told Otto he would not be allowed to finish his chemistry degree: that line of education was now barred to German students. German had been the language of chemistry in the earlier decades of the twentieth century, but the indelible stain of products like Zyklon B, used in the death camp gas chambers, put chemical experimentation off the syllabus for many able German students in the late 1940s.

With the route to becoming a research chemist blocked, Otto retrained as an architect. He made it home to the Pfalz, writing his doctoral thesis on the design features of wine houses in his home region. In 1948 Otto married Irmgard and they settled in her family's house in an eastern suburb of Berlin. In 1953, eight years before the communist regime built the Berlin Wall, many city workers rebelled against their 'paradise'. Under great pressure from an exodus of skilled workers, East German authorities persisted with unrealistic production quotas, heaping more and more demands on workers earning far less than their equivalents in the western part of the city.

When the inevitable backlash against the repressive authorities occurred, in mid-1953, Otto was one of the strike leaders in the state architecture workshop in East Berlin. The Stasi – the secret police – had infiltrated the workforce and identified him as a ringleader. Otto, tipped off just minutes before police entered the building to arrest him, escaped down a back stairway and fled to West Berlin. His wife, Irmgard, and her daughter, Renate, joined him, abandoning the house. Russian tanks took to the streets of

East Berlin, firing on protesters and suppressing the '17 June' uprising. The Frieses started a new life in the west.

Paul Zorner, who had flown to intercept the bombers the night Col died, faced a much harsher exposure to the historical reckoning of victor and victim. Though his wife and daughter lived in Germany's south-west – the French zone – Zorner ended the war stationed near Vienna. When he heard of the German surrender on 8 May 1945, he travelled with an English-speaking colleague and a driver through a series of American checkpoints to a large compound and walked through its gates past scores of redundant, high-ranking German officers. There he offered to surrender the 80-strong fighter group under his command to the US Army. The ranking American officer said they would take Major Zorner but not his men. 'I can't leave my men.' Then he would have to take his chances with the thousands of German soldiers being kept nearby in an open field. Zorner and his men remained penned in the open without food for a week. Then the Americans turned them over en masse to the Russians, who immediately separated Zorner and all other officers from the lower ranks.

Thus began the 25-year-old Zorner's 55 months of captivity in a Soviet labour camp in the Caucasus, though he had never fired a shot against a Russian. He spent much of his time in the prison camp mining limestone in the Soviet Socialist Republic of Georgia. Zorner returned to Germany in 1950, to his wife and a six-year-old daughter he had not seen since she was a tiny baby. Despite the hardship he had endured, he told me he was 'fortunate' in that he had remained healthy. His childhood home in Silesia is now part of Poland.

The family farm where Otto Fries's wife, Irmgard, had spent many happy times as a child with her grandparents – and some not-so-happy times escaping the wartime bombing with her daughter – is also in modern-day Poland. But the loss of her family's property did not end with the division of Europe in the immediate post-war years. After Germany reunited in 1990, Frau Fries expected to regain ownership of a large apartment building in eastern Berlin that her father had bought in 1935. She still had the deeds of sale and title, all registered with the authorities. Her father bought it from a willing Jewish vendor nine months before the Nazis introduced the anti-Semitic laws that persuaded many Jews of the need to sell up quickly and get out of Germany. Frau Fries said her father and the vendor agreed to lessen the transaction tax by declaring the sale price as below what was actually paid, and with the remaining portion paid under the table.

But there was no documentary proof of this supplement, and in 1996 the Jewish Claims Conference – an organisation set up to investigate the expropriation of Jewish property by the Nazis – determined that the house had been sold 'under duress'. By order, the JCC took ownership of the property and quickly sold it. The Frieses were given no opportunity to make up the small price difference to what the JCC deemed should have been paid back in 1935. Irmgard Fries remained bitter about this, but Otto Fries said it paled in comparison with what the Jews lost under Nazi rule. They did not shy away from the enormity of the Holocaust and the need for Germany to atone for it, but they believed their loss was a travesty committed as part of redressing that far bigger injustice.

But the Frieses bore a deeper wound. By early 1945, Irmgard had lost her first husband, also named Fries, a trainee doctor serving as an orderly with the Wehrmacht. He had been shot while attempting to escape from a British POW pen near Cassino, Italy, in January 1944. Then in April 1945, Irmgard was travelling through Berlin with their daughter Renate, not yet two years old, when they were forced into a shelter by an air raid. In the cramped, airless fug of the shelter the little girl caught measles which, because of the lack of medicine, developed into a deep-seated infection that permanently damaged her lungs. A doctor said her condition would be serious even if she were able to be treated in a clinic with the drugs she needed.

The doctor advised, however, against staying in Berlin. By mid-April 1945 the Russians were already at the eastern gates of the capital and horror stories about Red Army atrocities against German civilians were commonplace. The doctor could not promise that the clinic's nurses would stick around to meet them. Irmgard juggled the risks and decided to accept a ride in a car with others fleeing to the north-west. Renate, though afflicted by gasping for the rest of her life, lived until she was 13. Every Christmas Eve the Frieses lay a wreath on her grave near their home in western Berlin. Renate died in 1956, but was she a victim of the bombing? 'She was a casualty of war just as my first husband was,' Irmgard Fries said simply.

CHAPTER 16

UNSETTLED HISTORY

THE WESTERN ALLIES kept their part of Berlin as a showcase of capitalism during the Cold War – a contrast to the gritty reality of life for the East Berliners surrounding them. I was reminded, one spring morning in 2008, that the gap in living standards was still wide, even so many years after the Berlin Wall came down. The further east I drove, the more I became numbed by the unrelieved, packing case character of the Plattenbau block housing along my route. Much of this had been put up on the cheap and in a hurry, to accommodate the swelling numbers of Berliners repopulating the city after the wartime exodus to escape the bombing and then the Russian onslaught, though most at my destination, the suburb of Marzahn, had been erected in the 1970s.

I had spoken by phone to the woman in charge of administration at the Marzahn Cemetery, Frau Laubner, who had told me I had to turn up in person to check whether the records contained details of Col and his crew being buried there before their remains were reinterred at the new Commonwealth War Cemetery at Heerstrasse, near my home. Frau Laubner brought out two dusty volumes covering the mid- to late 1940s, one with names arranged alphabetically, the other by year of burial. Neither contained any details of Col or his crew. Frau Laubner phoned the person at Berlin city hall responsible for war graves, Frau Gutte, and handed the phone over to me. Frau Gutte sounded sympathetic but discouraging, and next day phoned me to say, most apologetically, that she could find no record of RAF crews ever having been buried at Marzahn. The conversations reinforced my impression that the German authorities took very seriously the matter of ensuring their country's former enemies were fully honoured in death.

It turned out I had been under a misconception about Marzahn, which an earlier inquiry had confused with 'Marihn', where Col's Lancaster came down. But my trip to Marzahn was not wasted. People walking through its cemetery gates are immediately reminded of the reason Col visited Berlin: a telephone box-sized monument carved to resemble a Schwurhand – a hand swearing an oath – remembers victims of the bombing buried in its grounds. It reads: 'To remind you living of 3330 victims of the bombing terror.' Apart from some preserved ruins, mostly churches, in various cities, this Marzahn stone was the first monument specifically to bombing victims that I had seen anywhere in Germany during seven years of travelling the country extensively. I later visited the mass grave for the 37,000 victims of the Hamburg bombings, but even this smaller one at Marzahn was a rare entry in the other side of the balance sheet of wartime suffering and remembrance.

Berlin's ghosts can be found in almost every neighbourhood. Closer to my home and not far beyond the rubble mound of Devil's Hill the affluent villa district of Grunewald begins. Here history has stopped in its tracks. One concrete-stepped pedestrian tunnel leading up from an underpass, and next to the others from which commuters come and go, leads to the memorial, Gleis 17. From this platform, more than 50,000 Berlin Jews were freighted off to death camps between October 1941 and March 1945. A stretch of rail tracks on weathered sleepers is lined with rusted iron duckboards, edged along both sides of the entire platform with dates, numbers deported, destinations. They detail a bureaucratic regularity that is robotic, and impossible to equate with a civilised human society. Platform 17 was an example of what German Jewish émigré and political theorist Hannah Arendt called the 'banality of evil' – running to timetables and output quotas. The most common destination is Theresienstadt concentration camp, Czechoslovakia. Most consignments, some on consecutive days, number exactly 100. From late 1942 the numbers of each deportation increase sharply to between 1000 and 1800 as Auschwitz enters the schedule. The Nazis agreed to this new dimension to the 'Final Solution', the extermination camps, in January that year at the Wannsee Conference, not far down the line from Grunewald. The size of the human consignments drops to the hundreds, then dozens, towards the end of the war as Berlin's Jewish community is eradicated.

Such monuments make it easier to understand why Germany still finds it so difficult to mourn or honour publicly those who died in uniform during the Second World War. Germany has an official remembrance day, Volkstrauertag, which is marked a week after the British observe Remembrance Day, on the Sunday closest to 11 November – the day the Armistice came into effect in 1918. I represented New Zealand at a Volkstrauertag ceremony in Berlin in 2006 – apparently the first time our embassy had been invited. I was one of only four civilian diplomats, rendered drab and invisible among at least two dozen military attachés from other embassies, in their braid and medal ribbons. The ceremony was a grand affair, with a brass band and a snappy naval detail bearing flaming torches in the twilight, casting angled shadow-giants against the imposing, tomb-like memorial behind. A sea of wreaths, including New Zealand's, filled a channel between us and the naval honour guard.

I recalled the first time I attended an Allied Remembrance Day service at Heerstrasse Commonwealth War Cemetery, where the graves of Col and his six fellow crew members are among 3695 from the Second World War. The Philip Hepworth-designed cemetery is a beautiful resting place, and on that November morning in 2004 I arrived well ahead of time. Overnight the first heavy frost of winter had fallen, creating a hush among the solid rows of white headstones. I felt as though I had been placed in the wordless company of the mourned – a spell that lifted gradually as the growing numbers of arrivals smudged green footfalls in the frost.

At the German ceremony two years later, I found the grandeur typical of the deadening effect of most military ceremonies I have attended around the world. The men in uniform far outnumbered the few city officials and the modest gathering of family who had turned out to pay their respects. Away from the bugler, the brass band and the torches, a flat field lay quilted with the concrete plaques marking the graves of hundreds of German soldiers – or more probably older men and teenage boys – who died defending the city from the advancing Russians in the early months of 1945. For me the point of this ceremony, what salvaged its personal dimension from the industry of ritual, came in one instant. Four old men – two German and two Russian – shuffled forward in their loosely fitting suits, linked arms around each others' backs and laid a wreath to their brotherhood and reconciliation – at the end, comrades in arms.

During my travels through eastern Germany I came across monuments to the Russian dead of that war much more frequently than I found German war memorials. Post-war East German ideology cast the Russians as liberators and portrayed the war as a Nazi travesty against the German worker. This flick of the historical cape placed the East Germans in league with the 'victors' of 1945 – with their Soviet brothers who had 'rescued' them. This self-deception helped East Germany not only to distance its citizens from their own role in supporting and sustaining Nazism, but also to justify a continuation of totalitarian rule as 'protection' against the common 'class enemy'.

The end of the East German state in 1990 left an awkward legacy, which many people who grew up under that regime would still prefer to ignore. The north-eastern town of Penzlin, where Col Jones met his death, reflects this ambivalence. Here I found this debate stirring after more than half a century of politically induced sleep. Pastor Hartmuth Reincke and Kurt Köhn were among a small group who wanted to establish a memorial to those from the town who died in the Second World War, just as the oak panels in the Marienkirche remembered the fallen of the First. Reincke and Köhn estimated the number from the later war would come to between 150 and 200 names.

In attempting to settle the waters of the past, however, their initiative was churning up a maelstrom in the town. The East

German authorities had prohibited any commemoration of 'war criminals' – meaning anyone in a wartime German uniform, from Wehrmacht stablehand to SS officer. But the end of that regime had not cleared up the difficulty of determining who was victim and who was perpetrator. Who would qualify for inclusion on the Penzlin memorial Pastor Reincke was proposing? This, he told me, was a vexing question: Should it include just members of the Marienkirche's congregation before the war? Some had left in the 1930s to join the Nazi Party, but should they be remembered officially in death? What about refugees from bombed western cities or those from the east who had fled the advance of the Russians? In many cases their names were not recorded officially at the time they died. Could the memorial possibly include the names of 'political' SS from Penzlin or others who did the Nazis' dirtiest work? If not, what about the Waffen SS, many of whom were no more than élite soldiers? What about the ordinary Wehrmacht foot soldier? Penzlin lost many men at Stalingrad and more in a single disastrous action in Romania late in the war. 'Our starting point is to remember all who fell,' Pastor Reincke said. 'The issue is the wording.'

Germany still finds it too difficult to separate the sacrifices of its old soldiers as individuals from the greater evil they helped to perpetrate. Otto Fries said he often asked himself after the war what he should have done – *could* have done – against the spiral of destruction gathering speed in Germany and Europe. 'Sabotage? Opposition? And if I had been a communist, should I have tried revolution, or become a saboteur? I couldn't answer it. I came to the conclusion I couldn't have done anything. My place was at the front. I had to fight for my country.' He saw himself as just one of millions of young men in uniform, yet fortunate enough to be indulging his love of flying. As the war turned against Germany he believed his duty to his country strengthened, and that breaking step with his country's doomed march would have been to desert the Fatherland at its hour of greatest need. Only when I pressed him about the death camps did he waver from this line. 'If I had known, I think I would have flown to England.'

I said I found it curious his contribution was viewed no more sympathetically today than that of invading German soldiers, of Luftwaffe bombers, of U-boat crew who had claimed so many civilian lives and laid waste to much of Europe, sometimes going well beyond the rules of war. Surely his job of shielding German civilians and their homes from the nightly onslaught of RAF bombers was as unambiguously defensive as any act of war committed by the Third Reich. In Britain, 'The Few' were lauded as heroes for the same self-sacrificing devotion to defending their homeland during the Battle of Britain; the German night fighters had stuck to their similar task till the end. Fries gave a short, dry laugh and held up his palms in resignation: 'Yes, but we *lost* the war – so we were the last idiots!'

CHAPTER 17

JOURNEYS ENDED

'THE LAST IDIOTS'? I had come to know Otto-Heinrich Fries, a defeated former enemy, because he had lived a full and rewarding life, while Col Jones and the thousands who lie about him knew neither victory nor the peace they had fought to win. I reflected on this at the Heerstrasse War Cemetery one October morning in 2008, shortly before I left Berlin to return to New Zealand. Trees aflame with autumn foliage defied the sombre mood as we gathered for the burial, with full military honours, of a 21-year-old English airman shot down over Berlin in January 1944, three weeks before Col. As the Union Jack-draped coffin bearing the remains of Jack Bremner was lowered to the grave by six young RAF pallbearers, I felt a tug of recognition: Col had done the same for a friend in 1942 at the Beck Row Cemetery beside their Mildenhall airbase. He wrote later: 'All about the day was vividly alive with sunlight and flowers. And so he joins the growing company of plain little white crosses.' These crosses have been replaced both at Beck Row and Berlin with the distinctive, white tablets found at all Commonwealth War Cemeteries in Europe – Col's and Bremner's are just 10 paces apart.

There cannot have been much left of Jack Bremner to bury 64 years after his death, but that did not seem to matter to his 89-year-old sister, nor to his former navigator, who had returned to Berlin in 2005 to begin the search that eventually unearthed the wreckage from suburban woodland. They were both at St George's Anglican Church for the service that preceded the graveside ceremony along the road. During the service the sister had seemed a diminutive, bird-like figure, hardly visible in the front pew. As the pallbearers carried the coffin from the church she was helped into a wheelchair and turned into the aisle to follow her brother, but lost a shoe in the process. A younger, grey-haired man – the son of another crew member who died in the plane with Bremner – stepped from between the pews and helped her with a gentle familiarity that spoke of something shared. She thanked him with a beautiful smile, then tears sprang to her eyes; and in those tears the years of waiting, hoping, grieving and now, finally, release seemed distilled.

Paths I had followed came together that morning: not just the parallels between Bremner's violent death and Col's, but also the importance of that particular cemetery as their final resting place. Berlin had been the ultimate target, the heart of the enemy; now it offered these young men enduring sanctuary, each ceremony of remembrance attended by German authorities with all the dignity and respect they would accord their own fallen – possibly more, from what I had seen on my travels. For me, the wartime target zones in Berlin and elsewhere in Germany were the communities I lived in while this country was my home. This terrible episode in Germany's history and our own has left physical reminders, like Devil's Hill, not far from the cemetery. But some of the scars become visible only rarely, such as with the farewell to Jack Bremner, which brought into full view the pain his family had carried for so long.

Interred in Berlin, Bremner joins new company and leaves the roll of more than 20,000 airmen with no known grave, including the last member of his crew not yet accounted for. They are commemorated at Runnymede, near Windsor. In an important way, Bremner's farewell also marked my own. It reminded me how fortunate I had been to discover in my own journey my great-uncle's fate – a man I had come to know through his writing, a precious legacy that keeps him alive in our family's memory. For many other families uncertainty weighs upon loss. Their journeys have not ended; their search continues.

NOTES AND REFERENCES

Chapter1: Journey Among Ghosts

1: Harris is said to have uttered these words to a fellow officer while watching fires near St Paul's, London, during the German Blitz, but he repeated the phrase when he took over Bomber Command.

Chapter 2: Ditching

1: Jörg Friedrich, *Der Brand: Deutschland im Bomberkrieg 1940–1945*, RM Buch und Medien Vertrieb GmbH, Munich, 2002, p.100. Essen was Germany's second most bombed city after nearby Duisburg, which sustained 299 bombing raids.

2: 'Ropey loop' refers to a radio signal reading from the rotatable loop aerial behind the Stirling's cockpit canopy and used to fix a position bearing. A ropey loop would give a bearing in exactly the opposite direction from the source of the signal. This 180 degrees-out bearing was also called a reciprocal bearing. Source: Jim Coman, former 149 Squadron wireless operator, in conversation with author, 17 May 2008.

3: CD41 Recordings, *RAF Bomber Command at War 1939–45 (Vol. 2): Broadcast and actuality recordings together with crew debriefs and war correspondent reports, including low level and precision strikes*, compact disc: www.ltmpub.freeserve. co.uk

4: Air Ministry, *Pilot's and Flight Engineer's Notes: Stirling I, III, IV & V* (3rd edition), AP1660A, January 1944, p. 51.

5: Theo Boiten, in *Nachtjagd War Diaries*, p.94, claims Oberleutnant Petersen rammed the Stirling's rear turret by accident when his ME110 came in to attack too fast. Petersen never recovered from his injuries and took a non-combat role as adjutant to the night fighter ace Helmut Lent (see p.150).

Chapter 3: Landfall

1: F.C. Jones, 'Thesis on the effect on the social life of the Maoris of the missionaries and their teaching', (121 leaves; 34 cm), Alexander Turnbull Library, call #pq572.9931 JON 1935, PA Collection 3207.

2: Jones, unpublished, untitled manuscript, p. 9.

Chapter 4: Home Bases

1: I am grateful to Joanna Caruth, of the Suffolk County Council Archaeological Service, for providing or checking this historical detail.

Chapter 5: A Lucky Enemy

1: The Messerschmitt 110 was technically called a BF110, owing to its manufacturing origins at the Bayerische Fabrik in Bavaria, but I have used the more common designation of ME110, which is also how both Fries and Col referred to it.

Chapter 7: Firestorm

1: Figure for number of raids on Cologne cited in Friedrich, *Der Brand*, p. 100.
2: Cited in Eric Taylor, *Operation Millennium: 'Bomber' Harris's Raid on Cologne, May 1942*, Spellmount Staplehurst, 2004 (2nd edition.), p. 203.
3: Reproduced in Taylor, inside leaf.
4: Martin Middlebrook and Chris Everitt, *The Bomber Command War Diaries: An Operational Reference Book, 1939–1945*, Viking, London, 1985, p. 268.
5: The so-called Butt Report concluded that one bomber crew in three did not even claim to have reached the target. Of those who did, only one in four crews that believed its bombs had fallen in the right place actually hit within 5 miles of the target. This summary of the report is quoted in James Taylor and Martin Davidson, *Bomber Crew*, Hodder & Stoughton, London, 2004.
6: Friedrich, *Der Brand* p. 400.
7: The citation for this and a posthumous MID of Col have since been disposed of by the United Kingdom National Archives, so cannot be quoted.
8: Two weeks later the Lancaster in which they had flown this op, KO-N 'Nuts', broke up in flight and crashed in England on return from raiding Nuremberg, killing all its new crew. Bazalgette subsequently joined the Pathfinder Force and won the Victoria Cross posthumously for bombing and marking a missile-launching site in France on 4 August 1944, even though his Lancaster was so badly damaged he then had to crash land, killing himself and two crew too badly injured to bale out.
9: Goebbels' speech is reproduced in German on the website of the German History Museum in Berlin: http://www.dhm.de/lemo/html/dokumente/ sportpalastrede/index.html. Translation by author.
10: Friedrich's *Der Brand* cites Hamburg authorities for this estimate, p. 194. For a detailed account of the Gomorrah campaign, see Martin Middlebrook, *The Battle of Hamburg: The Firestorm Raid*, first published by Allen Lane, London, 1980.
11: Volker Hage, *Zeugen der Zerstörung: Die Literaten und der Luftkrieg: Essays und Gespräche*, S.Fischer Verlag, Frankfurt am Main, 2003, pp. 136, 148. Self-translation. Reproduced with author's permission.

Chapter 8: On a Wing and a Prayer

1: Middlebrook, in *The Bomber Command War Diaries*, pp. 290–1, puts the loss rate slightly lower – 29 of 68 that actually reached the target, from 256 aircraft dispatched.
2: The National Archives, United Kingdom, catalogue reference AIR/50/219.
3: Extract from Air Ministry Bulletin No. 8375 (26 October 1943). With thanks to RAF Museum Hendon, London.

Chapter 9: Interceptor

1: McDowell's crew was Pilot Officer John Elliott Kirkup, second pilot, age 21, RAF Volunteer Reserve, married of Essex; Sergeant John Anthony MacNish Porter, Flight Engineer, age 18, RAFVR (Royal Air Force Volunteer Reserve), of Essex – one of the youngest men to die with Bomber Command; Pilot Officer Edward Laming Jackson, navigator/bomb aimer, age 21, RAFVR, of London; Flying Officer Leone Joseph Roberts, air bomber, age 21, RCAF (Royal Canadian Air Force), of Saskatchewan; Sergeant Lawrence Ivory, wireless operator/gunner, age 24, of Neath, Glamorgan; Flight Sergeant Ralph Gordon Dunn, air gunner, age 22, RCAF, of Codrington Ontario; Flight Sergeant William John Whitney, air gunner RCAF.

2: The captain, Flight Sergeant J.Y. Lee, and crew member, Sergeant H.L. Pike, were taken prisoner, while Sergeant A.F. Gunnell escaped back to England. Killed were Flight Sergeant K.S. Bell RAAF (Royal Australian Air Force), Sergeant L.H. Jones, Sergeant A.M. Wilkinson RCAF and Sergeant G. Johnson. All are buried in Weert (Tungelroij) Roman Catholic Churchyard. Source: http://www.lostbombers.co.uk/bomber.php?id=3470

Chapter 11: Coping With Loss

1: Reported in the *Auckland Star*, Thursday April 7 1949, Vol. LXXX – No. 82, p. 1

2: Cited in Max Hastings, *Bomber Command*, Michael Joseph, London (2nd edition), p. 336. Hastings derives these figures from John Milward, *The German Economy at War*, London University, 1965, p. 188. The 13,000 Luftwaffe aircrew killed from June to October 1944 compared with 31,000 from January 1941 to June 1944.

Chapter 12: Aboard the 'Flying Coffin'

1: Harris wrote this description of the Lancaster in a letter to Sir Roy Dobson of A.V. Roe & Co. (Avro), quoted on p. 50 of Max Arthur, *Dambusters: A Landmark Oral History*, Virgin, London, 2008.

2: The lower survival rate of crew in stricken Lancasters compared with those in Halifax or Stirling bombers was the subject of wartime research, quoted in Middlebrook and Everitt, *The Bomber Command War Diaries*, p. 807. This concluded that one in six crewmen survived the shooting down of a Lancaster, compared with one in four for the other two. Figures cited by one New Zealand former Lancaster pilot, Douglas Hawker DFC, claim an even greater disparity, putting successful escapes by parachute at three times higher from Halifax bombers than from Lancasters. See Douglas Hawker, *With Luck to Spare*, Compaid Graphics, Preston, 2004, p. 116. www.compaidgraphics.co.uk

3: Martin Middlebrook, *The Berlin Raids: RAF Bomber Command Winter 1943–44*, Viking, London, pp. 269–70.

4: Ibid. pp. 378–9. Middlebrook cites figures showing 460 Squadron lost two more aircraft, but six fewer men.

5: Douglas Hawker describes seeing several bombers shot down by schräge Musik and assumed the danger was well known among fellow bomber pilots, so was astounded when the RAF expressed surprise, on capturing Luftwaffe airfields after the Allied invasion in 1944, to find night fighters equipped with these upward-firing guns.

6: Middlebrook and Everitt, *The Bomber Command War Diaries*, pp. 272, 472.

7: Ibid., p. 708. These authors cite information provided by the Air Historical Branch of the RAF and Appendix 41 of the British Official History, Vol. IV, pp. 440–4.

8: The figure of 1850 New Zealanders killed serving with Bomber Command is the result of exhaustive research by Errol Martyn for his three-volume *For Your Tomorrow*. It is higher than the total of 1679 dead cited by Middlebrook and Everitt, p. 711, because it also includes New Zealanders recorded as RAF rather than RNZAF Bomber Command aircrew.

9: Source: Imperial War Museum, London: iwm.org.uk/server/show/nav.2186

10: The statistical calculation of the probability of survival is (1-percentage losses) to the power of the number of operations, e.g. for 4 per cent losses the formula would be (1- 0.04)^30, or (0.96)^30 = 29.4 per cent probability of survival.

Chapter 13: The Last Night

1: Paul Zorner, *Nächte im Bomberstrom: Erinnerungen 1920–1950*, NeunundzwanzigSechs Verlag, Moosburg, 2007, pp. 235–6. Self-translation, republished with permission.

2: Memorandum 1251/566/P2 from RNZAF Headquarters, The Strand, London, to Air Department Wellington, 25 September 1947.

3: Memorandum from Flying Officer C.F. Dugdale, Investigating Officer: Investigation Report from Berlin Detachment, MREU, RAF Germany to Air Ministry London, 18 October 1947. Dugdale took part in the exhumation at Marihn on 30 September 1947.

4: Col's Mention in Dispatches 294, dated 14 January 1944, was for bravery during the raid on Hamburg on 24 July 1943, when he dropped an 8000-pound bomb. He did not tell any of his family he had returned to operations to fly on this raid and I could find no written detail of it other than in his logbook and personal service record. The National Archives in the United Kingdom wrote in 2008 that the actual citation no longer existed. Jones's second Mention in Dispatches was posthumous: No. 2645 dated 8 June 1944.

SOURCES

Much has been produced about Bomber Command and the Luftwaffe, including many works I have accessed as part of my research. Though other works are mentioned in the notes section, the following are those readily available books, tapes and websites that I found particularly valuable and which I would recommend to others interested in the events, the motivations, the way people felt at the time and the impact on the lives of those who survived. For this reason I comment on why I found them so useful.

Works in English

Air Ministry (UK), *Pilot's and Flight Engineer's Notes: Stirling I, III, IV & V* (3rd edition), AP1660A, January 1944.
_____ *Pilot's and Flight Engineer's Notes: Lancaster Mks I, II, VII, X* (3rd edition), AP2062A, C,F & H-PN, May 1944.
Technical manuals for Stirling and Lancaster that provide extensive 'anatomical' drawings of these aircraft, descriptions of the various crewmen's stations and detailed instructions on procedures for both normal flight and emergencies.

Arthur, Max, *Dambusters: A Landmark Oral History*, Virgin, London, 2008.
Though focusing on a celebrated single operation, this book is a model of oral history that also says much about life in Bomber Command more generally.

Boiten, Theo E.W., *Nachtjagd War Diaries: An Operational History of the German Night Fighter Force in the West*, Vol. 1: Sept 1939-March 1944, Red Kite, Surrey, 2008.

Chorley, W.R., *Bomber Command Losses*, Midlands Counties Publications, 1992–8.
In six volumes, one each for 1939–40 and each subsequent year, Chorley lists the names of crew members on each of the lost aircraft listed.

Falconer, Jonathan, *Stirling in Combat*, Sutton edition, Gloucestershire, 2006.
A thorough account of the development of this aircraft, from its arrival as the RAF's first four-engined 'heavy' in 1941 to its relegation to transport duties later in the war.

Hastings, Max, *Bomber Command*, Michael Joseph, London (2nd edition), 1980.
A rigorous and well-paced account of the action and politics around Bomber Command's contribution to winning the war.

Hinchliffe, Peter, *The Other Battle: Luftwaffe Night Aces Versus Bomber Command*, Airlife, Shrewsbury, (2nd edition), 1997.
A detailed study, with excellent technical explanations, of the men and their machines on both sides of the night war over Germany.

Johnston, John and Carter, Nick, *Strong by Night: Histories and Memories of No.149 (East India) Squadron Royal Air Force 1918/19–1937/56*, Air-Britain, Wiltshire, 2002.
A history of the squadron on which Col flew his first tour of operations, in 1942.

Lambert, Max, *Night After Night: New Zealanders in Bomber Command*, HarperCollins, Auckland, 2005.
The most thorough operational account yet of New Zealanders in Bomber Command, rich in anecdote as well as factual context. This first edition includes an index of names.

Martyn, Errol, *For Your Tomorrow: a record of New Zealanders who have died while serving with the RNZAF and Allied Air Services since 1915*, Volplane, Christchurch, 1998–99.
In three volumes Martyn profiles every New Zealand airman who died on active service during more than eight decades of last century, most during the Second World War. A meticulous record of the men who left these shores to fight in the air but never returned.

Middlebrook, Martin and Everitt, Chris, *The Bomber Command War Diaries: An Operational Reference Book, 1939–1945*, Viking, London, 1985.
An exhaustively researched volume that claims to catalogue chronologically every operation by Bomber Command during the war, including numbers involved and losses suffered by Bomber Command and often also casualties on the ground. An essential reference book for researchers of this subject.

Middlebrook, Martin, *The Battle of Hamburg: The Firestorm Raid*, first published by Allen Lane, London, 1980.
Detailed description from both sides of Operation Gomorrah, the destruction of Hamburg in July–August 1943.
_____ *The Berlin Raids: RAF Bomber Command: Winter 1943–44*, Viking, London, 1988.
Similar to his book on the Hamburg raids.

Neillands, Robin, *The Bomber War: The Allied Air Offensive Against Nazi Germany*, Overlook, New York, 2001.
A well-balanced account of RAF and USAAF bombing offensive and the German response.

Taylor, James and Davidson, Martin, *Bomber Crew*, Hodder & Stoughton, London, 2004.
Produced from a BBC series of the same name, this book describes life and death in Bomber Command through the personal stories of airmen.

Taylor, Eric, *Operation Millennium: 'Bomber' Harris's Raid on Cologne, May 1942*, Spellmount Staplehurst, 2004 (2nd edition.)
A thorough account of the first thousand-bomber raid of the war, carefully researched and with an immediacy provided by eye-witness accounts.

Works in German

Friedrich, Jörg, *Der Brand: Deutschland im Bomberkrieg 1940–1945*, RM Buch und Medien, Munich 2002.
A seminal German book on the Allied bombing of the Third Reich, rich in detail and staggering in its account of the suffering on both sides.

Volker Hage, *Zeugen der Zerstörung: Die Literaten und der Luftkrieg: Essays und Gespräche*, S.Fischer, Frankfurt am Main, 2003.
Reflective, first-hand accounts by German writers and artists who experienced the bombing, interviewed by the arts editor of the weekly news magazine, *Der Spiegel*.

Zorner, Paul, *Nächte im Bomberstrom: Erinnerungen 1920–1950*, NeunundzwanzigSechs Verlag, Moosburg, 2007.
A detailed and sobering account by one of Germany's most successful night fighter pilots of his time in the air and his subsequent years as prisoner in a Soviet labour camp.

Leiwig, Heinz, *Deutschland Stunde Null: Historische Luftaufnahmen 1945*, Motorbuch Verlag, special edition, 2005.
A volume of US and RAF aerial photographs taken mostly at the war's end, cataloguing the destruction of German cities by Allied bombing. Though the text and captions are in German, the photographs make the most powerful statement about the effects of the bombing.

Archives

New Zealand Defence Force, Trentham, holds personnel records of servicemen and women. Col's file contained a wealth of information not known to our family until then. Write to Enquiries, Personnel Archives Enquiries Unit, New Zealand Defence Force, Private Bag 905, Upper Hutt, or email: personnel.archives@nzdf.mil.nz

Royal Air Force

The Air Historical Branch, Bentley Priory, helped with details of what happened to crew members mentioned in Col Jones's diary and correspondence.

Officers' Disclosures, Room 5, Building 248a, RAF Innsworth, Gloucester GL3 1EZ, provided details of Col Jones's service record, though this was far less extensive than the records I obtained from the New Zealand Defence Force (above). Information on non-commissioned airmen and women is held also held at RAF Innsworth, by writing instead to 'Airmen's Disclosures'.

The National Archives (TNA), based at Kew, London, is the central archive of RAF operational records and is therefore a must for serious research into the RAF. TNA responded slowly to my queries and I was able to glean information only via its website.
Email: enquiry@nationalarchives.gov.uk

RAF Museum Hendon, London.

Websites

www.cwgc.org.uk
Details of service personnel who died on active service and descriptions and locations of Commonwealth War Cemeteries around the world.

www.lostbombers.co.uk
Gives the history of bombers lost on operations, including their previous operations and names of crew on board at the time they were destroyed.

www.luftarchiv.info
Useful information and bulletin board in German and English.

www.luftwaffe.cz
> Profiles of prominent Luftwaffe fighters, including times and locations of shootings-down attributed to them.

www.luftwaffe-experten.org/forums/
> Message board in English on air war, particularly Luftwaffe.

www.michael-reimer.com/CFS2/CFSU_Aircraft_Profiles.html
> Useful for its extensive aircraft illustrations and information on Nachtjagd squadrons and their stations. Also information on USAAF and French and Russian air forces.

www.nationalarchives.gov.uk/documentsonline/ww2aircombat.asp
> Contains original, scanned documents of combat reports filed by airmen on returning from operations.

www.rafcommands.com
> Provides details of the activities and locations of individual squadrons.

APPENDIX ONE

FRANK COLWYN JONES:
KEY DATES IN LIFE AND SERVICE

21 April 1908	Born in Auckland to Frank and Emma Jones
1915–21	Northcote Primary School, Auckland
1922–6	Auckland Grammar School
1927–35	Auckland University College, University of New Zealand
	1930: Diploma in Journalism
	1932: Graduates Bachelor of Arts in History
	1936: Graduates Master of Arts (Hons) in History
1929	Reporter (temporary job) on *New Zealand Herald*, Auckland
1929	Employed as cadet on *Auckland Star*
1937–40	Follows the building of six Maori war canoes (waka)
June 1939	Joins New Zealand Army as a Territorial (intelligence) with 1st Brigade, Auckland Regiment
Dec 1939	Applies to RNZAF
Sept 1940	Enters RNZAF Initial Training Wing, Levin
5 Nov 1940	Departs Auckland for Canada aboard USSC vessel *Awatea*
24 Nov 1940	Arrives at Vancouver, British Columbia
Dec 1940–Feb 1941	No. 4 Air Observers' School, bombing and gunnery, Fingal, Ontario
Feb–Mar 1941	No. 4 Air Observers' School, London, Ontario
Mar 1941	Awarded flying badge, promoted sergeant
Mar 1941–Apr 1941	Air Navigation School, Rivers, Manitoba
May 1941	Departs Halifax Novia Scotia in Atlantic convoy

Jun 1941	Arrives Scotland
	Posted to 20 Operational Training Unit, Lossiemouth
Oct 1941	Posted to 149 Squadron, Mildenhall, Suffolk
1 Oct 1941	Promoted flight sergeant
14 Jan 1942	First operation against the enemy
Feb 1942	149 Squadron transferred to Lakenheath, Suffolk
4 June 1942	Promoted pilot officer
27 Oct 1942	Awarded Distinguished Flying Cross
7 Nov 1942	Final (33rd) op with 149 Squadron
4 Dec 1942	Promoted flying officer
Dec 1942	Posted to No. 1651 Conversion Unit, Waterbeach, Cambridgeshire as squadron bombing leader
14 Dec 1942	Promoted acting flight lieutenant
9 Feb 1943	Receives DFC from King George VI at Buckingham Palace
June 1943	Posted to 115 Squadron, East Wretham, Norfolk, as navigation officer
24-5 July 1943	Bomb aimer on 115 Squadron Lancaster in first Gomorrah raid against Hamburg
Aug 1943	Moves with 115 Squadron, still as navigation officer, to Little Snoring, Norfolk
4 Jan 1944	Mentioned in Dispatches
29 Jan 1944	Posted to 7 Pathfinder Squadron, Oakington, Cambridgeshire
15 Feb 1944	Missing on operations to Berlin
8 June 1944	Posthumous Mention in Dispatches

LIST OF OPERATIONS
FLOWN BY FRANK COLWYN JONES DFC

Op No.	Date	Take-off	Aircraft	Pilot	Target	Duration
1	14-1-42	17.00 hrs	OJ-N	Gibb	Emden	5h55m
2	17-1-42	17.30 hrs	OJ-A	Gibb	Bremen	6h20m
3	13-3-42	19.55 hrs	OJ-T	Knocker	Dunkirk	2h35m
4	25-3-42	21.20 hrs	OJ-R	Turtle	Essen	returned
5	6-4-42	00.50 hrs	OJ-T	Turtle	Essen	2h00m
6	15-4-42	00.05 hrs	OJ-A	Watt	Dortmund	5h20m
7	19-4-42	21.25 hrs	OJ-A	Watt	Mine-laying	4h25m
8	22-4-42	21.20 hrs	OJ-A	Watt	Cologne	4h55m
9	23-4-42	23.05 hrs	OJ-A	Watt	Rostock	7h20m
10	28-4-42	22.15 hrs	OJ-D	Watt	Kiel	7h00m
11	2-5-42	23.16 hrs	OJ-C	Watt	Kiel Bay*	6h50m
12	8-5-42	21.55 hrs	OJ-F	Watt	Warnemunde	7h30m
13	29-5-42	23.59 hrs	OJ-E	Watt	Paris	5h05m
14	30-5-42	00.05 hrs	OJ-Y	Watt	Cologne	4h10m
15	2-6-42	00.15 hrs	OJ-E	Watt	Essen	3h45m
16	5-6-42	23.55 hrs	OJ-T	Whitney	Essen	3h20m
17	19-6-42	23.40 hrs	OJ-E	Potts	Emden	5h15m
18	22-6-42	23.20 hrs	OJ-E	Potts	Emden	5h20m
19	25-6-42	23.15 hrs	OJ-E	Watt	Bremen	5h15m
20	29-7-42	22.40 hrs	OJ-B	Greenslade	Hamburg	6h05m
21	10-8-42	22.30 hrs	OJ-A	Charlton-Jones	Denmark*	7h50m
22	12-8-42	21.40 hrs	OJ-A	Watt	Mainz	5h25m
23	20-8-42	20.45 hrs	OJ-A	Greenslade	Bordeaux*	8h15m
24	24-8-42	21.20 hrs	OJ-E	Greenslade	Frankfurt	4h50m
25	28-8-42	20.55 hrs	OJ-E	Greenslade	Nuremberg	6h45m
26	1-9-42	23.30 hrs	OJ-C	Greenslade	Saarbrücken	5h45m
27	3-9-42	Not given	OJ-B	Hartford	Emden	returned
28	4-9-42	00.05 hrs	OJ-B	Greenslade	Bremen	5h05m
29	6-9-42	01.05 hrs	OJ-G	Greenslade	Duisburg	4h15m
30	14-9-42	19.50 hrs	OJ-G	Greenslade	Wilhelmshaven	4h35m
31	15-9-42	19.35 hrs	OJ-G	Greenslade	Bordeaux*	6h50m
32	23-10-42	18.25 hrs	OJ-T	Wasse	Genoa	8h40m
33	7-11-42	17.50 hrs	OJ-E	Patrick	Genoa	8h15m
34	24-7-43	22.30 hrs	KO-N	Bazalgette	Hamburg	5h20m
35	15-2-44	17.09 hrs	MG-W	Barnes	Berlin	KIA

*mine-laying op

APPENDIX TWO

WHAT BECAME OF THEM?

Col Jones's diary and letters mention many friends and colleagues he came to know between enlisting in 1940 and his death in 1944. What follows is what I have been able to find out about what happened to some of them. Unless otherwise stated, it is assumed they are British. As most of them did not survive the war, they are listed by date of death.

Peter Jarrett, Sergeant, an early room-mate of Col's, Jarrett died on 13 or 14 October 1941 when his 115 Squadron Wellington bomber was lost on a raid to Munich. He is buried in the Dürnbach War Cemetery, south of Munich. After Jarrett's death, Col became very friendly with his sister, Cecily.

Ian Gordon Harrowby, 21, Flight Sergeant, navigator, Aucklander and friend of Col Jones since training in Levin and Canada. Killed on 7 November 1941 with all his crew when their Wellington bomber crashed near Assen, Holland, for reasons unknown. All are buried at Beilen General Cemetery, Drenthe, Netherlands.

Peter John Paine, 24, Flight Sergeant, pilot, one of Col's early room-mates and a friend who invited him to spend leave with him in Kent. After Paine died in the wreckage of his Wellington bomber on 26 March 1942, Col stayed in touch with his mother and wife, Ruth, both of whom wrote to Col's mother after his death. Paine is buried in the Reichswald Forest War Cemetery, Germany.

Keith Roderick, 21, Sergeant, rear gunner, killed when his rear turret was sheared off by a German night fighter plunging out of control – part of the dramatic chain of events that led to Col's Stirling crash-landing in the English Channel on 6 June 1942, as described in Chapter 2. Roderick's body was washed ashore on the French coast and is buried in the Parish Cemetery at Riykeyorsel, near Antwerp, Belgium.

William George 'Crasher' Barnes DFC, 29, Flight Lieutenant, second pilot, killed when his 149 Squadron Stirling was shot down by a night fighter on 29 June 1942 and crashed near the northern coast of Holland. He is buried in Wonseradeel (Makkum) Protestant Churchyard, Ijsselmeer.

Cecil Charlton-Jones, 28, Wing Commander, pilot, who flew down to Kent to take Col and his crew back to Lakenheath after they had been rescued from the English Channel on 6 June 1942. The Stirling piloted by Charlton-Jones was shot down by a night fighter on 28 August 1942, north of Mannheim. He is buried in Dürnbach War Cemetery, south of Munich.

William Roy 'Al' Greenslade DFC, AFC, Squadron Leader, a Canadian, one of Col Jones's regular pilots, with whom he had narrowly escaped death over Hamburg in July 1942, as described in Chapter 8. Greenslade's 149 Squadron Stirling was shot down by a night fighter over Holland, near the border with Germany, on 2 October 1942. Col was close friends with all of this, his second regular crew: **F.L. 'Bill' Hughes**, 21, Sergeant, wireless operator; **W. Frederick Leonard 'Bill' Orange**, Flight Sergeant, air gunner; **Earnest Les Moore**, 21, Sergeant, wireless operator/air gunner; **Marshal Kenneth Smith**, 21, Sergeant, flight engineer; **R.F. McIntyre**, Sergeant, observer; **Benjamin Frederick Goldsmith**, 22, Flight Sergeant, air gunner. All are buried at Jonkerbos Cemetery, near Nijmegen, Netherlands.

John Herbert 'Jack' Ekelund, 23, Flight Sergeant and one of Col's pilots while at 149 Squadron. Ekelund, a Canadian, died on 16 October 1942 with his whole crew when they crashed into the sea south of St Nazaire, France, while laying mines. All are buried at Port Joinville Communal Cemetery, L'Ile-d'Yeu, France.

Victor Mitchell DFC, Wing Commander, pilot whom Col Jones knew at 149 Squadron in 1942. Mitchell transferred to 75 (NZ) Squadron as commanding officer and died when his Stirling was one of four from the squadron lost in bad weather on operations on 17 December 1942. Mitchell and his crew are commemorated at Runnymede Memorial, near Windsor.

Reginald W.A. Turtle DFC, 26, Flight Lieutenant, pilot of the Stirling in which Col Jones experienced serious icing before aborting a mission to Essen in April 1942. Turtle was shot down by a night fighter on 7 June 1942, well into his second tour of operations, and is buried in the Vredenhof Cemetery, Schiermonnikoog, Holland.

Kenneth Duke Knocker, 35, Wing Commander, pilot serving with 149 Squadron when Col Jones joined it, but was killed flying with 214 Squadron on 3 July 1942 and is buried at Westernieland General Cemetery, de Marne, Netherlands. Though Col refers to him as a New Zealander, he was born in Marlborough, England. His mother, the Baroness de Serclaes, was awarded the Military Medal for her work as a nurse in the First World War trenches. Col also knew Knocker's wife Pauline who, in 1931, became one of the first women to qualify as a pilot in New Zealand.

Eric Pierce Wynn, 20, Pilot Officer, pilot, a Canadian friend of Col Jones, and one of Barry Martin's pilots at 149 Squadron. Col Jones was a pallbearer at Wynn's funeral at Beck Row Cemetery, after he died when his Stirling crashed while taking off from Lakenheath on 24 August 1942, as described in Chapter 11. Other friends of Col's killed in the same crash were **D.A. Pebworth** and **Jim Trotter**, an Australian.

William Cyril Hutchings DFC, 29, Squadron Leader, pilot, killed on 10 October 1942 when his 149 Squadron Stirling caught fire and crashed near Mildenhall during an air display for a visiting Russian delegation. He was cremated at Golders Green, London.

Rawdon Hume 'Ron' Middleton VC, 26, Pilot Officer, pilot, an Australian friend of Col's from 149 Squadron. Middleton was awarded the Victoria Cross posthumously for his heroic actions on 29 November 1942, described in Chapter 11. He is buried at Beck Row Cemetery, St John's Churchyard, beside Mildenhall Airbase and in the row next to Eric Wynn's grave.

Barry Martin, 31, Flight Lieutenant, navigator, from Christchurch, Col Jones's closest wartime friend, killed when his 7 Squadron Pathfinder Stirling was shot down on 2 February 1943 near Rotterdam. He is buried in the Crooswijk General Cemetery, Rotterdam. Martin's DFC was gazetted two days after his death.

Tom Benson Blackburn, 25, Pilot Officer, navigator, from Christchurch. Col Jones was best man at his wedding in Liverpool in November 1941. Blackburn broke his back in a flying accident in 1942, made it back into the cockpit but was killed in another flying accident at his airfield in April 1943. His South African wife, Patricia, settled in Christchurch after the war. He is buried at Helston Cemetery, England.

Les Martin, Flying Officer, pilot, English friend of Col Jones and died on 14 May 1943 when his 149 Squadron Stirling was shot down near Antwerp. He is buried in the Schoonselhof Cemetery, Antwerp.

John Milton Patrick Riordan, 32, Sergeant, family friend of Col's from Auckland, was killed when his 75 (NZ) Squadron Stirling was shot down and crashed into the sea off the Belgian coast on 26 May 1943. His body was not recovered and he is commemorated at Runnymede Memorial.

Ian Willoughby Bazalgette VC, DFC, 25, Squadron Leader,

Canadian pilot of the Lancaster in which Col Jones was bomb aimer during the first 'firestorm' raid on Hamburg in July 1943. Bazalgette subsequently joined the Pathfinder Force and won the Victoria Cross posthumously. On 4 August 1944, while Bazalgette was flare marking a German rocket launch site in France, flak knocked out both starboard engines of his Lancaster. He tried to crash-land after four of his crew parachuted but he and the other two crew died when the bomber exploded on impact.

L.O. 'Tony' Tugwell, 26, Flight Lieutenant, pilot with whom Col flew while serving with 149 Squadron. Tugwell was killed when his 101 Squadron Lancaster was lost on an operation to Braunschweig on 13 August 1944. He is buried with seven other crew at Hanover War Cemetery, Germany.

The Survivors

The following details are among the few I could find about wartime colleagues Col wrote about and who survived the war.

Dave Gibb, a New Zealander whom Col knew in Auckland before the war and with whom he flew his first two ops with 149 Squadron, transferred from 149 Squadron to 75 (NZ) Squadron. He settled in Banks Peninsula after the war, but kept in contact with Col's family.

Stan Galloway DFC, an air gunner from Lancashire, with whom Col flew early ops. Their pilots included Dave Gibb. Galloway flew a second tour, as a wireless operator with 75 (NZ) Squadron and won the DFC. After the war he married a pilot colleague's sister and they had eight children together, one of whom, Gordon, made available valuable family material for this book. Stan Galloway became a quarry manager in Lancashire after the war. He visited Dave Gibb in New Zealand in the 1980s and died in 2007, aged 85.

Charles Lofthouse, OBE, DFC, English friend who invited Col home on leave to meet his family. Col went to Buckingham Palace for Lofthouse's investiture of the OBE (military), awarded after the young officer helped to rescue five trainee crew from a burning bomber that had crashed at Waterbeach airbase in November 1942. Squadron Leader Lofthouse was on his 37th operation when he was shot down by a night fighter in August 1943, during the first raid of the Battle of Berlin. Lofthouse and his entire crew of seven baled out and were taken prisoner. He was interned at the POW camp immortalised in the film *The Great Escape*, Stalag Luft Sagan, and helped to forge maps and identity documents for the mass breakout. He became a school teacher after the war and also served as President of the 149 Squadron Association. The London *Daily Telegraph* published a lengthy obituary when Lofthouse died in October 2002, aged 80.

Al Shoreman, wireless operator with whom Col Jones flew 17 ops, including the first 'thousand bomber' raid on Cologne in May 1942. Shoreman had an eye blown out by shrapnel during his second tour, but put it back again. Despite the injury he remained in the RAF after the war. His daughter, Jan Burke – one of four children – lent me his logbook and other personal records to help with my research. At 94, Shoreman was still able to see with both eyes, but was too ill to interview.

Johnny Brittain, whose wedding Col attended at Church Stretton in 1942, and whom he replaced on Jock Watt's crew, settled in Canada after the war and remained friends with Al Shoreman, another guest at the wedding.

Eric Whitney, the pilot of the Stirling in which Col Jones crashed in the English Channel in June 1942 and whose BBC recording of the episode is quoted in Chapter 2, lived in Warwick after the war. His logbook is held at the RAF Museum at Hendon, London.

Also mentioned

Noel Parker, DFC and bar, from Goulburn, New South Wales, was on his 10th op as pilot of a 75 (NZ) Squadron Stirling when it fell to Otto Fries's guns in November 1943. After escaping back to England via Spain following this shooting down, Parker joined 97 Pathfinder Squadron. After the war he flew passengers for Trans Australian Airlines and Qantas and, after retiring from that job, ferried light aircraft solo from Italy to Melbourne well into his sixties. According to a family website he died in 1996, aged 80.

Jack Hyde, one of Parker's crew, seriously wounded when shot down by Otto Fries, was released from a German POW camp in April 1945 and returned to Christchurch where he died in 2007, aged 85.

The Germans

Otto-Heinrich Fries and **Fred Staffa** helped to rebuild Germany after the war – Otto as an architect and Fred as a construction engineer. In August 1945 Otto, barred from crossing the Rhine, instead crossed the Neckar at Heidelberg when, with Fred, he helped to rebuild one of the many destroyed bridges over the river. They studied together at Darmstadt University, razed with much of the old city by a firestorm bombing in September 1944. Otto married Irmgard in 1948 and they settled in Berlin, where he eventually became Professor of Architecture at the city's technical university. Irmgard's child by her first marriage, Renate, died in 1956, but she and Otto had two children and three grandchildren. The Frieses celebrated their 60th wedding anniversary in 2008, shortly after Professor Fries's 90th birthday.

Fred worked as a construction engineer in Frankfurt and Essen, moved to Berlin to become the city's construction director and then joined Otto on the teaching staff of the technical university. He and his wife, Inge, had four children. When I met them Otto, Fred and their wives were still meeting every Monday at each other's homes in the west of Berlin to play bridge.

Paul Zorner, after his return from 55 months in a Soviet labour camp, had soon to leave his wife and daughter again for two and a half years while he retrained in Stuttgart as an engineer. He rejoined them to move to Bonn in the early 1950s, and while there he applied unsuccessfully to become a pilot in the post-war German air force, established in 1955. After that, until his retirement in 1988, Zorner worked for the large German chemicals company, Hoechst, including spending seven years in the Netherlands. He and his wife, Gerda, had three children, five grandchildren and a great-grandchild. In 2008 they celebrated their 65th wedding anniversary in Homburg-Saar, south-west Germany.

INDEX OF NAMES AND PLACES